The Mafia

Recent Titles in
Guides to Subcultures and Countercultures

Guides to Subcultures and Countercultures

The Mafia

A Guide to an American Subculture

Nate Hendley

GREENWOOD

AN IMPRINT OF ABC-CLIO, LLC
Santa Barbara, California • Denver, Colorado • Oxford, England

Library of Congress Cataloging-in-Publication Data

Hendley, Nate.
    The Mafia : a guide to an American subculture / Nate Hendley.
        pages cm. — (Guides to subcultures and countercultures)
    Includes bibliographical references and index.
    ISBN 978–1–4408–0360–4 (hardcopy : alk. paper) — ISBN 978–1–4408–0361–1 (ebook)
    1. Mafia—United States—History. I. Title.
HV6446.H393   2013
364.1060973—dc23   2013013396

ISBN: 978–1–4408–0360–4
EISBN: 978–1–4408–0361–1

17 16 15 14 13   1 2 3 4 5

This book is also available on the World Wide Web as an eBook.
Visit www.abc-clio.com for details.

Greenwood
An Imprint of ABC-CLIO, LLC

ABC-CLIO, LLC
130 Cremona Drive, P.O. Box 1911
Santa Barbara, California 93116-1911

This book is printed on acid-free paper ∞

Manufactured in the United States of America

This book is dedicated to New York police lieutenant
Joseph Petrosino,
a very brave policeman.

Contents

Series Foreword

From Beatniks to Flappers, Zoot Suiters to Punks, this series brings to life some of the most compelling countercultures in American history. Designed to offer a quick, in-depth examination and current perspective on each group, the series aims to stimulate the reader's understanding of the richness of the American experience. Each book explores a countercultural group critical to American life and introduces the reader to its historical setting and precedents, the ways in which it was subversive or countercultural, and its significance and legacy in American history. *Webster's Ninth New Collegiate Dictionary* defines counterculture as "a culture with values and mores that run counter to those of established society." Although some of the groups covered can be described as primarily subcultural, they were targeted for inclusion because they have not existed in a vacuum. They have advocated for rules that methodically opposed mainstream culture, or they have lived by their ideals to the degree that it became impossible not to impact the society around them. They have left their marks, both positive and negative, on the fabric of American culture. Volumes cover such groups as Hippies and Beatniks, who impacted popular culture, literature, and art; the Eco-Socialists and Radical Feminists, who worked toward social and political change; and even groups such as the Ku Klux Klan, who left mostly scars.

A lively alternative to narrow historiography and scholarly monographs, each volume in the *Subcultures and Countercultures* series can be described as a "library in a book," containing both essays and browsable reference materials, including primary documents, to enhance the research process and bring the content alive in a variety of ways. Written for students and general readers, each volume includes engaging illustrations, a timeline of critical events in the subculture, topical essays that illuminate aspects of the subculture, a glossary of subculture terms and slang, biographical sketches of the key players involved, and primary source excerpts—including speeches, writings, articles, first-person accounts, memoirs, diaries, government reports, and court decisions—that offer contemporary perspectives on each group. In addition, each volume includes an extensive bibliography of current recommended print and nonprint sources appropriate for further research.

Preface

The Mafia is the best-known and arguably most feared criminal organization in the United States. Whether it's illegal gambling, prostitution, labor racketeering, extortion, loan sharking, drug trafficking, or, during the years of Prohibition, selling bootleg liquor, the Mafia has had a hand in it. New scams include credit card fraud and online sports betting from websites located abroad.

Also called La Cosa Nostra (LCN), the Mafia is not an easy organization to join. To get "made" (that is, to become a formal member of the Mafia), you must be male and of clear Italian/Sicilian lineage. You have to put the Mafia ahead of family, friends, and any other considerations. Consider the Mafia like the army—a unique subculture that demands total obedience, devotion, and an obsessive adherence to rituals and customs. In the Mafia, greed and a proclivity toward violence are considered positive attributes that might lead to promotion and wealth.

While the earliest leaders of the American Mafia started out as street-corner thugs, La Cosa Nostra has come to epitomize organized crime. Unlike a street gang, in which leadership roles are blurry and constantly in flux, the Mafia is organized into "families" that preside over various cities. Some locales such as New York City are large enough to support multiple Mafia clans. Each family has carefully demarcated territories in which it can operate its "rackets." A racket is simply a scheme, scam, or service that is usually illegal and that brings in money.

Mafia families are generally structured the same way: at the top, there is the boss or don, who works closely with an underboss and a consigliere, or adviser. Beneath the boss and underboss are a handful of capos—the Mafia equivalent of middle managers. Capos command roughly 10 "soldiers" each. Assisting the soldiers is an army of "associates"—criminals from any ethnic background who aren't official members of the Mafia, but are happy to help.

Orders flow downward, from the bosses to the capos, then to soldiers and associates. This system was designed to make it difficult for authorities to hold the man at the top responsible for crimes committed by his underlings. Profits, on the other hand, flow upward, with the greatest share going to the family bosses.

FBI agent Joseph Pistone successfully infiltrated the Mafia in New York in the 1970s. In the process, he picked up some fascinating insights into the mindset of "wiseguys" (the term Mafia members use to describe themselves). "Wiseguys exist in a bizarre parallel universe, a world where avarice, violence and corruption are the norm, and where the routines that most ordinary people hold dear—working good jobs, being with family, living an honest life—are seen as the curse of the weak and the stupid," wrote Pistone, after leaving the Mafia.[1]

"Wiseguys are not nice guys," Pistone continued. "Wiseguys aren't even close to being nice guys. In fact, wiseguys are the meanest, cruellest, least caring people you'll ever meet. They have zero regard for other people's feelings, rights and safety. They will end your life with all the forethought required to flick off a light switch."

Most wiseguys live entirely in the moment, with little thought to past or future. "They are basically street people, street thieves, ruling through fear and intimidation ... the majority of them, might have $100,000 in their pocket today and tomorrow they are borrowing from the shylock (loan shark)," Pistone told a U.S. Senate subcommittee.[2] "They fit into their own environment very well. They do not fit into the straight world at all, because they cannot fathom doing anything legitimate as a first means of making any type of money ... from the

The funeral of Mafia leader Vito Genovese. (Associated Press/Wide World Photo)

time he wakes up until the time he goes to bed, he is a 24-hour Mafia member and all he is thinking is Mafia, how to make scores, how to get money, how to maintain whatever position he has in that family," he added.

In general, Mafiosi also tend to have a fatalistic outlook. "All wiseguys fully expect to either go to jail or get whacked . . . wiseguys know they are entering a dangerous profession when they sign up," wrote Pistone.[3]

This book profiles famous "wiseguys" such as Salvatore Maranzano, Frank Nitti, and Al Capone. Also included are Italian American thugs such as Ignazio Saietta (aka "Lupo the Wolf") and "Big Jim" Colosimo. Saietta and Colosimo didn't formally belong to the Mafia but can be considered LCN pioneers. Major Mafia players from Charles "Lucky" Luciano to John Gotti are also scrutinized, as are Mafia rituals (such as the induction ceremony for made members) and secrets.

This book examines Mafia geography—the cities and locales where the U.S. Mafia has traditionally felt most at home. In addition to obvious choices such as Chicago, New York City, and Las Vegas, the Mafia's presence in Philadelphia, New England, Los Angeles, and the Midwest is also cited.

This book does not glorify the Mafia or its leaders. Mafia crimes are looked at in detail, as are underworld rackets. The common thread running through all Mafia activities is fear and intimidation. The Mafia has never hesitated to use violence to further its goals and silence critics. Sometimes, the Mafia turns against its own, as in the strange case of mob boss turned civil rights crusader Joseph Colombo Sr.

Mafia adversaries are also covered, including turncoats such as Joseph Valachi and Salvatore "Sammy the Bull" Gravano. FBI agent Pistone's undercover experience is examined at length. Also covered are various tactics and strategies used to take down major Mafia players, from tax laws to the RICO (Racketeer Influenced and Corrupt Organizations) Act, wiretaps, and the witness protection program.

The book looks at pop culture depictions of the Mafia, in movies such as *The Godfather* and *Goodfellas* and television programs such as *The Sopranos* and *Boardwalk Empire*. Mafia books, movies, and TV programs are probed for accuracy and authenticity.

If there is a theme to this book, it comes in the form of a question: How did an organization with roots in distant, poverty-stricken Sicily come to dominate the underworld in the United States for so many decades? The answer is found by looking into the mythologized past, major personalities and uncertain future of America's most notorious criminal organization.

Notes

1. Joseph Pistone, *The Way of the Wiseguy* (Philadelphia: Running Press Book Publishers, 2004), 9–18.
2. Joseph Pistone, testimony before the U.S. Senate Permanent Subcommittee on Investigations, 1988.
3. Pistone, *The Way of the Wiseguy*, 194.

Acknowledgments

I wish to thank: ABC-CLIO for asking me to write this title, the FBI for making so many of their files available, the *Chicago Tribune*, the *New York Times*, and *Time* magazine for having such extensive online archives, and Jeanne Enright for being the world's finest research assistant, neighbor, girlfriend, and partner.

Timeline

1880	Giuseppe Esposito becomes first Sicilian Mafiosi to immigrate to the United States, according to the FBI. Esposito settled in New York but was arrested in New Orleans and sent back to Italy.
October 1890	New Orleans police chief David Hennessy is murdered, possibly by Sicilian American gangsters. The press and public blame "the Mafia" (although an organized Mafia had yet to take shape in America). A mob storms a prison and lynches 11 Sicilian-Americans being held in connection to the Hennessy murder.
January 1899	Alphonse Capone is born in Brooklyn.
1899	Ignazio Saietta, aka "Lupo the Wolf," arrives in New York City from Sicily. With his brother-in-law Giuseppe Morello, Lupo becomes a notorious gangster specializing in the pre-Mafia "Black Hand" scam.
March 1909	New York police lieutenant Joseph Petrosino is murdered in Sicily while investigating possible

	Mafia links to Black Hand bandits in the United States.
March 1915	Harrison Narcotics Act, ostensibly a revenue bill, comes into effect. The Act outlaws nonmedical use of drugs such as morphine, cocaine, and opium. The same year, Charles "Lucky" Luciano becomes one of the first (future) Mafiosi to be arrested on drug charges.
January 1920	Alcohol is outlawed in the United States as Prohibition takes hold. Gangsters throughout the U.S. become fantastically wealthy selling illegal liquor.
May 1920	"Big Jim" Colosimo, top Italian American crime boss in Chicago, is murdered. His death was arranged by rising mob star Johnny Torrio.
1921	Al Capone arrives in Chicago, to work with Johnny Torrio. Capone rises quickly to become Torrio's right-hand man.
1925	Italian dictator Benito Mussolini launches a brutal crackdown on the Sicilian Mafia, leading hundreds of mobsters to flee to the United States.
March 1925	After being shot in an ambush, Chicago crime boss Johnny Torrio willingly hands over his underworld kingdom to his protégé, Al Capone.
1927	Salvatore Maranzano arrives in the United States from Sicily. He has been sent by Sicilian Mafia boss Don Vito Cascio Ferro to unite the Italian American underworld.
1928	The brutal "Castellammarese War" breaks out in New York City, as Salvatore Maranzano and Giuseppe Masseria battle for underworld control.
February 1929	Six members of the George "Bugs" Moran gang and one unlucky hanger-on are murdered in the so-called St. Valentine's Day Massacre in Chicago. The massacre was ordered by Al Capone to crush one of his main rivals.

Fall 1929	The New York stock market crashes, triggering the nationwide Depression.
April 1931	Giuseppe Masseria is shot dead in a Brooklyn restaurant. His death was arranged by rising mobster Charles "Lucky" Luciano in order to make Salvatore Maranzano the top gangster in town. Maranzano ends the bloody Castellammarese War.
Spring 1931	Salvatore Maranzano holds a mass meeting in New York City, outlining his vision of a structured, organized Italian American underworld divided into "families" with clearly delineated hierarchies and territories. Maranzano calls the organization "La Cosa Nostra" ("our thing" in Italian) and outlines the importance of "Omerta" (staying silent in the face of arrest). The meeting marks the birth of an organized American Mafia.
1930s	Italian American underworld forces in cities across the United States begin to structure themselves into organized, hierarchical Mafia families, along the lines suggested by Salvatore Maranzano.
September 1931	Salvatore Maranzano is murdered in his Park Avenue office. While Italian American mobsters embrace Maranzano's vision of an organized Mafia, gangsters resent his dictatorial ways. The assassination is organized by Charles "Lucky" Luciano, who now becomes the most powerful Mafia boss in New York City.
October 1931	Chicago mob boss Al Capone is found guilty in federal court of tax evasion, sentenced to 11 years plus fines.
1933	Prohibition is repealed. With alcohol legally available again, Mafiosi turn to other sources of revenue, such as gambling, drugs, labor racketeering, extortion, and prostitution.
May 1936	Charles "Lucky" Luciano, top Mafia boss in the United States, goes on trial on prostitution-related

	charges in New York City. He is found guilty and sentenced to 30–50 years in jail.
1942	U.S. government seeks imprisoned Mafia boss Charles "Lucky" Luciano's help in investigating possible sabotage and espionage by Italian American dock workers during World War II.
January 1946	Charles "Lucky" Luciano is released from prison in return for aiding the U.S. government. He is exiled to Italy one month later.
March 1946	Ground is broken for the Flamingo, an upscale casino in then desolate Las Vegas. The Flamingo is bankrolled by Jewish American mobsters and the Mafia. Erratic gangster Benjamin "Bugsy" Siegel oversees construction.
January 1947	Al Capone dies of a heart attack in Miami, Florida.
1950	U.S. senator Estes Kefauver leads a nationwide investigation into organized crime in which the Mafia features prominently.
October 1957	Gambino family boss Albert Anastasia is murdered in New York City. His death was arranged by rivals Vito Genovese and Carlo Gambino.
1957	The U.S. Senate Select Committee on Improper Activities in the Labor or Management Field launches a probe into labor racketeering. The Mafia again features prominently in the hearings.
November 1957	Police break up a major Mafia gathering in Apalachin, New York.
1958	The FBI releases an internal report called the "Mafia Monograph" that finally acknowledges the existence of a U.S. Mafia.
April 1958	Mafia "soldier" Johnny Stompanato is stabbed to death by his lover's teenage daughter in Beverly Hills, much to the embarrassment of the Los Angeles mob.

Early 1960s	After a shaky start, Las Vegas is flourishing as a casino destination. Several casinos/hotels are backed by Mafia money.
September–October 1963	Mafia turncoat Joseph Valachi spills mob secrets before a Senate subcommittee.
1960s–1970s	As illegal drug use explodes, the Mafia becomes increasingly involved in trafficking operations. Some Mafia leaders remain wary of drug-dealing, however, due to the severe penalties associated with narcotics.
1969	Mario Puzo's epochal book *The Godfather* is published.
1970	Organized Crime Control Act of 1970 establishes a federal witness protection program and the RICO (Racketeer Influenced and Corrupt Organizations) Act, which gives prosecutors a powerful weapon to use against the Mafia and similar groups.
June 1971	Mafia boss turned civil rights crusader Joseph Colombo Sr. is shot and critically wounded at a rally of the Italian-American Civil Rights League in New York City.
1972	Movie version of *The Godfather* becomes a huge hit and garners top Oscars. Some critics say the movie glorifies the Mafia.
Mid-1970s	Cleveland, Ohio, is dubbed "the bombing capital of America" thanks to the frequent use of explosives in a vicious war between the Mafia and Irish American gangsters.
September 1976	FBI agent Joseph Pistone goes undercover as jewel thief "Donnie Brasco" in order to infiltrate the New York Mafia.
March 1980	Long reigning, peace-loving Philadelphia Mafia boss Angelo Bruno is murdered, leading to years of violence-drenched intra-Mafia warfare.

February 1985	All five bosses of the top New York City Mafia families are arrested under the RICO Act. The arrests were orchestrated by U.S. attorney and future mayor Rudolph Giuliani.
December 1985	Gambino family boss Paul Castellano and underboss Thomas Bilotti are murdered in New York City. The assassination was arranged by John Gotti, who takes over as Gambino boss.
September 1986	"The Commission" trial of top New York Mafia leaders begins.
1990	Martin Scorsese's movie *Goodfellas*, which offers a lurid look at low-brow Mafia life, is released. Some film critics say it is the greatest gangster movie ever made.
Fall 1991	Top Gotti henchman Salvatore "Sammy the Bull" Gravano agrees to become a federal witness and testify against his boss.
April 1992	Thanks in large part to surveillance recordings and the testimony of Salvatore Gravano, John Gotti is found guilty of a slew of charges and sentenced to life in prison.
January 1995	New England Mafia leader Frank "Cadillac" Salemme discovers at his trial that two codefendants, Irish American mobsters Stephen Flemmi and James "Whitey" Bulger, are longtime FBI informants.
1999	Widely acclaimed TV show *The Sopranos*, which follows the life of a neurotic New Jersey Mafia boss, goes on the air.
September 2002	Mafia turncoat Salvatore Gravano is sentenced to 20 years for running a major drug ring with friends and family members.
April 2003	Appearing in federal court in Brooklyn, Genovese family boss Vincent "the Chin" Gigante finally concedes he has been playacting at being insane for years to evade punishment.

	Gigante pleads out to various charges and dies in prison two years later.
February 2004	New York State Gambino family members are arrested for phone "cramming" (placing unauthorized charges on phone bills), a new Mafia moneymaker.
2004	*The Changing Face of Organized Crime in New Jersey*, a report that examines Mafia activity in the eastern United States, is published. The report suggests the Mafia's glory days are long gone.
June 2007	Start of the "Family Secrets" trial in Chicago of the leadership of "The Outfit" (Chicago's homegrown version of the Mafia).
January 2011	Over 90 members and associates of seven Mafia families in New York, New Jersey, and New England are arrested in what Attorney General Eric Holder calls the "largest single day operation against La Cosa Nostra" in U.S. history.
May 2012	Alleged members of the Genovese family in New York State and New Jersey arrested for involvement in an online sports betting ring conducted from websites in Costa Rica. Police see the arrests as a sign that the Mafia has gone high-tech.
November 2012	Voters in Colorado and Washington State approve referendums legalizing recreational marijuana use and sale, possibly signaling the beginning of the end of the so-called War on Drugs.

CHAPTER ONE

History of the Mafia

The origins of the Mafia, in sunny Sicily, are shrouded in legend and myth. A strategically placed island in the Mediterranean, Sicily has been repeatedly conquered by foreigners. At different times in its history, Sicily was ruled by Greeks, Arabs, Romans, Normans, Byzantines, Austrians, the French, and the Spanish. Most of these groups ruled badly and treated the island's peasantry like slaves, fit only for generating wealth for the ruling class. Making things even more inhospitable was the island's geography. Western Sicily in particular is mountainous, with many isolated villages.

Not surprisingly, the Sicilian population began to develop certain cultural traits to endure foreign occupation. Sicilians learned to distrust all forms of government and anyone in authority. The rule of law meant nothing in Sicily; citizens were encouraged to take personal revenge for crimes against kin and clan, rather than seek justice in court. This of course, led to a never-ending series of blood feuds (vendettas). Helping authorities in any way was taboo. It was considered far better to remain silent than to assist the police, even if someone in your family had been murdered.

There is no consensus on where the actual name "Mafia" came from. "Scholars disagree on whether the term came from 'maehfil'

A street peddler hawks his wares in Montelepre, Sicily, May 30, 1949, where police are concentrating a search for Salvatore Giuliano, an outlaw blamed for scores of robberies and the killing of 70 policemen. The small town is nestled among the mountains of western Sicily and is reportedly the gang's stronghold. A strict curfew was clamped on the town and all stores were closed for several days in an effort to drive Giuliano into the open. (Associated Press/Wide World Photo)

meaning union in the language of the 9th Century Arab conquerors of Sicily or from the Tuscan word 'maffia' signifying poverty or misery," stated an October 15, 1984, article in *Time* magazine.

One legend suggests that in 1282, Sicilians rebelled against French rule. As their battle cry, these rebels used the slogan, "Morte all Francia Itala anela" ("Death to the French is Italy's cry"). The letters to this slogan spell out "Mafia."[1]

Sicily was freed from foreign oppression in 1860, with the unification of Italy. The central Italian government was weak, however, and generally ignored the poor south, including Sicily. Conditions were perfect for the rise of a violent underworld. Accounts vary as to how exactly this underworld came to be.

In one version, organized bands of armed men (who were primarily related by blood) were formed in the nineteenth century to fight off various oppressors. While these groups were initially founded for self-defense, they quickly resorted to blatant thuggery.

These armed bands practiced something of a protection racket. They demanded money from landowners and businessmen to guard their properties and ensure their personal safety while in Sicily. They also started extorting merchants, insisting on a share of their profits. These criminal organizations became something of a quasi-government in parts of Sicily, doling out raw justice and controlling the economic lives of the peasantry. Such brigands were lumped under the generic term "Mafia."

A different story points to absentee landlords, particularly in isolated western Sicily. These absentee landlords would typically let an overseer actually run their property. The overseer would collect rents from the peasantry, keep some for himself, and forward the rest to the absentee landlords. The overseers typically relied on a clutch of toughs with guns to enforce their rules and guard the landlord's property. In addition to guarding rich people's property, these toughs began to terrorize the population. In this manner, the Mafia was born.

In Italy, the Sicilian Mafia was merely one of several organized crime groups. Other groups included the Camorra or Neapolitan Mafia, based in Naples, which first emerged in the mid-1800s as a prison gang. The 'Ndrangheta, or Calabrian Mafia, was also formed around the same time in Calabria. The fourth major organization was the Sacra Corona Unita or United Sacred Crown, based in the Puglia region. Generally, all these groups shared a proclivity toward violence, avarice, and thuggish behavior.

Mafia clans in Sicily were not united. There was no single, monolithic "Mafia" organization with a central command and supreme leader. Various Mafia factions fought each other as much as the police or carabinieri (paramilitary peace officers). Needless to say, when the opportunity to emigrate arrived, millions of people took advantage of it.

The vast majority of Sicilian immigrants to the United States wanted nothing more than to work, improve their living conditions, and raise their families in peace. Unfortunately, a small minority of Sicilian newcomers had less peaceful ambitions in mind.

The Battle of New Orleans

According to the FBI, Giuseppe Esposito "was the first known Sicilian Mafia member to immigrate to the United States." Esposito journeyed to New York City in 1880 "after murdering the chancellor and a vice-chancellor of a Sicilian province and 11 wealthy landowners," states the FBI.[2] He was arrested one year later in New Orleans and shipped back to Italy. Other accounts mention nothing about wealthy land-lords and murder, but merely state that Esposito was eager to escape one of the periodic crackdowns on the Mafia in his homeland.

Esposito first journeyed to New York City and then went to New Orleans, which had a burgeoning Sicilian American population. The immigrants liked the warm climate and the city's Catholic ambience. Esposito was captured in 1881 then extradited back to Sicily.

A decade after Esposito's visit, New Orleans was the site of what the FBI called "the first major Mafia incident in this country." On October 15, 1890, New Orleans police chief David Hennessy was shot, execution-style. Before he died, Hennessy blamed "the dagoes" for his shooting, "dago" being a derogatory name for anyone hailing from a Mediterranean nation. Police found four "luparas" (double-barreled, sawed-off shotguns with retractable stocks) near the scene of the crime. Such weapons were extremely common in Sicily.[3]

At the time, two prominent Sicilian American factions in New Orleans—one led by Charlie Matranga, the other by Joe Provenzano—were feuding over who would win the right to unload fruit boats at the docks. Hennessy (who was rumored to favor the Provenzano side) had been investigating this low-intensity conflict. In the aftermath of Chief Hennessy's death, scores of Sicilians were arrested. A total of 19 men (from the Matranga faction) were indicted for murder, but only nine ended up going on trial.

When the case came to court, six of the defendants were acquitted outright. As for the other three, the jury said it couldn't make up its mind. In a city already tense with racial strife and rumors about a mysterious group called "the Mafia," the verdict triggered an explosive reaction. A mob of several thousand people stormed the prison where the six acquitted defendants (who were still in jail, pending the outcome of some other minor matters) plus the other 13 men from the original indictment were being held. Prison staff let the Sicilians out of their cells and told them to hide. The mob surged inside the prison and grabbed as many of the Sicilians as they could find. Two were hung and nine shot dead. The other eight men managed to get away. It was one of the worst mass lynchings in American history.

It's unclear whether any of the 19 men indicted for killing the chief were actually connected to the Mafia (or had anything to do with Hennessy's murder for that matter). No matter; the assassination of Chief Hennessy and subsequent lynching of his accused killers marked the first time Americans faced the specter of Mafia violence on home soil.

Lupo the Wolf, and the Black Hand

Born in 1877 in Sicily, Ignazio Saietta acquired the nickname "Lupo the Wolf" for his criminal proclivities in his homeland. He fled Sicily in 1899 after killing a man and settled in New York City. There, he connected with his brother-in-law, Giuseppe Morello, who had established himself as a successful crime boss in East Harlem. Morello worked with his brothers Tony and Vincent and a half-brother named Ciro.

Lupo and Morello combined forces to head up an extremely feared criminal group. In general, Morello worked in the background while Lupo handled street action. Media accounts of the day depicted Morello as the head of the Mafia in the United States, with Lupo as one of his trusted officers.

Lupo specialized in the primitive "Black Hand" scam. This racket was simple; an anonymous note would arrive at the home of an Italian emigrant threatening all manner of torture and violence unless a large fee was paid. The extortionist sending the letter would typically "sign" it by dipping their hand in black ink and pressing their palm against the paper. This would leave the impression of a black hand, which is how the scam got its name.

There was no central Black Hand "organization." The racket was practiced by con artists in any city with a large Italian population. Many new Italian immigrants were poorly educated, were deeply superstitious, and had an inbred mistrust of police (who tended to be very corrupt in their homeland). Italians were unlikely to report Black Hand intimidation to authorities.

In many respects, the Black Hand was an embryonic Mafia—a violent crime ring run by Italian Americans. The difference was, Black Handers preyed upon their countrymen only in specific neighborhoods, while the American Mafia would be national in scope and have far greater impact.

A snappy dresser and something of a dandy, Lupo liked to ride around New York's Little Italy in a horse-drawn carriage. A cold-blooded thug at heart, Lupo was a feared presence on the street. He still answered to his brother-in-law Morello, however, who was on his way to becoming the top Sicilian mobster in New York.

Lupo and the men who worked for him ran a "Murder Stable" in Italian Harlem. This was a former horse stable where anyone who crossed Lupo was tortured and murdered. Some sources estimate Lupo killed 60 people in his career, mostly rival gangsters and people who balked at paying Black Hand tribute. When he wasn't victimizing his countrymen, Lupo was employed as a wholesale grocer.

In April 1903, Lupo and Morello were arrested as part of a wide sweep of Italian gangsters following an infamous "barrel murder." The mutilated corpse of a man named Benditto Madonia had been found stuffed in a barrel. It was known that Madonia was trying to collect money owed him by Morello when he disappeared.

Police ended up focusing their investigation on one member of the Lupo/Morello gang. This sole suspect was put on trial, but no one would testify against him, so he was set free. While they weren't put on trial themselves, it was strongly suspected that Lupo and Morello were involved in Madonia's murder.

A few brave souls fought back against Lupo the Wolf. A *New York Times* article from November 23, 1909, examined a court case in which Lupo (identified as "Ignazio Lupo") was "charged with extorting $4,000 from Salvatore Manzella ... under threats of death." Manzella failed to appear in court and Lupo was discharged, only to be immediately hit with a federal warrant for other crimes.

Those other crimes included counterfeiting. Lupo and Morello set up a counterfeiting operation in which they supplied criminal contacts in other cities with fake greenbacks. Lupo, Morello, and a handful of others were arrested in 1910 by the Secret Service (the branch of the U.S. Treasury Department responsible for protecting politicians and the nation's currency). Lupo was found guilty and, on February 19, 1910, sentenced to 30 years in federal prison in Atlanta. Morello got 25 years.

The trial garnered huge coverage, much of it wildly inaccurate. A *New York Times* article from April 3, 1910, for example, described the Lupo/Morello gang as "the most dangerous band of foreign criminals ever known in this country." Other stories in the *Times* credited Morello with being the head of the American Mafia and Lupo "the reputed treasurer of Mafia society." Ironically, these comments occurred two decades before a structured, organized American Mafia even existed. Such reportage is an example of the media's indiscriminate use of the word "mafia" at the time. For good measure, the *Times* also called Lupo "proud and haughty."

Lupo served 10 years and was paroled in 1920. Upon release, Lupo visited Italy, then went into the wholesale fruit and baked goods business with his son.

By this point, the Black Hand scam had pretty much run its course. The Italian community had become more sophisticated and less likely to fall for Black Hand threats. With the advent of Prohibition, gangsters found a much more lucrative source of income than simple extortion.

On top of his grocery business, Lupo ran a few low-key rackets, such as illegal lotteries, after getting out of prison. This proved to be a mistake. In 1936, New York State governor Herbert Lehman asked President Franklin Roosevelt to have Lupo rearrested for racketeering. This was done, and Lupo was once again put behind bars in Atlanta's federal penitentiary. When he was released for a second time, he was a powerless figure who soon died in obscurity.

A thug at heart, Lupo wasn't much of an organizer and couldn't put together the kind of vast, multilevel underworld organization that later criminals such as Al Capone or Charles "Lucky" Luciano established.

Mussolini's Fascist Fury Sparks a Mafia Exodus

In the mid-1920s, a dictator in Italy decided to rid his nation of the Mafia. In doing so, he greatly empowered what was to become the American Mafia.

The dictator was Benito Mussolini, and his National Fascist Party seized power in Italy in the early 1920s. The Fascists opposed Communism and "class war," preaching instead a doctrine that stressed unity, nationhood, and class cooperation. The Fascists supported dictatorship over democracy and brute force over the rule of law. Mussolini and his Fascists believed in Social Darwinism and brooked no rivals.

According to legend, Mussolini decided to pay a visit to Sicily in 1924. The dictator toured a town called Piana dei Greci, where the mayor admonished him for having so many bodyguards. The Mafia-connected mayor assured Mussolini that no harm would come to him; he was under the mayor's personal protection. The implication was the Mafia-linked mayor had more power in the region than the tyrant who ran the country. Another version of the tale suggests that the mayor ordered everyone in town, except village idiots, drunks, and beggars, to stay indoors and ignore Mussolini's arrival.

In any case, Mussolini was infuriated and ordered Cesare Mori, prefect of Palermo, to root out the Mafia by any means necessary. Some historians state that Mussolini's hatred was more political than personal; condescending mayors aside, Mussolini viewed the entrenched Mafia as a threat to his own power.

Mori was a particularly accomplished henchman who set about his task with great energy. He relied on a huge army of police and para-military security forces and earned himself the nickname "The Iron Prefect."

Mori's campaign featured the widespread use of torture, preventive detention, mass arrests, violence, and public humiliation (arrested Mafiosi were displayed in cages during their trials). The wives and family members of Mafiosi were kidnapped and held hostage until the gangsters Mori pursued gave themselves up. Farm animals belonging to members of the Mafia were seized, slaughtered, and then sold at markdown prices.

The crackdown was highly successful, largely because the Fascists, like their Mafiosi opponents, didn't hesitate to break the law to achieve their goals. In the end, over 1,000 Mafia members were convicted, for terms ranging from a few years to life behind bars.

The downside to this brutal crackdown was that an estimated 500–1,000 Mafiosi left Sicily for the more welcoming climes of America. Fleeing Mafiosi typically entered America in one of two ways: via Marseilles, where they would ship out to Canada or New York, or via Tunis, then Cuba, and then Miami or other southern cities.

Mussolini's crackdown was a windfall for American underworld leaders. Hundreds of mobsters joined their ranks, all at the perfect time. With Prohibition still the law of the land, gang bosses required larger and larger armies to control the transportation, manufacture, and sale of illegal alcohol.

One Mafiosi who made the trek to America prior to the war had a vision and a plan. His name was Salvatore Maranzano, and initially he was an emissary for Sicilian Mafia boss Don Vito Cascio Ferro. Ferro had a dream of uniting the Italian American underworld and putting himself in command. By the late 1920s, however, Ferro found himself languishing in a Fascist prison cell. His emissary Maranzano decided to co-opt his boss's plan for himself. Maranzano established himself in New York City and forged alliances with leading gangsters. He would go on to become the father of the modern American Mafia.

Salvatore Maranzano, the Castellammarese War, and the Founding of the American Mafia

Salvatore Maranzano established the internal structure of the American Mafia in the early 1930s but was too tyrannical to enjoy the benefits of his creation. In addition to creating the template for organized crime, Maranzano's life serves as a cautionary tale for wannabe mobsters on how not to behave.

Equal parts visionary and megalomaniac, Maranzano was born in 1868 in Castellammare del Golfo, Sicily, a part of the world that has birthed an unusually large number of crime bosses. It is said Maranzano studied in a seminary to become a priest or even attended college. He never served as a man of the cloth, however, preferring to plunge into Sicily's thriving criminal culture.

Maranzano came to America in 1927 at the behest of Sicilian mob boss Don Vito Cascio Ferro. Ferro had dreams of organizing the U.S. underworld and putting it under his command. Once established in New York, Maranzano became more interested in bootlegging than empire-building for a distant boss. He allied himself with rising gangsters such as Joseph Bonanno, Joseph Profaci, and Stefano Magaddino, all of whom hailed from Maranzano's hometown. Ferro was imprisoned during Mussolini's crackdown, which gave Maranzano an excuse to sever ties. Maranzano was quick to profit from his mentor's misery. In addition to bootlegging, he got involved in the people trafficking business—smuggling his Mafia comrades into the United States.

There are opposing views on Maranzano's personality and character. A recent Mafia history claimed that Maranzano's underlings were awed by his presence: "The first thing they noticed about Maranzano was his physical appearance. He was tall for a Sicilian and powerfully built giving the impression that he could snap a man's neck with his fingers. But his greatest asset was his voice. According to Bonanno, it was clear and pleasant with an 'echo like' quality. A former seminarian who spoke five languages and could quote the Latin poets, he held audiences in rapt attention," stated this account.[4] It was also said Maranzano was an amateur historian who was fascinated by the history of Imperial Rome.

Other descriptions are considerably less flattering. They describe a man who could barely speak a word of English, much less master five languages. Turncoat Mafia soldier Joseph Valachi certainly wasn't awed by Maranzano. "He looked just like a banker. You'd never guess in a million years that he was a racketeer," wrote Valachi.[5]

If there are discrepancies about his character, no one disputes that Maranzano had nerve. Not only did he spurn the instructions of his mentor, he blatantly encroached on the territory of fellow Sicilian gangster Giuseppe "Joe the Boss" Masseria in New York City.

Masseria was a powerful mobster who was not pleased by Maranzano's cheek. Maranzano remained defiant, in spite of Masseria's growing wrath. His men began hijacking trucks, containing illicit liquor belonging to the Boss, and taking over speakeasies he controlled.

Not surprisingly, the rivalry between the two hot-headed Sicilian American gangsters soon erupted into outright warfare. The struggle was dubbed "the Castellammarese War" in honor of the town where most of the men involved came from.

At the outset of the war, in 1928, it appeared that Masseria was bound to win. He had more gunmen and clout, but he was hobbled by an unlikable personality. In the eyes of the Young Turks in Masseria's organization, the Boss was a "Moustache Pete"—a contemptuous term for an old-fashioned, Old World–style underworld leader. Moustache Pete's were clannish and closed-minded. They refused to do business with non-Sicilians, were dismissive of new ideas, and were more concerned with preserving "honor" than with making money.

As the Castellammarese War ground on, younger members of Masseria's gang quickly grew disenchanted. The younger soldiers didn't see any point in pursuing a personal, bloody vendetta for the benefit of "the Boss." They were primarily interested in getting rich, not getting even.

Charles "Lucky" Luciano—one of Masseria's youngest, most able lieutenants—was particularly annoyed. Luciano was chums with Meyer Lansky, a Jewish criminal mastermind. Luciano and his peers had no problems doing business with Jews or Irish gangsters—something Masseria frowned upon. They resented Masseria's narrow worldview and obsessive blood-lust. Luciano contacted Maranzano and struck a deal. Luciano would arrange for his boss to be killed. In exchange, Maranzano would end the costly Castellammarese War.

On April 15, 1931, Masseria was murdered in a restaurant in the Coney Island section of Brooklyn. Luciano (who was conveniently in the washroom when a hit team burst into the eatery and shot his boss) told investigators he had no idea why anyone would want to kill Masseria.

Maranzano quickly took charge of Masseria's troops following the death of Joe the Boss. True to his word, Maranzano ended the Castellammarese War. The strife had resulted in an estimated 50 deaths, though an exact total would be difficult to calculate.

Maranzano's vastly expanded gang was unhappy to discover their new leader shared many of the same traits as the despised Masseria.

They perceived Maranzano as arrogant and pretentious. If it is true that he barely spoke English, Maranzano would have faced a massive communications gap with the mobsters under his command. Like Masseria, Maranzano was clannish, set in his ways, and more interested in amassing personal power than in making his followers rich.

For all his faults, Maranzano was a man with big ideas. He borrowed Ferro's grandiose vision, of a united underworld, and put a historical twist on the notion. Maranzano's concept was to organize the New York mob like a military unit, with clear chains of command. The goal was to bring order to the inherently chaotic world of crime.

Maranzano divided the main gangs in New York City into five "families." Each family would have a boss and an underboss. He appointed five of his closest allies—Luciano, Bonanno, Profaci, Vincent Mangano, and Thomas Gagliano—to lead these families.

The bosses would be in charge of a group of capos or caporegimes (i.e., lieutenants). Each capo would command a unit of roughly 10 "soldiers" (gunmen and thugs). The soldiers in turn could rely on the help of "associates"—men who carried out the mob's bidding but weren't formally part of the family. Associates could be Italian, Irish, Jewish, or any other nationality. They could not rise any higher in the family's ranks, however, unless they could prove pure Italian lineage.

This orderly structure was designed to provide maximum protection for the leaders at the top. Family bosses would deal only with capos and underbosses. They would have no personal relationship with the men who did the family's dirty work. Any felonious activity within the family would be performed by disposable soldiers and associates.

Maranzano outlined his vision at a mass meeting of several hundred mobsters held two weeks after Masseria's death. The mobsters met in a banquet hall in upstate New York (Valachi said it was a rented hall in the Bronx and estimated that 400–500 gangsters were in attendance).

In his remarks, Maranzano defended Masseria's assassination on the grounds that Joe the Boss was out of control and killing people for no good reason. It was a hypocritical stance, but no one challenged Maranzano on it. During his speech, Maranzano used the expression "Cosa Nostra" ("our thing" in Italian) to refer to the criminal organization he envisioned. He avoided using the word "Mafia" (a loaded term that, for Maranzano, referred specifically to the Sicilian underworld).

Semantics aside, this meeting marked the birth of a structured, organized American Mafia.

Maranzano laid down several operating principles. Talking about Cosa Nostra to outsiders was forbidden, punishable by death. Random killings of family members were out (all major hits were supposed to be cleared by the bosses first) as was having sex with another member's wife. Adultery among the ranks of Cosa Nostra would be a capital offense.

In the organized family structure he put together, Maranzano envisioned himself as capo di tutti capi—Boss of the Bosses. It was the same role that Ferro had wanted for himself. Like Caesar, Maranzano wanted to rule without any checks or balances.

While gangsters readily agreed to Maranzano's organizational model, they resented his position at the apex of power. It didn't help that Maranzano bossed around his subordinates like serfs and refused to countenance any views but his own.

Maranzano suspected that his subordinates were unhappy with his tyrannical leadership and were plotting against him. He hired notorious hit-man Vincent "Mad Dog" Coll to eliminate his rebellious underlings. A former employee of Jewish gangster Dutch Schultz, Coll had acquired his nickname after callously firing into a crowd of children playing on the street in order to shoot a rival gangster. Maranzano wanted Coll to murder Luciano and Vito Genovese. He later expanded his death list to include Schultz, Capone, Frank Costello, Willie Moretti, and Joe Adonis, among others.

Before Coll could do any killing, however, Luciano caught wind of Maranzano's plans and hatched a plot of his own. On September 10, 1931, in mid-afternoon, four men pretending to be U.S. Treasury agents burst into Maranzano's headquarters, which was located on the ninth floor of the Eagle Building on Park Avenue. A sign outside the offices said "Real Estate" to conceal the real nature of the transactions that went on inside.

The hit team disarmed bodyguards on the scene. Two of them stood watch over the bodyguards while the other pair burst into an inner office. Inside the inner office, they found Maranzano sitting behind a desk. The two assassins shot and stabbed the gang leader to death. Then, all four members of the death squad raced out of the building. Legend has it that the foursome ran into Mad Dog Coll, who was arriving for a meeting. The four men yelled a warning that a police raid was taking place, and Coll took off.

Maranzano had served as "Boss of Bosses" for only four months. After his death, Luciano emerged as top New York Cosa Nostra leader. Luciano wisely refused to take on the capo di tutti capi position. He retained the basic structure of the organization Maranzano had put into place, but made the top level more egalitarian. Luciano thought the Mafia should be run as a corporation, with a board of directors setting policy rather than one dictatorial boss.

While incompetent as a leader, Maranzano was still an enormous influence on organized crime. His Five Families structure (now enlarged to include a sixth family, based in New Jersey) remains intact today. Since Maranzano's time, an organized, structured Mafia has expanded far beyond New York, taking up root in cities across the country. The hierarchical structure Maranzano set up for each Mafia family (boss, underboss, caporegime, soldiers) also remains in place—testament to the strength of an idea from a flawed but visionary mobster.

Notes

1. Thomas Reppetto, *American Mafia: A History of Its Rise to Power* (New York: Henry Holt and Company, 2004), 4.
2. Federal Bureau of Investigation, "Italian Organized Crime," http:/www.fbi.gov/about-us/investigate/organizedcrime/italian_mafia.
3. Reppetto, *American Mafia*, 2.
4. Reppetto, *American Mafia*, 135.
5. Peter Maas, *The Valachi Papers* (New York: HarperCollins, 1968), 74.

| # Rackets

Prohibition

If one single factor spawned the emergence of an organized American Mafia, national in scope and international in reach, it was Prohibition—the U.S. government's ill-fated attempt to legislate sobriety.

"Mafia operations in the United States were still comparatively limited at the time the 18th Amendment to the Constitution became effective in 1920. The advent of Prohibition brought the Mafia to fruition. The wealth and influence achieved by Mafiosi before 1920 were insignificant compared to what they had achieved by the end of Prohibition. To Mafiosi, the manufacture and sale of illegal liquor was the ring on which they cut their teeth," reads the *Mafia Monograph*, a report put together by the FBI in 1958.

Prohibition lasted from 1920 to 1933 and was intended to stamp out alcohol by force of law. It was the end result of decades of lobbying by church groups, feminists, progressives, business owners, and bigots. These forces were responding to the United States' alcohol-saturated culture. They blamed liquor for a slew of social problems, including violent crime, juvenile delinquency, poverty, mental illness, and spousal and child abuse.

New York City deputy police commissioner watches agents pour liquor into the sewer following a raid during the height of Prohibition, ca. 1921. (Library of Congress)

On December 18, 1917, the House of Representatives took up the Eighteenth Amendment to the U.S. Constitution, which banned the manufacture and sale of beer, wine, liquor, and other spirits. The amendment was approved then passed to the states for ratification. If three-quarters of the states ratified the amendment, it would become law.

Meanwhile, Congress was also debating a piece of legislation called the Volstead Act, which spelled out the details covered by the Eighteenth Amendment. Under the Volstead Act, it would become a crime to manufacture, sell, barter, transport, import, export, deliver, furnish, or possess intoxicating liquors. Introduced on May 27, 1919, the Volstead Act was passed by Congress and vetoed by President Woodrow Wilson, who said it was unconstitutional. Congress easily overrode the president's veto.

By July 16, 1919, some 36 states had ratified the Eighteenth Amendment, making it part of the Constitution. Prohibition came into effect at midnight, on January 16, 1920. "Dry" forces were overjoyed. Popular preacher Billy Sunday, addressing a rally in Norfolk, Virginia, famously observed, "The reign of tears is over. The slums will soon only be a memory. We will turn our prisons into factories and our jails into storehouses and corncribs. Men will walk upright now; women will smile and children will laugh. Hell will be forever for rent."[1]

Prohibitionists naively believed that by passing a law, they would change everyone's behavior. Congress set up a Prohibition Unit (later called the Prohibition Bureau) to enforce the Eighteenth Amendment, but set aside only $3 million for enforcement. The Prohibition Unit had only 1,500 officers, for the entire United States. Agents were poorly paid ($2,300 a year, a low salary even for the era), which encouraged them to take bribes.

These agents had their hands full: in 1921, authorities seized over 95,000 illicit distilleries, stills, and fermentation facilities. This rose to 170,000 in 1925 then to over 280,000 in 1930. Some 35,000 people were arrested in connection with these seizures in 1921, rising to 62,000 in 1925 and 75,000 in 1928. Clearly, the public still wanted to drink, even though liquor was illegal.

"Bootlegging" (i.e., trafficking alcohol) became extremely common. It's unclear where the term came from, although some sources suggest it referred to criminals who hid supplies of illicit spirits in their boots. Alcohol was smuggled into the United States from Canada (where it was still legal to manufacture), the Bahamas (where many distillers set up shop), and Europe.

Speakeasies (illegal bars) opened up in major cities almost immediately. By the early 1920s, there were 5,000 speakeasies in New York City alone. By 1927, there would be over 30,000. What is remarkable is that this was double the number of bars, restaurants, and saloons that sold liquor legally *before* Prohibition.

Prohibition served as a demarcation line for organized crime. In Chicago, rising Italian American mobster Johnny Torrio was frustrated by the reluctance of his boss, "Big Jim" Colosimo, to jump into the bootlegging racket. Torrio correctly perceived that Prohibition offered incredible opportunities for gangsters. Colosimo wasn't interested, however, so Torrio had him murdered on May 11, 1920. A good judge of criminal talent, Torrio brought his protégé, Al Capone from New York, to help him run rackets in Chicago. The pair soon controlled one of the largest gangs in the country.

The underworld that furnished illegal alcohol had a multicultural cast. Jewish gangsters, from Meyer Lansky and Benjamin Siegel to Dutch Schultz and Arnold Rothstein, were prominent, as were Irish American mobsters such as Dion O'Banion, the O'Donnell brothers, and Jack "Legs" Diamond.

The emerging Italian American underworld proved more enduring then either of these ethnic-based gangs, however. Prohibition served as a training ground for an entire generation of Mafia leaders, including Torrio, Al Capone, the Genna Brothers, Frank Costello, and Charles "Lucky" Luciano.

Thanks to a lax administration and impressive criminal talent pool, Chicago became the epicenter of organized crime activity. "At the start of Prohibition in Chicago, thousands of residents of the Italian community were organized into a veritable army of alcohol makers. It has been claimed that at one time 80 percent of the families in the Italian colony of that city were involved in the production of alcohol by home stills. The easy money to be realized from bootlegging appealed to these people and was a major cause of conflict between the many gangs of Italians and other nationalities," reads the *Mafia Monograph*.

While Prohibition had been sold in part as a public health measure, people began dying and becoming sick in huge numbers from tainted liquor. There were no health warnings or quality controls on bootleg alcohol. Consumers took a chance every time they sampled illicit spirits. Cocktails—that is, drinks containing alcohol and a mix of other beverages and flavors—became hugely popular during Prohibition to mask the taste of inferior liquor.

Far from reducing crime, Prohibition spawned law-breaking the likes of which the United States had never seen before. Gangs battled it out with rapid-fire machine guns and hand grenades. On February 14, 1929, gunmen acting for Capone murdered seven men connected to the rival "Bugs" Moran gang, in a cold garage in Chicago. The so-called St. Valentine's Day Massacre made headlines around the country. Chicago wasn't alone in terms of lawlessness. By the early 1920s, New York City had basically given up trying to enforce federal Prohibition laws.

Politicians began coming out against Prohibition. Al Smith, governor of New York, ran for president in 1928, against Prohibition. He lost, but one year later, the fiery Fiorello La Guardia became mayor of New York. As a congressman and then mayor, LaGuardia was extremely opposed to Prohibition. Lobby groups started to coalesce against the Eighteenth Amendment. The criminal underworld was one of very few groups that wanted to maintain Prohibition. As long as alcohol was illegal, gangsters could charge exorbitant prices for inferior liquor.

In the fall of 1929, the New York Stock Exchange crashed, which led to economic unraveling known as the Great Depression, which further turned people off Prohibition. It seemed pointless to spend money chasing down bootleggers when millions of people were out of work. Desperate farmers yearned for the profits they could make growing hops, wheat, and barley once again. Critics also pointed out that governments were losing a big source of tax revenue by keeping liquor illegal while enriching bootleggers.

In the presidential election of 1932, Democratic Party candidate Franklin Roosevelt promised to repeal Prohibition. Once elected, Roosevelt modified the Volstead Act to allow for 3.2 percent alcohol beer (up from 0.5 percent). Congress easily passed this measure into law, which relegalized "real beer."

A measure to repeal the Eighteenth Amendment was introduced in the Senate on February 14, 1933. After winning approval in the Senate and House of Representatives, the amendment was passed to the states for ratification. In late 1933, Utah became the 36th state to ratify the Twenty-first Amendment (which gutted the Eighteenth Amendment). On December 5, 1933, it became legal once again to purchase hard liquor under federal law. People no longer had to buy dangerous, overpriced alcohol from gangsters. They could purchase quality-controlled spirits at reasonable prices from respectable outlets.

Reducing crime had been a key motivating factor for temperance leaders who promoted Prohibition. On this count, Prohibition was a complete failure.

Violent crime skyrocketed during Prohibition. In 1900, the murder rate in the United States was under 2 per 100,000 people. By the early 1930s, this had reached nearly 10 per 100,000 people. When Prohibition was repealed, the murder rate dropped sharply, to roughly

5 per 100,000 by the mid-1930s. The homicide rate didn't rise to Prohibition-era levels again until the 1970s.

Enforcement of Prohibition was abysmal. The Prohibition Bureau was riddled with corruption and incompetence. At most, Prohibition agents were never able to stop more than 5 percent of illicit alcohol coming into the United States.

Prohibition generated a general disrespect for law and order. Ordinary citizens began to think nothing of flouting the law by drinking at speakeasies or buying liquor from criminals. Citizens began to lose faith in policemen, judges, politicians, and other forces of authority who were perceived as being in the pay of mobsters.

The worst effect of Prohibition, however, was that it turned petty thugs into millionaires. If Prohibition hadn't happened, chances are that Capone, Torrio, Luciano, Costello, and other budding Mafiosi would have remained small-time players, running local neighborhood scams. Instead, bootlegging made minor mobsters rich beyond their wildest dreams. Bloated with wealth from illegal liquor, a structured, organized American Mafia took root in the early 1930s. This home-grown Mafia was organized, disciplined, and far more powerful than "the Black Hand" or other Italian American organized crime groups that preceded it.

"Prohibition brought Mafia operations out of the Italian community and into the community at large in order to satisfy the desire of many citizens to quench their thirst. The 18th Amendment endowed the Mafia with fabulous funds and took it from the isolated Italian quarters and bestowed it on the cities as a whole," reads the *Mafia Monograph*.

This powerful underworld continued to thrive even after Prohibition was repealed. While unhappy about losing bootlegging revenue, the post-Prohibition Mafia found new sources of income in prostitution, drugs, labor racketeering, extortion, and illegal gambling.

Drugs

There is a long-standing myth that the American Mafia won't sell illegal drugs. This myth is based on a partial truth—some Mafia bosses have vehemently opposed drug trafficking—but it doesn't tell the whole story. Many Mafiosi have no problem selling heroin, cocaine, marijuana, and methamphetamine. There is also a huge discrepancy between what Mafia members say and do.

Turncoat Joseph Valachi epitomized the American Mafia's complex relationship with illicit drugs. In testimony before the U.S. Senate Permanent Subcommittee on Investigations in the fall of 1963, the Mafia soldier turned government witness trotted out the usual party line about drugs. "No narcotics. You are in serious trouble if you were arrested for narcotics. After [Mafia boss Albert] Anastasia died in 1957, all families were notified—no narcotics," said Valachi.[2]

Valachi admitted, however, that many Mafiosi simply ignored this stricture, dazzled by the lure of enormous profits. Valachi himself was arrested numerous times on drug charges. At the time Valachi spoke to the subcommittee, the Lucchese family of New York City was involved in drug trafficking, as was the Magaddino family, based near Buffalo.

Harsh penalties are the main reason why the American Mafia pays occasional lip service to the notion of "no drugs." When faced with decades of prison time on drug charges, Mafia minions might be tempted to talk to police, goes the reasoning. To prevent such an unthinkable violation of "Omerta" (the Mafia code of silence), family bosses have often counseled against drug dealing.

Initially, organized crime had little to do with drug trafficking. This was largely because, in the decades after the Civil War, opiates, cocaine, marijuana, and other drugs were legally available and cheaply priced across the United States.

The Consumers Union Report on Licit and Illicit Drugs, published in 1972, has described nineteenth-century America as "a dope fiend's paradise." Drugs could be purchased legally from doctors, at drugstores (over the counter, without a prescription), in grocery and general stores, and even by mail. Hard drugs could also be found in "patent medicines"—compounds of dubious medical merit, sold as cure-alls for vague ailments.

The move to ban drugs began to pick up steam in the early 1900s out of concerns about health and blatant racism. Antidrug groups and sensationalist reporters associated drug use with visible minorities. Newspaper headlines told the story: "Drug Crazed Negroes Start a Reign of Terror and Defy Whole Mississippi Town" read a

September 29, 1913, piece in *the New York Times*. Another story, from February 8, 1914, was tagged, "Negro Cocaine 'Fiends' Are a New Southern Menace." An April 30, 1905, *New York Times* article, with the headline "Cocaine Habit's Horrors" noted that, "In the south, some of the worst crimes committed by the negroes result from the use of cocaine."

Racism was not limited to African Americans. A March 15, 1906, article in *the New York Times* headlined, "Patent Medicine Bill to Curb Drug Users" stated that "of the 250 white girls, some no more than 14 years old, now living in Chinatown, New York, 60 percent of them were cocaine and opium fiends."

Cocaine was associated with African Americans, opium with Asians, and marijuana with Mexicans. All three groups were said to go berserk when on these drugs. Minorities were also accused of using drugs to seduce unwitting white girls.

States began restricting the legal availability of drugs, followed by the federal government. On December 17, 1914, partly to fulfill international treaty obligations, Congress approved the Harrison Narcotics Act. The act came into force March 1, 1915. Technically, the Harrison Act was a tax and licensing bill that merely called for some paperwork on the part of people who sold or prescribed opiates or cocaine.

In reality, the federal government used the act as a bludgeon to end the easy availability of narcotics. From this point forward, state and federal penalties on illicit drugs would become increasingly harsh. In time, states such as Texas would impose life sentences for simple marijuana possession. While federal, state, and municipal laws on illegal drugs, particularly marijuana, have been greatly relaxed in recent years, trafficking penalties remain steep. Hence, the continued wariness about drugs on the part of Mafia bosses.

Charles "Lucky" Luciano was one of the first members of the Mafia to get involved in illegal drugs. In 1915, the 18-year-old mobster-in-training purchased a supply of drugs, either opium or morphine (accounts vary), and sold it to addicts in his neighborhood. Luciano was caught and spent six months in a reformatory.

After his release from reformatory, the teenage Luciano went to work for Arnold Rothstein, the gray eminence of organized crime. In addition to bootlegging, Rothstein funded drug smuggling operations.

In this manner, Rothstein became one of the first major traffickers in illegal drugs. Jewish Rothstein was not part of any Italian American underworld but worked closely with figures who did belong.

As drugs became less available, their value shot up dramatically in price while their purity declined (criminals aren't concerned with quality control). Federal narcotics commissioner Harry Anslinger, for example, noted that heroin, which cost $25–50 an ounce in the 1920s, was retailing for $3,000 an ounce by the 1950s.

For decades, Anslinger was the main government official fighting illicit drugs. J. Edgar Hoover, at the Federal Bureau of Investigation (FBI), wanted nothing to do with narcotics. It is believed Hoover worried that his agents might be prone to bribery or addiction if they pursued undercover drug cases. Unlike Hoover, Anslinger readily acknowledged the existence of a homegrown American Mafia, although he mistakenly insisted it was controlled by Sicilian crime bosses.

The trade in illegal drugs remained miniscule until the mid-1960s, when young people began to embrace LSD, amphetamines, and, especially, marijuana. In the 1970s, powder cocaine became hugely popular in chic, urban circles. The 1980s marked the advent of crack cocaine (a cheap, concentrated version of the drug, prevalent in African American communities), while the 1990s saw the rise of methamphetamine (a powerful version of the stimulant amphetamine, primarily made, used, and sold by rural whites).

As drug use exploded, the underworld stepped up to provide a supply for boosted demand. In 1973, for example, Harlem mobster Leroy "Nicky" Barnes organized drug dealers into a citywide syndicate called "the Council." Barnes received his supply of drugs from Mafia wholesalers belonging to the Lucchese family and other clans, who were happy to let African Americans retail their product on the streets of New York City.

The American Mafia sometimes took a more hands-on approach to drugs. Rising mob boss John Gotti and his peers were heavily involved in drug trafficking in the 1980s, despite a ban on such behavior from family boss Paul Castellano. It is believed Gotti arranged Castellano's death in part because he feared retribution should the Gambino family boss discover that his underlings sold drugs. Henry Hill, the longtime Mafia associate whose life story formed the basis of the classic gangster film *Goodfellas*, was also a major drug trafficker and user.

The Gambinos remain active participants in the drug trade. In the mid-1980s, mobster Rosario Gambino, of the crime family that bears his name, was found guilty of a conspiracy to sell heroin and given 45 years in jail. Gambino was linked to the "Pizza Connection" investigation, which centered on a heroin-and-cocaine-smuggling venture involving pizzerias as fronts. He was deported to Italy in May 2009. On September 17, 2009, a Gambino family soldier named Charles Carneglia was given life in prison for various charges including murder, kidnapping, robbery, and marijuana distribution conspiracy. And, on February 17, 2012, four members of the ill-fated Gambino family pled guilty in Manhattan federal court to a variety of offenses, including racketeering and narcotics trafficking.

If the American Mafia dabbles in drugs, it certainly doesn't control the trade. The *National Drug Threat Assessment 2011*, a report by the U.S. Department of Justice, excludes the American Mafia from its list of "transnational criminal organizations (TCOs)" that traffic drugs. According to the report, "Mexican based TCOs dominate the supply, trafficking and wholesale distribution of most illicit drugs in the United States."

The American Mafia will retain a degree of involvement in the drug trade, however, as long as drugs remain a valuable commodity. The National Drug Threat Assessment report pegs the mid-2010 price of a gram of cocaine at over $150. A gram of meth went for an average of $82 in the same time period. Heroin retailed for $157 a gram on U.S. streets in 2009, according to the United Nations' *World Drug Report 2011*.

Drug policy is one of the most hotly debated topics in North American political discourse. Some critics say the drug war has failed; they point to the failure of Prohibition as an example of the negative consequences of trying to ban popular intoxicants. Drug law reformers believe that criminalizing drugs keeps their price artificially high (thus making them a desirable commodity for gangsters) while providing zero quality controls or health warnings. Organized crime groups, including the Mafia, will lose interest in illicit drugs when their value decreases, say reformers.

Drug war supporters think this is nonsense and that any move toward loosening drug laws would increase addiction. They argue that if mobsters stopped selling drugs, they would simply move to other rackets (as what happened when Prohibition was repealed in 1933). Tougher enforcement and greater drug education, they believe, is the answer.

This argument might soon be settled by real-world examples. In November 2012, voters in Colorado and Washington State approved referendums to legalize the possession and sale of marijuana. Similar referendums and legalization legislation are widely anticipated for additional states. Policymakers will be watching closely to see how legalization plays out in those states in part to see what role—if any—organized crime will play in a legal marijuana milieu.

Gambling

"Gambling is probably the most important source of income for the Mafia ... although narcotics trafficking may be a major money-maker for various members of the mob, not every member of the family may be involved in it. On the other hand, every Mafia member was involved in gambling and used the profits from it to sustain his other activities," undercover FBI agent Joseph Pistone told a Senate subcommittee in 1988.[3]

The Mafia used to be heavily involved in "the numbers" racket, which was basically an illegal lottery. Hugely popular in poor districts, numbers offered people a cheap, relatively safe way to gamble. Players would bet a few pennies on a three- or four-digit number. The gangsters who ran the game would select a winning number from an objective source, such as sport scores. Anyone who picked the winning number would receive a small cash prize.

In the 1930s, Jewish mobster Dutch Schultz became one of the first major crime figures to take an interest in numbers, which was particularly popular in Harlem. At the time, the New York numbers racket was dominated by African American hustlers. The Mafia looked down upon numbers as a fringe racket not worthy of serious consideration. Schultz proved the mob wrong. He muscled into numbers and seized control. He allowed black operators to remain in business, provided they gave him most of their profits. Schultz began taking in millions of dollars a year from numbers. His peers in the Mafia and the Jewish American underworld took note. After Schultz was killed in 1935, his criminal counterparts took over New York numbers.

Numbers continued to be popular until legal lotteries became common. Today, anyone can buy lottery tickets at a convenience store, with no need to gamble with gangsters. As a result, the numbers racket has largely disappeared.

For decades, the Mafia was also involved in casino gambling in Las Vegas. Mobsters would typically siphon off undeclared profits at casinos in which they had a stake. Tighter controls and investigations by law enforcement have largely driven the Mafia out of Vegas. At the same time, legal casino gambling has become widespread across the United States. In spite of all this, the Mafia still has a major presence in the gambling underworld.

Casinos require winners to pay taxes on their earnings and file paperwork. This is generally too much hassle for "degenerate" gamblers (Mafia-speak for gambling addicts). Such people often prefer to take their chances at illegal gaming halls, where winnings aren't taxed and no paperwork is required.

Hand in hand with gambling is the age-old practice known as loan sharking. A loan shark is a criminal who gives out loans at exorbitant rates of interest. Sometimes, the amount of interest paid exceeds the actual principal of the loan. Nonetheless, recipients of such loans usually pay up, out of fear of incurring a beating or worse at the hands of the loan sharks and his comrades.

If Mafia involvement in casino gambling (at least in Las Vegas) has diminished, the mob still runs extensive sports betting operations. Some of these operations rely on websites run in foreign countries in an effort to evade the law.

It's safe to say that as long as there are people willing to place wagers to win cash or prizes, gambling will remain a Mafia mainstay, in one form or another.

Notes

1. Edward Behr, *Prohibition: Thirteen Years That Changed America* (New York: Arcade Publishing, 1996), 82–83.
2. Joseph Valachi, testimony before the U.S. Senate Permanent Subcommittee on Investigations, 1963.
3. Joseph Pistone, testimony before the U.S. Senate Permanent Subcommittee on Investigations, 1988.

| # Chicago

If New York City was the birthplace of the U.S. Mafia, Chicago was one of the mob's main proving grounds. As an urban center, Chicago is very new. It wasn't incorporated as a city until the early nineteenth century. By 1850, barely 30,000 people lived in Chicago. Explosive growth pushed the city to 300,000 residents by 1870. Even a massive city fire in 1871 didn't slow Chicago's expansion. By 1890, the population topped one million. At the start of Prohibition, some 2.7 million people called Chicago home.

Chicago residents of the nineteenth century had a laissez-faire attitude about law enforcement. In the first decades of the city's existence, there was virtually no official police force to maintain law and order. Needless to say, crime, particularly prostitution, thrived.

Even Chicago's legal businesses had an aura of violence. The city became synonymous with the slaughter of animals. Pigs, sheep, and cows raised on midwestern farms were shipped to Chicago to be dispatched in one of the city's countless abattoirs. The slaughterhouse was an all-too-apt metaphor of what the city would become in the twentieth century.

Chicago has always been extremely commercially minded. In addition to abattoirs, the city's leading industries in its early years included railroads and lumberyards. Getting rich was the order of the day. Working the slaughterhouses, the railroads, and the lumberyards was an army of poor slum dwellers.

Political corruption was another Chicago tradition. By the early 1900s, the city had a thriving red-light district, to which municipal officials turned a blind eye. City politicians happily took payoffs from the pimps, madams, and gangsters who controlled the underworld.

Such was the environment that produced "the Outfit," Chicago's homegrown version of the Mafia.

Big Jim Colosimo: Diamond in the Rough

Big Jim Colosimo was one of the first major Italian American crime bosses in Chicago. He could have ruled the Windy City for decades but was undone by love and the good life. As it is, he laid the groundwork for one of the most powerful, deep-rooted American Mafia factions in the country.

Born in Cosenza, Italy, in 1877, Colosimo immigrated with his family to Chicago in 1895. Like many immigrants, Colosimo had to settle for a series of menial jobs. While primarily employed as a street sweeper, he showed a flair for organization. Colosimo organized the city's sweepers and helped set up social and athletic clubs for their benefit. Colosimo, who had no moral compunctions about breaking the law, moonlighted as a pimp and pickpocket.

Colosimo's organizational abilities and criminal hustle soon drew the attention of two powerful—and extremely corrupt—city aldermen, Michael "Hinky Dink" Kenna and John "Bathhouse John" Coughlin. The pair represented the First Ward, which is where the city's red-light district (called the Levee) was based, and took a cut from vice operations in the area. Kenna and Coughlin started giving Colosimo patronage appointments.

Colosimo ran a poolroom and a saloon, and then became a "bagman" for Kenna and Coughlin. It was his job to make the rounds of local brothels and collect money from the pimps and madams for the two aldermen. In 1902, while performing these duties, Colosimo encountered a plump, middle-aged madam named Victoria Moresco. She was drawn to Colosimo's swarthy good looks and Mediterranean charm. He in turn was attracted to her wealth and position as a top procurer of flesh. Colosimo and Moresco entered into a whirlwind romance. Within weeks, the brothel keeper (who was twice her paramour's age) and the bagman were married.

Moresco gave her new husband a job as manager of her relatively upscale brothel. Colosimo quickly opened up a series of new, cut-price establishments in the Levee. These were dives where the going rate for a brief encounter with a prostitute was $1 or $2. Colosimo also launched a few classier bordellos. Colosimo didn't neglect his mentors and made sure Kenna and Coughlin got a cut of his proceeds.

Colosimo had a good eye for marketing. He established gambling dens and saloons near his brothels, so patrons could enjoy multiple vices in one convenient location. Prostitution, however, remained the mainstay of the burgeoning Colosimo/Moresco empire. The pair soon owned dozens of brothels across the city.

At the time, prostitution was even less glamorous than it is today. Penicillin hadn't been invented, and sexually transmitted diseases were rife. Effective contraception didn't exist (and, in some jurisdictions, was illegal); for many prostitutes, illicit abortion was their main form of birth control.

Being a prostitute was a very short-term vocation. Most girls lasted only a few years, their physical and mental decline abetted by drugs, drink, abuse, and STDs. Because turnover was so high, a constant supply of fresh talent was required. Colosimo and his fellow pimps relied on "white slavers" to bring in new hookers. These unscrupulous businessmen lured naïve country girls and new immigrants with fake ads for housekeepers and nannies. Girls who responded to the ads would be abducted, raped into submission, and then sold like cuts of beef to pimps and madams. Prostitutes were kept in line by threats, physical beatings, and the occasional murder of one of their members.

Colosimo grew hugely wealthy off such misery. He took to encrusting himself in expensive stones. He wore diamond rings, diamond-studded belts and suspenders, and diamond cufflinks. People started calling him "Diamond Jim." Colosimo was also fond of finely tailored, all-white suits.

Colosimo was no run-of-the-mill criminal; he had political connections and controlled a vast underworld network. These two factors elevated him from street thug to organized crime boss.

As powerful as Colosimo was, a few brazen mobsters tried to extort money from him. Annoyed, Diamond Jim contacted Moresco's cousin, a young striver named Johnny Torrio. A rising star in New York City's gang firmament, Torrio was cunning and cold-blooded.

Torrio moved from New York to Chicago in 1909 and quickly took the situation in hand. Torrio arranged for a death squad to murder the extortionists who were bothering Colosimo. Impressed, Diamond Jim asked Torrio to stick around. Put in charge of a brothel, Torrio proved to be an excellent manager. Unlike most gangsters, Torrio didn't smoke, drink, curse, or avail himself of the flesh he peddled each day. Colosimo kept ceding more authority to Torrio, until the up-and-comer was virtually running Diamond Jim's empire. By this point, Colosimo and his wife owned 200 brothels and employed hundreds of people. All was good.

Diamond Jim set up a nightclub, at 2126 Wabash Avenue, and named it after himself. Colosimo's Café was a high-end establishment with a full orchestra. The café attracted famous celebrities of the day such as opera singer Enrico Caruso and legendary defense attorney Clarence Darrow. The glitzy club served gourmet food and fine wine and was Colosimo's personal playground.

In 1912, pressure from civic groups led to the closure of the Levee. Colosimo simply opened new brothels in the suburbs outside the city. Two years later, William Hale "Big Bill" Thompson was elected mayor of Chicago. Reviled as the most corrupt mayor in American history, Thompson had no interest in being a crime-buster. The Levee soon reopened for business.

Torrio continued to be an effective manager. He expanded Colosimo's domain, opening new brothels, gambling dens, and saloons. Torrio hired new recruits as well. One of his future finds was a young gangster he had known in New York named Al Capone. Capone was brought to Chicago and given lowly tasks at first, such as standing outside brothels and pitching the services found within.

Colosimo paid little attention to Torrio's staffing decisions. He was content to sit back and enjoy the fruits of his labors. In 1918, Colosimo fell in love with Dale Winter, a young winsome singer who appeared at Colosimo's Café. Diamond Jim started squiring Winter about town, openly treating her as his escort. Moresco was told to pack her things and leave the family home.

Colosimo's fellow gangsters were appalled. As violent as they were, the gangsters held themselves to a certain standard. Family values were greatly honored. While it was perfectly acceptable to cheat on your wife, this was generally done in private. It was considered a shocking breech of underworld etiquette to humiliate your wife by accompanying a young siren in public.

Deeply in love, Colosimo paid no mind. He also stopped paying any attention to business. Prohibition was scheduled to come into effect at midnight, January 16, 1920. Far-seeing gangsters such as Torrio realized that Prohibition represented a bonanza for organized crime. People would still want to drink, despite the law. If they couldn't buy alcohol from a legal source, they would buy black-market booze sold by criminals. Despite Torrio's pleading, Colosimo didn't want to make a major investment in bootlegging. He was content with the way things were, and he was more interested in his new girlfriend anyway.

In March 1920, Colosimo divorced his wife, giving her a $50,000 settlement. One month later, Big Jim married Winter. The marriage lasted only a few weeks. As his boss enjoyed his nuptials, Torrio schemed. He decided Colosimo had to be eliminated. Torrio would take over Big Jim's empire once Colosimo was gone, and go into bootlegging in a big way. Torrio met with other city crime bosses and got their approval (more or less) for his plan.

On May 11, 1920, Torrio called Diamond Jim and told him a big whiskey delivery would be arriving at Colosimo's Café at precisely 4:00 p.m. that day. Torrio insisted that his boss be there for the delivery. Colosimo reluctantly agreed, but when he showed up, no one knew anything about the shipment. Colosimo chatted with a few befuddled staffers and then wandered into the cloakroom, where a gunman was waiting. The gunman fired twice, and Big Jim was killed instantly. The killer was Frankie Yale, a seasoned thug from New York City. He was almost certainly hired by Torrio.

Colosimo left the earth in the same way he lived—in a tawdry haze of flash and sparkle. "Big Jim had the first of the gangland funeral extravaganzas of the 1920s—a $50,000 affair," wrote journalist Paul Sann.[1] As part of the funeral procession, Colosimo's bronze casket was taken to the very café where he had been murdered. Some 2,000 mourners crowded outside to pay their respect, as two brass bands performed appropriately somber music. A funeral service was held at Colosimo's house, and all present appeared sufficiently mournful.

Everyone knew Colosimo was a pimp, but that didn't stop plenty of respectable people from attending his funeral, including judges, a congressman, several city aldermen, a district state attorney, and countless other worthies. Thousands of mourners and spectators alike turned out on the street to see Colosimo's bronze casket go by.

Torrio, of course, denied having any clue who would want to harm his boss. He appeared appropriately shaken and distraught. Torrio's mourning was brief; he quickly took the reins of power and appointed himself head of Colosimo's vast empire. There was a new crime boss in Chicago and, unlike his predecessor, he wasn't about to be sidetracked by a woman or a love of luxury.

"Scarface" Al Capone

On Valentine's Day, February 14, 1929, the most notorious "hit" in underworld history took place in a cold Chicago garage. Located at 2122 North Clark Street, the garage was used by the North Side gang, led by mobster George "Bugs" Moran, to receive shipments of bootleg alcohol. On the morning in question, seven men stood impatiently inside the unheated garage, waiting for an expected liquor delivery. Six of the men worked for Moran. One had brought his dog, a German shepherd, which was tied up. The seventh man was an optometrist named Dr. Reinhart Schwimmer, who liked hanging around criminals. All the men, save the eye doctor, were armed, with cash on hand to pay for the bootleg spirits whenever they arrived.

Around 10:30 a.m., the men received a surprise visit from members of the Chicago Police Department. Two men in uniform and two plainclothes cops entered the garage, guns drawn. They ordered the gangsters up against a brick wall. The seven men grumbled, but obeyed. Chicago was extremely corrupt, but police still occasionally made raids, if only to show who was boss. Moran's men lined up, facing the wall.

One of the cops methodically checked each man and removed their guns. Then, all four policemen raised their own weapons and began to shoot. They raked the backs of the helpless gangsters with machine gun, rifle, and pistol fire. Each man was hit multiple times. They collapsed, spraying blood over the concrete floor as the tied-up dog howled.

When the cops were through, the two plainclothes men put down their weapons and put up their hands. The uniformed officers stood behind them, guns drawn, and led them outside to a waiting police cruiser. The two men in police uniforms put the plainclothes cops in the back seats, and then got in the car themselves. Anyone looking on would assume police had just raided a known gangster hideout, shot it out with mobsters, and taken two prisoners. The four assassins raced off.

When real cops finally showed up, they discovered a scene that resembled the killing floor of one of Chicago's numerous abattoirs. Six men were dead. Amazingly, one man named Frank Gusenberg was still alive, despite being shot 22 times. True to the gangster code of ethics, Gusenberg refused to tell police what had happened. He died before authorities could get any useful information out of him.

The attack at the North Clark Street garage was an enormous success except for one thing: the main target—Bugs Moran himself—wasn't there. Moran had been running late that morning. When he showed at the garage, the four fake cops were already inside. Moran eyed the police cruiser by the curb, figured a raid was in progress, and hurriedly left.

The St. Valentine's Day Massacre (as the media called it) was a sensational story worldwide. The suspected perpetrator—Al Capone, head of one of the largest criminal organizations in Chicago—became a household name. Capone was residing at his luxurious mansion in Miami, Florida, when the massacre took place. Of course, he denied having anything to do with it. He said he harbored no ill will against the North Side gang and their leader, Bugs Moran. Moran for his part knew exactly who orchestrated the hit. "No one kills like that except Capone," a dazed Moran told reporters.[2]

The man who ordered the attack was born in 1899 in Brooklyn, to Gabriele and Teresina (called Teresa) Capone, immigrants from southern Italy. The Capone family faced poverty and prejudice (Italian immigrants were not popular among the Anglo-Saxon Protestant majority), but in this they were no different from millions of other immigrant families. Gabriele Capone was a hard-working family man who worked first in a grocery store and then as a barber in Brooklyn. Teresa Capone was a sober, family-minded matriarch. Son Al Capone seemed entirely average and unexceptional.

The only thing that really distinguished Capone was his close relationship with an older man, Johnny Torrio. Torrio was a local gangster who occasionally hired neighbor boys to run errands for him. Capone observed that Torrio—unlike his own father and those of his friends—always dressed in expensive clothes. He was flush with cash (some of which he doled out to favored errand boys, including Capone) and commanded respect. Torrio controlled illegal lotteries and brothels in the neighborhood. Unusually for a mobster, he was polite and quiet, returning home each day after work to spend the evening with his wife.

In 1909, Torrio left New York to work for Big Jim Colosimo in Chicago. Capone remembered Torrio's vivid example, however, particularly how he carried himself with quiet dignity in a community where most men were battered down from exhausting physical labor.

Capone joined with other local kids in a street gang. Capone's crew mostly just hung out, smoked cigarettes, and talked tough. He dropped out of school at age 14 and worked various menial factory jobs.

In 1917, while employed in a dingy Coney Island bar, Capone crudely complimented a female patron on the appearance of her derriere. The young woman's escort, who happened to be her brother, took umbrage and slashed Capone with a knife. For the rest of his life, he bore three scars on the left side of his face. Interestingly, Capone never sought revenge against the man who maimed him (the prevailing underworld sentiment, by which Capone abided, was that the assailant was right to defend his sister's honor).

Knife wounds didn't prevent Capone from getting married. In late 1918, he wed an Irish American girl named Mae Coughlin, with whom he already had a son. Unbeknownst to his parents, the boy, whom they called Sonny, was born with congenital syphilis, passed on from his infected father. Capone had acquired venereal disease (probably from a prostitute) as a young man but never sought treatment for it. The disease went into remission, and Capone assumed it had gone away.

Capone worked briefly as a bookkeeper in Baltimore, but was lured to Chicago by his old mentor, Torrio. By the time Capone arrived in town in 1921, Torrio had become one of the Windy City's top mobsters. He achieved this through the simple expedient of murdering his boss, Colosimo, and seizing his underworld empire. While Big Jim had been reluctant to get involved in bootlegging alcohol, Torrio had no such compunctions. He was soon controlling thousands of speakeasies, brothels, and gambling dens. Torrio wanted Capone to help out by managing a handful of whorehouses.

Capone proved to be an able brothel manager and pimp. He was given a promotion, so to speak, and put in charge of a Torrio establishment called the Four Deuces. Located at 2222 South Wabash, the Four Deuces served as a combination speakeasy, brothel, and headquarters of the expansive Torrio crime empire. Once again, Capone showed a flair for management.

Capone soon became a near-equal partner to Torrio. With money coming steadily in, Capone bought a two-story, red-brick house at 7244 Prairie Avenue for his family. The home was relatively modest but had plenty of rooms (15 in total). Capone installed Mae and his boy Sonny there as well as his mother and other family members.

Torrio and Capone faced some stiff competition in Chicago. One of their main rivals was a mentally addled Irish gangster named Dion "Deanie" O'Banion who headed the North Side gang. When he wasn't taking care of bootlegging operations, O'Banion spent time arranging flowers in a florist shop he owned. His gang was notoriously eccentric. After one of their members died when they were thrown from a horse, O'Banion's troops tracked the horse down and killed it.

The horrible Genna brothers were another major power. This Sicilian-born clan of bootleggers was allied with Torrio, more or less. In 1920, with the advent of Prohibition, the Gennas somehow acquired a government license to make industrial alcohol. They used this poisonous brew to produce batches of bootleg liquor. The latter was doused in chemicals and coloring to make it look and taste more like real whiskey. The product was still highly dangerous, and possibly even fatal to those who consumed it, a fact that bothered the Gennas not one bit. The brothers also paid hundreds of poor Italian families $15 a day (a generous sum at the time) to brew cheap liquor in their residences. As awful and dangerous as the Gennas' product was, they couldn't keep up with the staggering demand for bootleg spirits.

Torrio managed to establish a shaky truce with O'Banion and the Gennas. Torrio argued that there was more than enough cash to go around, and that there was no need for rival gangsters to be at each other's throats. Each gang would stick to its territory and not intrude on anyone else's turf. Torrio favored diplomacy over underworld warfare.

The Chicago underworld benefitted from the fact that the city government was in the hands of corrupt, buffoonish Mayor "Big Bill" Thompson. Thompson opposed Prohibition and did little to halt the spread of organized crime. He made florid, bizarre speeches in which he mused on conspiracy theories involving English royalty (a topic that went over extremely well with anti-British Polish and German voters).

Unfortunately for the gangs, Thompson decided not to run for another term in 1923. He was replaced by a wannabe reformer named William Dever who hoped to bring the underworld to heel.

Torrio and Capone (who by this point was Torrio's main lieutenant and a powerful mobster in his own right) saw the writing on the wall. They moved some operations from Chicago to a small, neighboring city called Cicero. The Torrio/Capone organization purchased a Cicero property called the Hawthorne Inn and set about taking over the city. They came to completely dominate the municipal government, one of the few times in American history when an entire town was run by mobsters.

At this juncture, Torrio decided to take his aging mother back to Italy for a visit. He left Capone in charge of things during his absence. In the spring of 1924, Torrio returned from Italy and immediately faced a major problem. The delicate truce Torrio had established was starting to unravel. O'Banion accused the Gennas of flooding his turf with cheap, substandard liquor. Bootleg alcohol made by O'Banion came at a premium price but was of far better quality, in that it was less likely to blind or kill anyone who drank it.

The Gennas were gearing up for war with O'Banion. At the last minute, the wily Irishman pulled back from the brink. He announced he wanted to retire, saying he was tired of being a gangster and wanted to live in peace. As a sign of his good faith, he offered to sell his share of the Sieben Brewery, which was operating illegally under the joint ownership of O'Banion, Torrio, and Capone, for $500,000.

Torrio was wary but eager to take greater control of the brewery. He agreed to meet O'Banion at the brewery on the night of May 19,

1924. The mobsters chatted as their minions loaded trucks with boot-leg alcohol. Suddenly, the facility was invaded by a small army of policemen. The police were led by federal authorities. O'Banion and Torrio were placed in federal custody instead of the municipal jail. Torrio had reason to be concerned. He already had one Prohibition-related offense on his record. A second federal offense might bring serious jail time.

It dawned on Torrio that he had been set up by O'Banion, who had a clean record. As a first-time offender, O'Banion's punishment would be much milder than anything handed to Torrio. The erratic Irishman laughed uproariously at Torrio's misfortune. He had tipped off the police and knew the raid was coming. O'Banion regarded the episode as a marvelous practical joke.

As the cliché goes, Torrio had the last laugh. In November 1924, three men entered O'Banion's florist shop and shot him dead as he arranged flowers. The trio was almost certainly sent by either Torrio or the Gennas.

O'Banion had a splendidly gaudy funeral featuring 26 cars carry-ing funeral flowers, three bands, and a police escort. An estimated 10,000 people joined the funeral cortege to see the dead gangster off.

Torrio and Capone feigned grief, but were delighted that one of their biggest rivals was gone. Now they could move in on O'Banion's turf. What Torrio and Capone didn't appreciate was that they had made bitter enemies out of O'Banion's loyal followers. The North Siders were now led by Earl Wajciechowski (aka "Hymie" Weiss), who had been close friends with O'Banion. Another North Side asso-ciate waiting in the wings was George Moran (better known as "Bugs" Moran—"bugs" being period slang for crazy).

Over the next two years, O'Banion's former followers would try to kill Capone at least a dozen times. Capone by this point traveled with a minimum of two bodyguards (one for each side) and rarely walked in public, preferring to move about by car, flanked by more bodyguards. His chauffeur was armed and, to make his travel even safer, Capone journeyed only at night.

Torrio was much less security conscious. Two months after O'Banion was killed, the North Siders ambushed and shot him outside his Chicago residence. Torrio survived but decided to quit. In March 1925, he turned his entire criminal empire over to his protégé,

Capone. All Torrio wanted was a share of the profits. He moved to Italy in retirement, giving Capone free reign in Chicago.

Now that he headed a huge criminal network, Capone began living like an emperor. He installed himself in a high-end suite of five rooms at Chicago's swanky Metropole Hotel, at a cost of $1,500 a day. He could afford it. Some estimates peg his annual income at around $100 million (worth approximately 10 times as much today). Almost every day, Capone—escorted by bodyguards and lieutenants—would travel to a Chicago building that housed municipal offices and do business with city officials. At his peak, Capone controlled an army of 1,000 gangsters and offered the usual underworld smorgasbord of alcohol, brothels, and gambling.

While arguably the most powerful mob boss in the city, Capone was smart enough to bring reliable subordinates into his leadership circle. One of his top lieutenants was Frank Nitti, who was a decade older than Capone and of a very different temperament. Nitti's nickname was "The Enforcer" (a reflection of his supposed tough-guy image), but in fact he was a somewhat nervous, high-strung man who avoided unnecessary confrontation.

Jake Guzik was another important member of Capone's team. An orthodox Jew and definitely not a thug, Guzik was a money wizard who provided financial advice. Capone also placed some of his brothers in leadership positions—an action that would have tragic results in the case of one sibling. In 1924, Capone's brother, Frank Capone, was killed by police during a violence-drenched municipal election in Cicero.

As Capone rose in power, his rivals were cut down or disappeared. In the mid-1920s, three of the Genna brothers were assassinated in a row by North Side gunmen. The remaining brothers took the hint and fled, leaving their bootlegging empire behind for their rivals. In 1926, Capone's men killed Hymie Weiss, a move that propelled Bugs Moran into the leadership of the North Side gang.

In a 1927 civic election, Chicago voters brought "Big Bill" Thompson back to office. Dever was seen as well-intentioned but weak. Thompson at least, was more entertaining.

In May of the same year, the Supreme Court issued a ruling that would have enormous consequences for Capone and fellow gangsters. The Court ruled that criminals had to declare all their revenue— legally earned or not—to the government. Even if the income in question was generated by vice, murder, and corruption, it still had to be reported. Failure to file a proper return could result in charges of tax evasion.

Capone paid no heed to this development. He continued to live it up and hit the town. He frequented concerts and boxing matches and struck up a friendship with famed pugilist Jack Dempsey.

By decade's end, Capone decided the time had come to deal with his rival Bugs Moran once and for all. In early 1929, Capone met with "Machine Gun" Jack McGurn, a hit man-for-hire, in Florida. Capone told McGurn he wanted Moran dead. It was McGurn's job to figure out how best to make this happen.

McGurn gathered together a team of assassins and began observing his prey. Some sleuthing revealed that Moran used a garage on North Clark Street for liquor shipments. One of McGurn's men put a call through to Moran claiming to be a bootlegger with a supply of high-end liquor for sale. Moran took the bait and offered to meet the bootlegger on Valentine's Day morning, at North Sider headquarters. Moran never made the appointment.

Accounts differ as to Bugs Moran's career after the Valentine's Day Massacre. Some crime historians say Moran fled Chicago, a move that allowed Capone to take over his underworld businesses and territory. Other accounts indicate Moran stayed on, despite the slaughter of six of his men. It has been confirmed that Moran eventually became a bank robber, was caught and convicted, and died in federal prison in 1957.

In retrospect, the St. Valentine's Day Massacre can be seen as the appalling pinnacle of Prohibition-era violence in Chicago. According to FBI research, over 700 gangland murders—few of them solved— occurred in the Windy City between 1920 and 1933.[3]

The massacre made Al Capone the leading gangster in Chicago— and fatally raised his national profile. Among his new detractors was President Herbert Hoover in Washington, D.C. Hoover was infuriated by the seemingly endless violence in Chicago and Capone's position as gangster kingpin. Hoover demanded that Capone be stopped. Authorities began working on two fronts against Capone. In Chicago, an incorruptible lawman named Eliot Ness and a small team of police officials harried Capone by raiding his distilleries and seizing trucks and other equipment that belonged to him. Officials within the

Internal Revenue Service (IRS), meanwhile, began putting together a tax case against the head of the Chicago underworld.

In 1931, Capone was slapped with nearly two dozen charges of federal tax evasion for the years 1925–1929. The IRS estimated he had earned a net income of over $1 million in this period (a gross underestimate) and thus owed $200,000 in unpaid taxes.

Spring brought more bad news for Capone. On April 8, 1931, the gangster-friendly Mayor Thompson was defeated by Democrat Tony Cermak. While something of a party hack, Cermak had no love for the underworld. With Cermak in charge, Chicago would no longer be an open city for gangsters.

On October 17, 1931, a jury found Capone guilty of tax evasion. He was given a stiff sentence of 11 years in jail plus fines. Capone was shipped off to a federal penitentiary in Atlanta, then to an unpleasant new prison on Alcatraz Island, just off San Francisco.

In their efforts to incarcerate Capone, authorities didn't neglect his subordinates. Nitti and Guzik were also charged with tax evasion. They were convicted but given much lighter sentences than their boss.

In prison, Capone's health soon deteriorated. He was finally diagnosed with syphilis and given treatment, but by this point it was too late. Capone began to suffer brain damage from syphilis, becoming confused and disoriented. He spent the last year of his sentence in a prison hospital.

Capone was released early for good behavior. In November 1939, he left prison and was placed in a Baltimore hospital by his wife. He received more treatment and then convalesced at his Palm Island mansion in Florida, fishing, playing cards, and avoiding work. Now muddle-headed, Capone no longer ran the criminal empire he once dominated.

On January 25, 1947, Capone suffered a fatal heart attack. His family could take cold comfort in the fact that, unlike most of his underworld peers, Alphonse Capone died of natural causes.

Frank Nitti, the Outfit, and the Family Secrets Trial

If Big Jim Colosimo founded an underworld empire that Johnny Torrio expanded and then bequeathed to Al Capone, Frank Nitti is the man who consolidated various criminal elements to create the Outfit, Chicago's version of the Mafia.

Nitti served time for tax evasion, just like Capone. Upon his release from jail in 1932, Nitti took control of Capone's underworld kingdom. Nitti's reign was supposed to be temporary. He would serve as caretaker boss until Capone got out of prison and took back command. Capone, however, languished for years in jail and was far too sick with syphilis to lead when he was released.

If Capone had been a high-profile leader, given to flaunting his power and wealth, Nitti was nearly invisible. He took up residence in Chicago's Lexington Hotel and kept a very low profile.

Low profile or not, Nitti did not enjoy the best of relations with Chicago mayor Tony Cermak. In December 1932, Nitti was shot and wounded in his office by a detective said to be employed by the mayor. The detective claimed self-defense and had a rather dubious hand wound (most likely self-inflicted) to show reporters. Unsurprisingly, the detective was later hunted down and killed by Nitti's men.

In February 1933, it was Cermak's turn to be shot. He was wounded by gunfire in Miami while meeting with President-elect Franklin Roosevelt. Cermak died three weeks after being hit. His assassin was Giuseppe Zangara, a deranged political nihilist. It was assumed Zangara really meant to shoot Roosevelt and only hit Cermak because his aim was off. A headline in the February 16, 1933, *Milwaukee Sentinel*, for example, reads, "Attempts to Slay Roosevelt; Wounds Cermak and 4 Others." To this day, speculation remains that Cermak was the real target and that the demented assassin had been unleashed by Nitti and company.

The repeal of Prohibition in 1933 forced the underworld to seek out new money-making ventures. With liquor legally available again, demand for bootleg spirits plummeted. People could purchase drinks legally, at a fraction of the price of illegal spirits and many times the quality.

Nitti's minions moved into labor and business racketeering and expanded gambling and loan-sharking operations. The Chicago mob also spread out to other cities, establishing criminal connections in Milwaukee and Madison, Wisconsin; Rockford and Springfield, Illinois; Kansas City; and even as far afield as Los Angeles.

While he had none of his predecessor's flair, Nitti was not lacking for vision. Around 1934, Nitti united disparate elements in Chicago's Italian American underworld to serve under his command, in one big

Mafia gang. The gang acquired the name "the Outfit" and dominated organized crime in Chicago for decades.

Unity was the Outfit's key signature. While New York City was presided over by five separate Mafia families jostling for control, Chicago's Mafia crews belonged to one big family run by Nitti. This was partly due to simple demographics: in the early 1930s, with 3.3 million people, Chicago's population was less than half that of New York City.

Nonetheless, the Outfit proved to be powerful and far-reaching, with connections that extended all the way to Hollywood. In the 1930s, the Outfit established a foothold in the movie capital through the efforts of two associates, George Browne and Willie Bioff. Browne and Bioff were involved with the International Alliance of Theatre and Stage Employees (IATSE), a union that included film projectionists and movie crews. The Outfit threatened film studios with labor strife unless they offered a share of their profits. The Chicago mob also extorted money from theater owners by threatening a projectionist strike.

The Hollywood link proved lucrative but treacherous. Browne and Bioff were indicted and agreed to testify for the government against Nitti and other Outfit leaders. Nitti and some of his subordinates were indicted on March 18, 1943. Faced with the possibility of spending years in jail—a prospect the claustrophobic boss simply could not handle—Nitti committed suicide the day after his indictment was handed down. Other Outfit leaders indicted in the case were convicted in October 1943 and given 10-year prison sentences.

With Nitti dead, leadership in the Outfit went to Tony Accardo, a former Capone bodyguard with the curious nickname "Joe Batters." Accardo allegedly earned this moniker because of his habit of using a baseball bat as an instrument of pain and persuasion.

The Second World War presented new opportunities for the Chicago underworld. Upon American entry into the fray, the Outfit began counterfeiting ration coupons for gasoline and other items in short supply.

The Outfit had other ways to earn money as well. Under Accardo, the Chicago Mafia hiked the "street tax" it imposed on small-time hoods in the city. The latter were now required to kick back more of their revenue to the Outfit. Anyone who didn't pay up faced the prospect of violence or regulatory pressure from city politicians owned by the Outfit.

Like Mafia gangs in other cities, the Outfit relied on a "sports wire service"—that is, a telegraph network that transmitted horseracing results—to fuel its gambling operations. By the mid-1940s, the Continental Press was the largest wire service in the country.

The Outfit decided to take ownership of the Continental Press. This wire service was controlled by James Ragen, who resisted Outfit entreaties to sell his business. Unable to persuade Ragen, the Chicago mob created its own racing wire service, which it called Trans American. The Outfit did its best to steal results and clients from Continental for its own wire service.

Ragen tried to hold on. He hired bodyguards and gave a nearly 100-page statement to the Cook County state attorney offering details about underworld gambling. The statement cited Accardo and Jake Guzik (who still helped the Outfit with money matters) by name and included information about mob payoffs to city politicians. In a stunning move, Ragen complained to the Chicago FBI that he was being pressured by mobsters.

None of these actions were looked upon with favor by the Outfit. On June 24, 1946, while driving in traffic, Ragen was ambushed and shot. His bodyguards, driving behind him, returned fire, but their employer was mortally wounded. Ragen died six weeks after the ambush. His successor quickly cut a deal with Accardo and the wire service war ended.

"Numbers" or "policy" proved to be another new moneymaker for Accardo. Numbers was basically an illegal lottery, particularly popular in black neighborhoods in the South Side of Chicago.

The Outfit's foray into numbers was spearheaded by small-time mobster Sam Giancana. While serving time in the mid-1940s, Giancana made the acquaintance of a black inmate named Ed Jones, who controlled "policy" operations on the South Side. Jones apparently explained to Giancana how the racket worked and who the key players were. Giancana expressed his gratitude by repeating all of this information to a very attentive Accardo.

Around 1946, the Outfit began moving in on African American gangsters running the numbers racket. Through intimidation and violence, the Mafia came to dominate Chicago's numbers scene by the early 1950s. Around the same time, the Outfit also got involved with casino gambling, investing in gaming houses in Cuba. In 1959, however, Communist guerrilla Fidel Castro took power in Cuba and closed the casinos, chasing the Mafia out of the country. The Outfit turned its gaze to Las Vegas, which was beginning to boom as a casino/entertainment destination. By the early 1960s, the Outfit had a stake in several Vegas casinos, including the Fremont, the Desert Inn, and the Riviera.

Perhaps with visions of Johnny Torrio's exit in mind, Accardo voluntarily stepped down as mob boss in 1957. Numbers man Giancana became boss, though he still reported to the semiretired Accardo.

Giancana proved to be a handful. Nicknamed "Mooney," Giancana was notoriously hot-headed. He started romancing Phyllis McGuire, a member of the clean-cut pop singing group, the McGuire Sisters. This high-profile romance gave the FBI plenty of opportunities to stalk Giancana and to provoke and unnerve the high-strung mob boss.

During the early 1960s, the Outfit faced greater scrutiny from the forces of law and order. As attorney general, Robert Kennedy began focusing on the Mafia and the corrupt unions with which it was involved, such as the Teamsters. In Chicago, a new, incorruptible police boss began raiding Outfit gambling dens and harassing the city's underworld.

In 1965, federal authorities ordered Giancana to testify before a grand jury or face contempt charges. Giancana refused to play along and was duly incarcerated on June 1, 1965. By this point, Giancana had been acting erratically for some time. His subordinates organized a coup and removed Giancana from the top spot. After getting out of jail in May 1966, Giancana fled the country rather than quibble with his rebellious underlings. He took up residence in Mexico.

At this juncture, Sam "Teets" Battaglia began a short-lived career as Outfit boss. Battaglia was jailed for racketeering in 1967 and replaced by Phil Alderisio, who himself was jailed in 1969 and consequently replaced by Jackie Cerone. Cerone was promptly convicted for gambling offenses in May 1970 and sentenced to five years in jail. After this, three Outfit leaders—Gus Alex, the semiretired Accardo, and Joey Aiuppa—ran the mob as a sort of triumvirate for a brief period. The idea was to groom Aiuppa until he was competent enough to take charge all on his own. The power trio ruled for a few years and then ceded full command to Aiuppa.

The mob got involved in new ventures, such as the "chop shop" business. This involved taking stolen cars, cutting them up, and selling the parts individually (which made it almost impossible to trace them back to any one particular purloined vehicle).

At the same time, the political landscape in Chicago was changing. Old-school autocratic political bosses such as the infamous Mayor Richard Daley were on their way out. The rise of the civil rights movement saw African Americans electing local officials who were neither beholden in any way to the Outfit nor interested in working with the organization. During the 1960s and 1970s, legitimate investors, particularly eccentric tycoon Howard Hughes, began pouring money into Las Vegas. Casino operators no longer had to rely on the Mafia for funding.

At this juncture, Giancana was expelled by the Mexican government and decided to return to Chicago. His presence was unwelcome, and on June 19, 1975, Giancana was assassinated in his Oak Park, Illinois, home by an unidentified gunman.

By the 1980s, the Outfit had become a considerably leaner organization than back at its peak in the Eisenhower era. Arrests at the top didn't help matters. In January 1986, Aiuppa and four other mob bosses were convicted in a Kansas City, Missouri, trial of skimming $2 million in profits from the Stardust casino/hotel in Las Vegas. Government prosecutors claimed that the "skim" was taken to Kansas City where it was then divided up between crime families in Chicago, Milwaukee, and Cleveland. The case represented "the most significant prosecution of organized crime figures in the history of the United States," hyperbolic Chicago FBI chief Edward Hegarty told the *Chicago Tribune*.[4]

Following Aiuppa's conviction, Joe Ferriola took over as leader of the Outfit. Ferriola died three years later, and Sam Carlisi became boss. In 1993, Carlisi was himself convicted and replaced by John DiFronzo. By this point, long-time Outfit stalwart Accardo was dead and the Chicago mob was limping along. A decision was made by mob managers to keep a very low profile. The initiative proved so successful that by the mid-1990s, authorities weren't even sure who was in charge of the Outfit any more. It was believed DiFronzo was still boss, but other possible contenders for the throne included mob leaders such as Joey "the Clown" Lombardo and Joe "the Builder" Andriacci.

An unwritten "no trafficking" rule was somewhat relaxed following Accardo's death. Previous Outfit bosses had prohibited "made" members in their ranks from selling drugs. This was largely out of fear that stiff sentences would encourage members to break Omerta if caught by police.

The new policy, formulated in the 1990s, was that Outfit members could traffic drugs, but only on their "own" time. Trafficking was not considered "official" Outfit business. Anyone who wanted to sell drugs would have to do so as a freelance operator, in addition to their regular Outfit duties. In other words, Mafiosi would have to moonlight if they wanted to sell dope. The Outfit wouldn't help them if they were caught. "Unlike their New York counterparts, the Outfit has traditionally stayed away from drug trafficking, preferring instead crimes such as loan sharking and online gambling operations and capitalizing on other profitable vices," notes a recent FBI press release.[5]

This new line on drugs was in effect for only a few years when the Outfit was severely tested in a sprawling trial in federal court. In the summer of 1998, FBI offices in Chicago received a typewritten letter dated July 27, 1998, from an imprisoned mobster named Frank Calabrese Jr. Calabrese Jr. was serving time at a federal penitentiary in Milan, Michigan, for loan sharking. His father, Frank Calabrese Sr., and uncle, Nicholas, were both major Outfit players. "I am sending you this letter in total confidentiality. It is very important that you show or talk to nobody about this letter except who you have to. The less people that know I am contacting you, the more I can and will help and be able to help you," stated the introduction to the letter.[6]

No doubt the Chicago FBI read this letter in growing astonishment. In his communication, Calabrese Jr. offered to meet with the FBI and fill them in on his father's crimes. Calabrese Sr., who was also in jail at this point, had committed multiple homicides.

Calabrese Jr. agreed to wear a recording device disguised in a pair of headphones to catch his father in incriminating conversation. Calabrese Sr. didn't suspect a thing and cheerfully engaged in detailed conversations about Mafia matters during father-son prison visits.

"Soon our agents had collected enough information—and corroborated it with evidence—to build an iron-clad case against the senior

Calabrese for the 1986 murder of mobster John Fecarotta in Chicago. The evidence also clearly implicated Calabrese's brother, Nicholas W. Calabrese ... faced with overwhelming evidence, Nicholas decided he wanted to cooperate too. He started spilling more family secrets. A lot of them, in fact, including details about 18 previously unsolved mob hits," states an FBI press release.[7]

The FBI dubbed the case "Operation family Secrets." The FBI gathered a mountain of evidence and handed it over to a federal grand jury. In April 2005, the grand jury returned a 43-page indictment against more than a dozen men.

A total of 14 defendants were arrested for racketeering and involvement in 18 murders between 1970 and 1986. Authorities specifically named the "Chicago Outfit" as a criminal enterprise under the federal RICO (Racketeer Influenced and Corrupt Organizations) statute. RICO essentially acts as a force-multiplier: once identified as leaders of a criminal enterprise, defendants are subjected to heightened criminal and civil sanctions.

Those arrested included ranking Outfit members James Marcello, Joseph "the Clown" Lombardo, Michael Marcello, Nicholas Ferriola, Joseph Venezia, Thomas Johnson, Dennis Johnson, Frank Saladino, Michael Ricci, Frank "the German" Schweihs, Anthony "Twan" Doyle, Nicholas Calabrese, Frank Calabrese Sr. and Paul "the Indian" Schiro. Two defendants—Doyle and Ricci—were former Chicago police officers. Seven defendants—James Marcello, Lombardo, Frank Calabrese Sr., Nicholas Calabrese, Schweihs, Saladino, and Schiro— were accused of murder. Saladino was found dead in a hotel room before he could be taken to trial. Ricci also died before trial.

In a press release, Robert Grant, special agent-in-charge of the Chicago FBI office, described the charges as "a milestone event in the FBI's battle against organized crime here in Chicago ... while there have been many successful investigations during the past quarter-century resulting in the arrest and indictment of high-ranking members of the Chicago Outfit, never before have so many in lofty positions in the Chicago mob been charged in the same case."[8]

The Family Secrets trial began in U.S. District Court in Chicago in June 2007. Star witnesses included Nicholas Calabrese and Frank Calabrese Jr., both testifying against their kin. Some low-ranking defendants choose to plead guilty. This narrowed the prosecution down to five core defendants—Marcello, Lombardo, Doyle, Schiro, and Frank Calabrese Sr. On September 10, 2007, the jury (whose names were kept secret from both the defendants and the lawyers in the case for security's sake) found the five guilty of racketeering conspiracy. Specific charges included making usurious loans, illegal gambling, imposing "street taxes," and using violence and murder to further the Outfit's goals.

The jury was not done yet. Jurors still had to deliberate about the 18 murders involved in the case. On September 27, 2007, the jury decided that three defendants—Lombardo, Marcello, and Frank Calabrese Sr.—were responsible for 10 of the murders in the case. Jurors were unable to reach a verdict for the remaining slayings. In March, 2008, Michael Marcello received 8.5 years.

On July 23, 2008, Schweihs died of cancer. Three weeks later, Venezia (who pled guilty to gambling and tax charges before the trial proper began) was sentenced to 40 months in prison. That same month, Ferriola (son of reputed mob leader Joseph Ferriola and alleged godson of Frank Calabrese Sr.) received three years, while Dennis Johnson got six months.

In late January 2009, Schiro was sentenced to 20 years in prison for racketeering conspiracy. Two days after Schiro's sentence was handed down, Frank Calabrese Sr. got life in prison. Frank Calabrese would eventually die in federal prison, three years later. Lombardo and Marcello in turn also received life sentences. Former police officer Doyle was given 12 years for passing evidence to an imprisoned mob boss.

One sentence drew intense public criticism. Nicholas Calabrese admitted he had taken part in the murder of 14 people. He was only sentenced to 12 years in prison, however, for testifying against his fellow mobsters.

A gloating FBI press release described the trial as "one of the most successful organized crime cases in FBI history."[9] Crime writers have been quick to note the historic dimensions of the Family Secrets case. "The men on trial were relics and dinosaurs, the remnants of the Chicago syndicate of the 1920s. Their convictions heralded the end of the mob of the last century, men who had been links on the Outfit's chain from Capone to Accardo to Aiuppa," stated author Jeff Coen.[10]

In a press release, Special Agent Ted McNamara, head of the La Cosa Nostra organized crime squad for the Chicago FBI, surveyed what remained of the Outfit: "The Chicago mob does not have the power and influence it once had. But the mob still operates and its members still represent a potentially serious criminal threat."[11]

The Chicago Outfit has survived near-death experiences in the past. It remains to be seen, however, if it can shrug off this latest round of high-level convictions and the exposure of its inner workings in a Chicago courtroom.

Notes

1. Paul Sann, *The Lawless Decade* (New York: Bonanza Books, 1957), 37.
2. John Kobler, *Capone: The Life and World of Al Capone* (Cambridge, MA: Perseus Books Group, 1971), 246.
3. Federal Bureau of Investigation, "Chronological History of La Cosa Nostra in the United States: January 1920–August 1987," October 1987.
4. Ronald Koziol, "5 Convicted of Mob Skimming," *Chicago Tribune*, January 22, 1986.
5. Federal Bureau of Investigation, "The Chicago Mafia: Down but Not Out," June 27, 2011.
6. Jeff Coen, *Family Secrets: The Case That Crippled the Chicago Mob* (Chicago: Chicago Review Press, 2009), 13.
7. Federal Bureau of Investigation, "Family Secrets of the Murderous Kind," October 1, 2007.
8. United States Attorney, Northern District of Illinois, U.S. Department of Justice, "14 Defendants Indicted for Alleged Organized Crime Activities; 'Chicago Outfit' Named as RICO Enterprise in Four-Decade Conspiracy Alleging 18 Mob Murders and 1 Attempted Murder," April 25, 2005.
9. Federal Bureau of Investigation, "The Chicago Mafia: Down but Not Out."
10. Coen, *Family Secrets*, 396–97.
11. Federal Bureau of Investigation, "The Chicago Mafia: Down but Not Out."

CHAPTER FOUR

The Mafia across America

Cleveland

Cleveland played host to a vicious gang war between the Mafia and a wily Irish American mobster in the mid-1970s. Explosive devices were used so extensively in this fight pundits took to calling Cleveland "the bombing capital of America." Such violence was par for the course for the Cleveland Mafia, given its bloody origins.

Joseph "Big Joe" Lonardo was the city's top Italian American crime boss during Prohibition. Lonardo became wealthy and powerful selling corn sugar to bootleggers who used it to manufacture corn liquor. Cleveland fronts onto Lake Erie, so bootleggers also kept up a brisk trade in smuggled alcohol from Canada.

Lonardo was killed on October 13, 1927, by Salvatore Todaro, who then became top boss in town. Two years later, Todaro was killed by Lonardo's teenage son, Angelo Lonardo. A new hood named Joe Porello became Italian American underworld boss, only to be gunned down in a restaurant on July 5, 1930. At this juncture, Frank Milano took charge.

Milano stayed on top for five years. After being indicted for income tax evasion, Milano fled to Mexico, leaving Al Polizzi to take charge. Polizzi ushered in a relatively lengthy period of stability at the top. With the end of Prohibition in 1933, the Cleveland Mafia directed its energies to gambling, loan sharking, and slot machines.

On October 19, 1944, Polizzi pled guilty to charges of failing to pay federal liquor taxes and was jailed. After his release a year later, Polizzi voluntarily stepped down and retired to Florida. He handed the reins to former burglar and stick-up man John Scalish.

Scalish would rule for four decades, creating an underworld Mafia empire in Cleveland. In addition to gambling and loan sharking, Scalish earned money through pinball machines and other ventures. When Ohio governor Frank Lausche closed Cleveland-area gambling casinos in the early 1950s, Scalish invested in a vending machine business. The company was hugely successful, largely because of the violent tactics Scalish's minions used to eliminate competition.

During Scalish's era, the Cleveland Mafia became involved in Las Vegas, with a stake in the Desert Inn and other casinos. The Cleveland Mafia took a share of the "skim" from their Vegas interests. Somewhat old-fashioned, Scalish wouldn't allow members of his mob family to sell drugs or pimp women.

While he was an excellent businessman, Scalish neglected other aspects of his position, such as appointing a successor. When Scalish finally died, in May 1976, it was unclear who was supposed to succeed him. "Even as the last shovels of dirt covered [Scalish's] gold-inlaid casket, the Cleveland underworld was already in turmoil. Perhaps John Scalish was wreaking some kind of revenge on his old enemies or his weakened condition diverted him from making the one crucial decision a capo should make. He did not pick a successor—one who could keep the peace among warring lieutenants and decide, once and for all, who got what and when," reads a story in *Cleveland* magazine. "That sin of omission, if you will, led to the bloodiest and most tumultuous internecine gang wars here since the savage bootleg brawls some 50 years earlier—when Scalish, a teenager, was just getting his start in crime," added the magazine.[1]

Violence and chaos became ever more prominent thanks to the rise of Irish American mob boss Danny Greene. Greene had no respect for the Mafia and recklessly tried to seize control of illegal gambling operations and labor racketeering in the city (the Cleveland underworld was heavily involved with the Teamsters union). In September 1976, Leo

"Lips" Moceri, underboss to the Cleveland Mafia, disappeared and was presumed murdered by Greene's hoods.

A war of attrition ensued between Greene and the Mafia (now led by James Licavoli, who managed to become boss in the chaos following Scalish's death). Both sides were fond of using explosives. During a one-year period in the mid-1970s, there were 37 bombings in Cuyahoga County, including 21 just in Cleveland itself, more than in any other U.S. city at the time according to the Bureau of Alcohol, Tobacco, and Firearms. Greene was finally killed (by a car bomb) on October 6, 1977, and the war came to an end.

By the early 1980s, the Cleveland Mafia had become locked into a new battle with an even more tenacious foe as the FBI investigated the family's top leadership. Licavoli was convicted on gambling charges and involvement in Greene's death. On July 30, 1982, Licavoli was sentenced to 17 years in prison. He died of a heart attack in a federal penitentiary in Wisconsin two years later.

Licavoli wasn't the only prominent Mafiosi caught in the FBI's net. In April 1983, family underboss Angelo Lonardo was given a 103-year term for drug offenses (evidently Scalish's successors didn't adhere to his ban on trafficking).

Facing a lifetime behind bars, Lonardo began cooperating with federal authorities. He testified at various trials and on March 10, 1987, his sentence was reduced to time served plus five years probation.

On April 4, 1988, Lonardo gave a lengthy summation of his life in the Mafia before a Senate subcommittee. He discussed Cleveland underworld operations from the late 1920s to the present. He casually admitted to homicide. ("[M]y father was murdered by Salvatore Todaro in 1927. In revenge, my cousin, Dominic Sospirato and I killed Torado. This is one of the reasons that I was proposed for membership in La Cosa Nostra.") He also explained the inner workings of the Cleveland Mafia. According to Lonardo, the Genovese family represented Cleveland's interests on the Commission, the Mafia's quasi-administrative body.[2]

He also took the time to complain about the changing nature of the underworld: "Mr. Chairman, I have been in the Mafia most of my adult life. I have been aware of it ever since I was a child in Cleveland. It has changed since I first joined in the 1940s and especially in the last few years with the growth of narcotics. Greed is causing younger members to go into narcotics without the knowledge of the families. These younger members lack the discipline and respect that made 'This Thing' as strong as it once was," said Lonardo.

Since Lonardo's defection, the Cleveland LCN has struggled to regain the prominence it once enjoyed. The current boss of the battered clan is reportedly Russell Paplardo, of whom little is known.

Detroit

Prohibition enriched the Italian American underworld across the United States, leading to the emergence of a formal, structured U.S. Mafia in the early 1930s. In Detroit, however, bootlegging operations were dominated by the Purple Gang, a group of tough, mostly Jewish thugs. From the dawn of Prohibition in 1920 to the early 1930s, the Purples were the biggest, strongest gang in the Motor City. Italian American mobsters were minor street criminals by comparison. The Purple Gang had such a reputation for violence and mayhem that some of its key members were recruited to take part in the St. Valentine's Day Massacre in Chicago in 1929.

An organized Detroit Mafia came together in the early 1930s, under the guidance of William "Black Bill" Tocco. By this point, Prohibition was clearly on its way out and with it, the source of the Purple Gang's financial clout and power. Some of the Purples left the city to work for Jewish American gangsters such as Meyer Lansky in other locales.

By the time Tocco passed the leadership torch to Joe Zerilli, the Mafia had become the top underworld power in town. The long-reigning Zerilli had a clever way of cementing group loyalty. Zerilli decreed that Mafiosi under his command could only marry the female kin of other Mafiosi. Zerilli believed this would ensure stability and loyalty. In this, he was largely successful, a point even the FBI conceded. "Detroit La Cosa Nostra members are tightly bound through blood and marriage, making the organization extremely difficult to penetrate," notes an online history of the Detroit FBI.[3]

After Prohibition, Zerilli's crime family earned its keep through gambling, loan sharking, money laundering, drug trafficking, and infiltration of legitimate business, among other activities. Crime historians say the Detroit Mafia peaked in the 1960s, with roughly 100 "made" members and countless associates.

Zerilli's reign lasted all the way into the 1970s. He designated his son, Anthony "Tony Z" Zerilli, as his successor. In 1973, Anthony Zerilli was incarcerated for "skimming" Las Vegas casinos (i.e., collecting undeclared revenue). As a result, Joe Zerilli demoted his own flesh and blood and made his nephew, Jack Tocco, second-in-command.

The Detroit Mafia was involved in a long-lasting underworld mystery: the disappearance of controversial labor leader Jimmy Hoffa. From the late 1950s through to the early 1970s, Hoffa headed the International Brotherhood of Teamsters. He was jailed in 1967 and released in 1971 with the proviso that he abstain from Teamsters work for several years. Hoffa was having none of that and attempted to regain control of his heavily mobbed-up union. On July 30, 1975, Hoffa was scheduled to meet with Detroit Mafiosi Anthony Giacalone and a Teamsters official named Anthony Provenzano. Hoffa was seen that day near a restaurant in Bloomfield, Michigan. Then, he disappeared off the face of the earth. Hoffa's fate had been widely speculated on with the general consensus he was murdered and buried in parts unknown.

Two years after Hoffa vanished, legendary boss Zerilli died, of natural causes. Tocco took charge. One of Tocco's first moves was to appoint Anthony Z. Zerilli as underboss, a move intended to mollify the onetime heir apparent.

In April, 1990, the FBI opened a racketeering investigation into the Detroit Mafia. The investigation centered on loan sharking, extortion, and the collection of "street taxes" from various hustlers involved in illegal gambling. The FBI received court approval to install wiretaps, which they used to monitor Mafia conservations. The case was dubbed "Operation Gamtax" by the FBI.

After carefully gathering evidence for years, the FBI made a dramatic move in March 1996, arresting nearly the entire leadership of the Detroit Mafia. Family boss Tocco was convicted of racketeering and extortion and jailed in 1998. Intriguingly, one of the men indicted in the case was Anthony Giacalone—the same Mafia player scheduled to meet Hoffa on the day he disappeared. Giacalone died of kidney disease before his trial started, taking with him any secrets he might have had about Hoffa's fate.

Tocco was released from federal prison in 2002. According to a crime history posted on the Detroit CBS website, Tocco was still boss of the Detroit Mafia as of mid-2011.

Joe Zerilli's goal of creating a stable, cohesive Mafia clan appears to have worked. "Unlike most of the country's mob families in the last three decades that have been torn apart at the seams from within, overwhelmed by informers or 'rats' as they're called in underworld circles, the Detroit mob has been [almost] virtually free of turncoats," stated the CBS Mafia history.[4]

One of the few "turncoats" in the Detroit mafia, a "rat" named Nove Tocco, started cooperating with federal authorities after being convicted in the Gamtax case. The grandson of Zerilli, Nove Tocco proved less than loyal by testifying against his peers in open court.

Marriage ties might have also prevented the Detroit Mafia from slipping into internecine warfare of the kind that has shattered La Cosa Nostra families in other cities. In fact, there have been relatively few murders associated with the Detroit Mafia in recent years (possibly in part due to a deliberate strategy of avoiding violence whenever possible).

Detroit Mafia strength is currently pegged at around 40–50 members. It fell as low as 30–35 members during the Gamtax trial but appears to have risen slightly, as a venerable Midwest mob family recovers from a devastating FBI investigation.

Las Vegas

While Mafia money turned Las Vegas into a gambling Mecca, the city's true mob founder was Jewish American gangster Benjamin "Bugsy" Siegel.

Desperate to raise tax revenues during the Depression, Nevada legalized casino gambling in 1931. For years, however, the legal gambling industry remained underdeveloped. By the 1940s, there were a few casinos and gambling dens in Las Vegas, but it remained a sleepy backwater. The larger hotel/casino operations were relatively upscale but still exuded a hick cowboy air.

William Wilkerson wanted to break this mold. The founder of the *Hollywood Reporter* newspaper and a string of upscale nightclubs in

This is an exterior view of the Aladdin Hotel and Casino as it sits on the Las Vegas Strip Thursday, March 14, 1996, in Las Vegas. A 41-page federal indictment against the Detroit Mafia said the mob acquired or tried to acquire a hidden financial interest in the casino in the 1960s. (AP Photo/Lennox McLendon)

Los Angeles, Wilkerson planned to create a hotel/casino that would be different than anything in Vegas at the time. The hotel/casino he envisioned would feature the best amenities (restaurant, pool, café, tennis courts) and attract celebrities and high rollers. Guests would be entertained by top musicians and singers. There wouldn't be a hint of cowboy décor or ambience.

Wilkerson picked up some investment funds for this project from the underworld. In the mid-1940s, Jewish American gang leaders Meyer Lansky and Bugsy Siegel, along with Mafia boss Frank Costello and several other partners, founded the Nevada Project Corporation. The corporation would be the vehicle by which the mob helped fund Wilkerson's hotel/casino project. Lansky asked Siegel to oversee the corporation's investment in the Nevada sands. It was not a wise choice; while handsome and charming, Siegel was notoriously erratic (the term "Bugs," the basis of Siegel's nickname, was slang at the time for "crazy") and violent.

Back in Vegas, construction on Wilkerson's dream hotel/casino began in March 1946. Crews worked night and day at the massive site. Siegel became more closely involved in the project. Even though building supplies were hard to come by in postwar Nevada, Siegel managed to get his hands on black-market materials. Wilkerson was supposed to be Siegel's boss, but Bugsy was soon chafing under his leadership. Siegel started ordering changes without seeking Wilkerson's approval.

The hotel/casino was now dubbed the Flamingo (Siegel's pet name for his mistress, Virginia Hill). As Siegel gained more control over the Flamingo, he began spending money with manic glee. He insisted on the finest materials (such as rare wood and expensive marble) and was constantly altering plans and changing his mind about aspects of construction. Ironically, Siegel was likely the victim of petty racketeers. It was rumored that shady contractors sold goods to Siegel at inflated prices, only to steal them from the worksite and sell them back to the distracted gangster.

Costs for the Flamingo soared, eventually nearing $6 million, a staggering amount of money in the late 1940s. Siegel shuttled back and forth between Los Angeles and Las Vegas, all the while dealing with increasingly nervous mob investors, who now wanted to recoup their $6 million investment. The underworld was deeply unhappy with the cost overruns on the project and openly questioned whether the hotel/casino would be a success.

Throughout late 1946, Siegel and Wilkerson scrounged up cash from banks and mobsters alike to keep construction going. Under extreme pressure from his underworld partners, Siegel doubled the size of the workforce and paid extravagant overtime rates to encourage productivity. Siegel also foolishly moved up the opening date of the Flamingo from March 1, 1947 (the date Wilkerson preferred) to December 26, 1946.

Sure enough, the Flamingo opened the day after Christmas, even though the facility was not complete. A large crowd of local residents turned out (partly out of curiosity), but only a handful of celebrities.

Construction was still going on during the opening, and the dealers working the casino tables were raw and unsteady. The Flamingo lost money on its opening night, and continued losing money for several days after. The place might have recouped costs by renting out expensive hotel rooms, except the hotel wasn't finished and there was nowhere for guests to stay.

Far from being a cash cow, the Flamingo was draining mob coffers. Siegel shut the place down in late January 1947, so workers could finally finish construction. Lansky and his underworld partners were not happy.

On March 1, 1947, the Flamingo was reopened. The hotel was finally done and the operation began making money. Still, the mob wasn't satisfied. Lansky and other crime bosses wanted Siegel to promptly pay them back the millions he had borrowed, plus interest. Siegel refused, telling the bosses he would pay on his terms and schedule. It was typical, impulsive Siegel, thumbing his nose at some of the most powerful gang bosses in the country.

By this point, Siegel's checks were bouncing. In the spring of 1947, two huge checks—one for $100,000, the other for $50,000 were returned to him. The checks had been made out by Siegel to Del E. Webb Construction, the company that built the Flamingo. The $100,000 check had its payment stopped while the $50,000 check was returned for insufficient funds.

Siegel was sitting on a couch in his mistress's Beverly Hills mansion, reading a paper, when he was killed. On June 20, 1947, a sniper with a .30-caliber military M1 carbine snuck into Hill's backyard and shot Siegel four times. It was never clear who ordered Siegel's murder. Lansky always denied involvement, although he was one of the investors closest to Siegel.

In some ways, Siegel had the last laugh. The Flamingo quickly got over its growing pains and proved to be a massive draw. Lansky took over the management of the hotel/casino and made it a huge success. Soon, the underworld was pouring money in Las Vegas. By the early 1960s, the city was dotted with huge casinos/hotels that offered legal gambling amidst luxurious accommodations, just like the Flamingo.

The Cleveland Mafia came to have a share in the Desert Inn casino, while the Chicago Outfit had investments in the Stardust casino/hotel, Fremont, and Riviera. The Detroit Mafia also had their hand in Vegas. Mafia favorite Frank Sinatra was soon a top performer in Vegas, as a solo artist or with the gang of friends dubbed "the Rat Pack."

In return for their financial support, the Mafia expected casinos to allow them to "skim" from undeclared revenues. Mafia bagmen would enter casinos in which their organization had a stake and help themselves to some of the cash the house had won from unfortunate gamblers before it was declared for tax purposes. Needless to say, authorities regarded skimming as a form of tax evasion.

In 1973, Anthony "Tony Z" Zerilli, son of longtime Detroit Mafia chieftain Joseph Zerilli and the heir apparent in the Motor City, was jailed for skimming. As a result, Joe Zerilli demoted his own son and made his nephew, Jack Tocco, second-in-command.

Thirteen years later, Joey Aiuppa, boss of the Chicago Outfit, and four other Mafiosi were convicted in Kansas City, Missouri, of skimming $2 million in profits from the Stardust casino.

The same year Aiuppa was jailed, violent mob enforcer Anthony Spilotro was murdered. Spilotro was a notorious Chicago Outfit thug who ran amok after being assigned to Vegas. Spilotro drew too much police attention to underworld operations in Las Vegas, so he was marked for death by his peers. Martin Scorsese's movie *Casino* depicted Spilotro's end in grim detail. In the film, Spilotro and his brother, Michael, are lured to a cornfield, only to be set upon with baseball bats wielded by aggrieved Mafiosi. The two men are battered and then buried alive amidst the corn rows.

While this made for gripping cinema, this celluloid depiction wasn't accurate. During the so-called "Family Secrets" trial of the Chicago Outfit, it was revealed that the Spilotro brothers were actually murdered in the basement of a Chicago home, then buried in an Indiana cornfield.

In the 1960s and 1970s, legitimate entrepreneurs such as Howard Hughes began investing heavily in Las Vegas. Vegas businessmen realized that casinos backed with licit funds and run by respectable managers were more profitable than "mobbed up" casinos. Legitimate operations had lower overhead (fewer bribes to hand out, no need to pad the payroll with underproductive Mafiosi, and no skim) and weren't subject to police raids.

As the investment side of Vegas became cleaner, the gaming industry itself tightened regulations on the operation of casinos.

The new rules were designed to make the ownership of casinos more transparent and weed out underworld backers.

The growing spread of legal casino gambling across the United States and Canada took away some of Vegas' naughty allure. Atlantic City, New Jersey, legalized casino gambling in the 1970s. Countless other jurisdictions followed suit, and soon it was no longer necessary to go to Vegas for a high-rolling, legal casino experience. Las Vegas itself began to emphasize nongaming attractions, such as live entertainment, cheap meals, and luxury hotel accommodations. No doubt Bugsy Siegel would be delighted at the growth of the gambling industry in Vegas, though somewhat mystified by the city's eventual rejection of gangster money.

Los Angeles

If the New York City and Chicago Mafias are, respectively, the lead actor and understudy of La Cosa Nostra, then the Los Angeles Mafia has traditionally consisted of bit players, even comic relief. Despite being based in one of the largest American cities, the Los Angeles branch of LCN has been derisively dubbed "the Mickey Mouse Mafia."

There are several reasons why. For a start, Los Angeles has a smaller population of Italian Americans to tap into for Mafia recruits, compared to the cities of the East and Midwest. The Los Angeles Mafia has also had to deal with ferocious competition and an embarrassing, much-publicized murder of one of its members at the hands of a young girl.

The LA Mafia, such as it is, has its roots in the Little Italy section of the city. There, in the early decades of the twentieth century, a local Italian American crime boss named Tony "the Hat" Cornero reigned supreme. The area was a hotbed of violence, with a section of one street called "Shotgun Alley." In 1925, an underworld war broke out for control of the lucrative bootlegging business. Cornero was annoyed that ships and trucks transporting his liquor kept getting hijacked, despite hefty payoffs to city police and politicians. Cornero put together an army of 100 thugs but was eventually chased out of town by the LAPD, which had a reputation for both corruption and off-the-books brutality.

When the U.S. Mafia was formalized in the early 1930s, a gangster named Jack Dragna emerged as head of the Los Angeles branch of La Cosa Nostra. Dragna had to contend with pressure from authorities and competition from fellow hoods.

In 1938, law-and-order-minded Earl Warren became attorney general of California. Among other actions, Warren went after underworld-run gambling ships that moored off the coast, slightly past the three-mile international line. Mobsters believed the location of their fleet protected them from authorities looking to enforce anti-gambling laws. The gangsters who ran these ships were so cocky, they openly advertised on billboards and in newspapers. Ignoring the fact the ships were in international waters, Warren had the vessels boarded and raided.

The 1930s and 1940s saw the Mafia move into the movie business. Hollywood shakedowns of the period were largely directed by the Chicago Outfit, however, not the LA Mafia. The most high-profile gangster in town during this period—Benjamin "Bugsy" Siegel—wasn't even part of the Mafia. Siegel was a charming, Jewish sociopath with a predilection for attractive women and the highlife. In theory, Siegel was supposed to answer to Dragna, but he mostly went his own way. His real employer was Jewish mob boss Meyer Lansky.

Siegel partied with Hollywood celebrities for a while and then became obsessed with building an upscale casino in Las Vegas. Throughout the late 1940s, Siegel continued to live on and off in Los Angeles but put most his energy into his Vegas dream casino (no doubt to Dragna's relief).

In the same period, Los Angeles experienced a major economic upswing. "Post World War II Los Angeles was booming with the construction, aircraft and movie industries operating in high gear. There was so much loose money floating around that bookie joints, gambling parlors and brothels peppered the city like palm trees. And there to seize some of the action was the syndicate. It was not unusual to see East Coast hoods hanging out in fancy clubs that dotted the Sunset Strip in the late 1940s," states a rather colorful account on the LAPD website.[5]

While the city offered plentiful money-making opportunities, the Mafia found themselves pitted against a tough-minded police force. In 1946, LAPD police chief Clarence Horrall set up a "Gangster Squad" charged with collecting intelligence and harassing local mobsters, Mafia-affiliated or not. The squad, which numbered around 18 men at most, was not above using strong-arm tactics and nonauthorized electronic surveillance devices.

A retrospective article in the *Los Angeles Times* quoted former Sergeant Jack O'Mara, on the Gangster Squad's habit of taking mobsters up the hills of Mulholland Drive in Los Angeles at night. On these slopes police would "have a little heart-to-heart talk with 'em, emphasize the fact that this wasn't New York, this wasn't Chicago, this wasn't Cleveland. And we leaned on 'em a little, you know what I mean?" O'Mara told the *Times*.[6]

On top of police pressure, Dragna had to deal with competition from violent Jewish American mobster Mickey Cohen. The relationship between the two mob bosses was not especially cordial. At one point, Cohen held up a racing wire room run by Dragna. This was a large operation with dozens of phones. Cohen and company stole some $30,000 and refused to give the money back.

In 1948, Dragna's goons tried to shoot Cohen as he strolled outside a nightclub on the Sunset Strip. The hit men failed, but such gunplay alarmed Attorney General Warren. Warren set up a private commission to look into organized crime and corruption in California. Efforts were also made to weed out corruption in the LAPD.

On February 23, 1956, Dragna was found dead in a hotel room, apparently of natural causes. He was succeeded by Frank DeSimone, who proved to be an inept boss. A few months after becoming family boss, DeSimone's underboss, Girolomo (Momo) Adamo, shot and seriously injured his wife and then committed suicide in San Diego. Adamo's wife was having either a consensual or forced affair (accounts vary) with DeSimone. If true, DeSimone violated a central Mafia tenet not to engage in sex with the spouses and daughters of fellow LCN members.

Another sex-related Mafia murder—of LCN soldier Johnny Stompanato—would prove an even greater public relations disaster for the mob. A former Marine, Stompanato was a handsome but thuggish Mafia soldier who moved to Los Angeles and became the lover of Hollywood actress Lana Turner. By all accounts, the relationship was tumultuous and Stompanato was a brute. On April 4, 1958, Stompanato and Turner got into a ferocious argument at Turner's Beverly Hills home. Believing her mother was in physical danger, Turner's 14-year-old daughter Cheryl plunged a kitchen knife into Stompanato's stomach. Stompanato died, Cheryl was acquitted on grounds of justifiable homicide, and the LA Mafia became an underworld laughingstock.

Los Angeles boss DeSimone died in less dramatic fashion, of natural causes on August 4, 1967. He was succeeded by Nicolo Licata.

On July 9, 1972, family underboss Dominic Brucceleri (aka Dominic Brooklier) and several other LCN members and associates were indicted on charges of extorting cash from local bookies, loan sharks, pimps, and other hustlers. Three years later, Brooklier (who took over as family boss following Licata's death in October 1974) and other Mafia leaders were convicted, with punishments ranging from 15 months to four years in jail.

On February 28, 1978, Brooklier got indicted again, along with four other LA Mafiosi for extortion, obstruction of a criminal investigation and other charges. He was convicted and jailed in 1980, dying four years later in federal custody.

The LCN tried to rebuild under acting boss Peter Milano but continued to be battered by law enforcement. In October 1984, the LAPD cracked down on Mafia-run bookmaking and gambling operations. Adding insult to injury, the police called the investigation "Operation Lightweight." Police chief Daryl Gates contemptuously dismissed the LA LCN as the "Mickey Mouse Mafia."[7]

The Los Angeles Mafia again began to feel the pinch of fierce competition. The 1980s saw the emergence of powerful African American– and South American–based street gangs, battling for control of the city's crack cocaine market.

On May 21, 1987, Peter and his underboss brother Carmen were indicted by a federal grand jury in Los Angeles. The indictment accused the Milano brothers and a handful of other LCN members of conspiring to violate the RICO statute by being part of a criminal enterprise engaging in drug trafficking, extortion, and violence, among other offenses.

By this point, the media viewed the LA LCN with something approaching pity. A profile published on June 28, 1987, in the *Los Angeles Times*, noted that Carmen Milano drove a 1973 Buick and lived in a modest home. The piece was headlined, "Not Entrenched like Eastern Families: The LA Mob Eking Out of a Living Working Streets."

The article said the LA Mafia was "barely 20 members strong, loosely organized and frequently ignored by its more powerful East Coast associates." As evidence of the latter, the piece pointed out that the Los Angeles LCN didn't even control the city's billion-dollar pornography business. This trade was dominated by Mafia families from Chicago and New York.

"The federal government's most recent investigations make clear that the Los Angeles mob is still largely working the streets, meeting in restaurant back rooms and threatening to break heads over $25,000 drug deals and $500 a week Shylock loans," stated the *Times* article, contemptuously. The *Times* described Dragna as "perhaps the only classic 'Godfather' that the city has ever known" and said the LA Mafia went into decline following his death.

In late March, 1988, seven mobsters, including Peter Milano, pled guilty in court, "in a case that may have sounded the death knell for organized crime in Southern California," as the *Los Angeles Times* put it.[8] Milano's guilty plea on racketeering charges came "on the eve of what could have been a six-month trial targeting the entire hierarchy of the mob in Southern California—a case which Attorney General Edwin Meese III has called the most significant organized crime prosecution on the West Coast in more than a decade," continued the article. Prosecutor Richard Small boasted that authorities had effectively put La Cosa Nostra out of business in Los Angeles.

As of 2012, Peter Milano is still alleged to be boss of whatever remains of La Cosa Nostra in Los Angeles.

New England

For the past few years, the most distinguishing feature of the New England Mafia has been the frequency with which its leaders have been put in jail. The latest round of arrests stem from Mafia shakedowns of Rhode Island strip bars—an act of criminality so petty the New England media has taken to openly mocking La Cosa Nostra's declining fortunes.

By virtue of geography, the New England Mafia has never been as wealthy as the New York City mob. Aside from Boston, New England has few cities of any notable size. Despite this, a powerful Italian American underworld did operate in New England for decades.

Raymond L. S. Patriarca is usually identified as the main driver behind the emergence of an organized Mafia in the New England region. Born in 1908 in Worcester, Massachusetts, Patriarca's family moved to the state of Rhode Island when he was young. His father ran a liquor store while his mother worked as a nurse. His first arrest came in 1938, when he was picked up for a robbery at the Narragansett Race Track. Throughout his life, he would rack up dozens of arrests and serve almost 12 years in jail on four separate convictions.

By the mid-1950s, Patriarca was well established as top don of the New England Mafia. He based his headquarters in the offices of the "Coin-O-Matic" automated machine business in Providence, Rhode Island. He relied on typical Mafia mainstays such as illegal gambling, loan sharking, and dealing in stolen goods to earn his keep.

Patriarca's final arrest came in March 1980. He was accused of involvement in two murders that took place in 1968. The victims were Robert "Bobby" Candos (a career bank robber who was going to testify against Patriarca) and Raymond "Baby" Curcio. Curcio was a small-time hustler who had the spectacularly bad luck to break into a home belonging to Patriarca's brother. For this violation of underworld protocol, the burglar earned a far harsher punishment than he would have received in court.

By this point, Patriarca was in bad health. His defense attorney claimed he was too sick to go to trial. There was some truth to this: on July 11, 1984, Patriarca died of heart failure while visiting his mistress.

Following a brief power struggle, Patriarca's son, Raymond Patriarca Jr., took over the reins of the New England Mafia. Patriarca Jr. had the unflattering nickname "Rubber Lips" (from his less-than-impressive physical appearance). It was whispered he was never the real mob boss, merely its figurehead. Rubber Lips "couldn't lead a Brownie troop," sneered South Kingstown Police chief Vincent Vespia in an article posted on the website of Providence TV station WPRI-12.[9]

In 1989, a police wiretap provided authorities with an audio recording of a house full of Mafiosi in Medford, Massachusetts, inducting four new members into the fold. Needless to say, such rituals are supposed to be conducted in utmost secrecy. The existence of the wiretap was greatly embarrassing for Patriarca Jr., particularly when the recordings were played to a federal grand jury. In March 1990, Patriarca Jr. was indicted for racketeering, murder, extortion, and drug trafficking.

At trial, Patriarca Jr. was found guilty and given an eight-year sentence. He served his time and was released, but did not go back to his underworld ways. According to WPRI-12, Patriarca Jr. currently makes his living from legitimate real estate transactions, not organized crime.

Mafia observers believe that Nicholas "Nicky" Bianco was the real power behind the throne during Patriarca Jr.'s reign. Bianco operated from the shadows, where all successful Mafia leaders dwell. He took over for good once Patriarca Jr. was put away. Bizarrely enough, Bianco wasn't a "made" man when he assumed the top job. Bianco was quickly invested into the Mafia's ranks, so he could serve as mob boss in a formal capacity.

Bianco did not rule for long. He was convicted of racketeering charges in August 1991 and was given an 11-year sentence later that same year. Bianco came down with Lou Gehrig's disease and died in a federal penitentiary in Springfield, Missouri, in November 1994.

In Bianco's absence, his underboss, Frank "Cadillac Frank" Salemme became the top New England boss. Salemme's big move was to transfer the mob's locus of power from Providence to Boston.

Salemme's mob career was notable for an unusual act of kindness to an authority figure. In the late 1960s, Salemme was jailed for his role in the January 30, 1968, car bombing of a lawyer named John E. Fitzgerald. Fitzgerald survived the attack but was seriously maimed. Sentenced to 15 years in jail, Salemme became a hero when he helped a guard who had been shot and injured by an inmate. For this unexpected act of decency, Salemme got a commendation from then Massachusetts governor Michael Dukakis.

In 1989, Salemme was ambushed outside a pancake house in Saugus, Massachusetts, when he arrived, unarmed, for what was supposed to be a mob meeting. Salemme was shot in the leg and chest. Police believed a rival Mafia faction was behind the act.

Salemme was indicted on racketeering charges in January 1995 and arrested in August of the same year. Four years later, in a plea agreement, Salemme pled guilty to the charges and received an 11-year sentence.

Luigi "Baby Shacks" Manocchio took over the New England Mafia in 1996 after Salemme was imprisoned. Manocchio moved La Cosa Nostra's New England "headquarters" back to Providence.

Manocchio was dining in a Providence restaurant in 2008, when the FBI decided to pay him a visit. In the course of their investigation, FBI agents discovered an envelope stuffed with marked bills in Manocchio's possession. Through some sleuthing, the FBI determined the money came from the Cadillac Lounge strip club. It seemed that the New England Mafia had been reduced to extorting adult entertainment businesses for "protection" money. Mafiosi would demand cash from owners and threaten violence or vandalism if they didn't pay up. After the visit by the FBI, Manocchio voluntarily resigned as head of the New England Mafia.

For a brief period in 2009, the New England Mafia was led by Peter Limone, whose criminal career included 33 years spent in jail for a murder he didn't commit. Limone was boss for only a few months; the same year he took power, he was arrested on state gambling charges.

The year 2010 marked the ascent of Anthony DiNunzio. With his brother Carmen "the Big Cheese," DiNunzio got his start in the Chicago Mafia. The two brothers were convicted in 1993 of extorting gamblers in Las Vegas. The pair served their time and then headed to Boston. It is believed Anthony DiNunzio took power after Limone was arrested.

While DiNunzio consolidated his shrinking empire, a former family head tried to evade the law. Manocchio was arrested in January 2011 in Fort Lauderdale for extorting strip club owners. In March 2011, he was slapped with a superseding indictment. When it came to court, Manocchio pleaded guilty in February 2012. On April 25, 2012, DiNunzio was arrested by the FBI on racketeering and extortion charges, also in connection to the strip club "protection" racket.

Battered by arrests and convictions, the New England Mafia wasn't exactly thriving at this point, as the media gleefully pointed out. "New England Mafia a Shell of Its Former Self," stated a headline to a *Boston Globe* article published May 8, 2012. "This is the leadership of the New England Mafia, a skeleton of the organization glorified in novels and in Hollywood. No more than 30 made or sworn-in members make up an organization that in its heyday was more than 100 strong, law enforcement officials say ... investigators, legal observers and court records describe an organization that continues to erode, as made members and associates abandon the code of silence and cooperate with officials ... long-time Mafia observers said the arrest of DiNunzio was disappointing, embarrassing even, given that the once-proud organization had resorted to shaking down strip clubs," read the *Globe*.

More embarrassment was to come. On May 11, 2012, Manocchio was sentenced in federal court on extortion charges. The unofficial Mafia Code of Conduct calls for stoicism in the face of arrest or trial. Manocchio, for his part, tried to shift the blame to his peers. "By virtue of my position, I inherited the deeds of my associates," Manocchio told the court, according to an article in the *Boston Globe* published the day of the arrest. His lawyer, Joseph Balliro, was quoted as saying, "He is very sensitive to anyone, especially the public, thinking he is this very bad guy. That's not his reputation." No matter: Manocchio received a five-and-a-half year sentence, to be served in federal prison.

The convictions kept coming. Anthony DiNunzio pled guilty to racketeering and extortion conspiracy in U.S. District Court in Providence, Rhode Island, on September 13, 2012. Again, the extortion charges were based on threats to strip club owners. "Through their painstaking hard work, the prosecutors, agents and detectives have decimated organized crime in Rhode Island and, with his pleas today, have removed its leader in Boston," stated U.S. Attorney Peter Neronha, in a Department of Justice press release.[10] The press release also noted that DiNunzio—who remains boss for the time being—was the eighth member of the New England Mafia to plead guilty in charges relating to the strip club shakedown, a pathetic coda for a once strong LCN family.

New England Sidebar: The Strange Case of James "Whitey" Bulger and Stephen "The Rifleman" Flemmi

In January 1995, New England Mafia chief Frank "Cadillac" Salemme was indicted on racketeering charges, along with two codefendants—his best friend, Stephen "the Rifleman" Flemmi, and cunning Irish

American crime boss James "Whitey" Bulger. Flemmi and Bulger were both career criminals who had committed several murders.

Salemme was astonished to discover that his codefendants were also longtime FBI informants. Making things even more galling, Bulger had gone into hiding, having been tipped off a few weeks earlier by his FBI handlers about the coming indictments. The indictment against Bulger stemmed from crimes he committed while informing to the Boston FBI throughout the 1980s and early 1990s. Flemmi, who had been informing since the 1960s, did not flee and was taken into custody.

A much-chagrined Salemme was arrested for racketeering in August 1995. Four years later, in a plea agreement, Salemme pled guilty to the charges and received an 11-year sentence. As he was being led away, Salemme revealed the extent of his bitterness. "I learned my lesson," he told reporters, according to the *Boston Globe*. "Shame on me if I didn't know after what happened to me in the last 35 years with my best friend [Flemmi]. Shame on me if it happens again."[11]

Bulger, meanwhile, remained at large. In 1999, he was added to the FBI's Ten Most Wanted Fugitives list. In September 2000, Bulger was indicted for additional crimes including his part in 19 killings.

While Bulger remained on the lam, Flemmi was brought to justice. In October 2003, he took a plea bargain and pled guilty to 10 murders, plus drug dealing, extortion, and racketeering, in exchange for a life sentence.

Bulger was finally arrested on June 22, 2011, in Santa Monica, California. A month later, he pleaded not guilty to multiple counts of racketeering, extortion, money laundering, perjury, obstruction of justice, weapons violations, and the 19 murders from the previous indictment. As of spring 2013, the octogenarian crime boss remained behind bars, awaiting trial.

Philadelphia

In August 2009, *Philadelphia Magazine* published a lengthy feature with the provocative title, "What Ever Happened to the South Philly Mob?" The reporter noted there hadn't been any Mafia-related killings in Philadelphia for several years. This was quite a contrast from previous eras, which saw constant Mafia infighting in the City of Brotherly Love.[12]

The article suggested two reasons for the sudden drop in violence. First, the Philly Mafia had been greatly reduced in size, thanks to internal strife and intense police pressure. (The *Philadelphia Magazine* claimed there were only 20 active Mafiosi left in the city as of 2009, with roughly 130 associates. Other sources cite 50 "made" members and around 270 associates. In either case, these are relatively small numbers for a city of 1.5 million people.)

The second factor centered on the placatory personality of Joe "Uncle Joe" Ligambi, the top Mafia boss in town. Ligambi was credited with toning down the violence that used to curse the city's Italian American underworld. Ligambi worked from the shadows (like traditional Mafia bosses) and lived a low-key lifestyle.

This is not to say Ligambi was a wimp: he was convicted in 1989 for murdering a Mafia associate named Frankie "Flowers" D'Alfonso and placed in jail. At a retrial in 1997, the conviction was overturned and Ligambi was acquitted and released.

Nor has Ligambi managed to avoid run-ins with the law; two years after the *Philadelphia Magazine* article came out, he was arrested by the FBI for racketeering and other crimes and is currently in jail.

Ligambi is one in a line of Mafia bosses in Philadelphia stretching back to the early 1930s. Prominent Philly dons include Angelo Bruno, who was in power from 1959 to 1980, a staggeringly long tenure by Mafia standards. His longevity probably had something to do with his negotiating skills: Bruno's nickname was "the Gentle Don." He preferred diplomacy over gunplay and frowned on drug trafficking. Bruno was "an avuncular man who took a decidedly low profile ... [he] dressed in nondescript business suits bought off the rack at local department stores and rode around town in Plymouths and Chevys. He avoided the limelight and generally got along with everyone, even those who had been investigating him for years," wrote crime author George Anastasia.[13]

Bruno's charming personality wasn't enough to prevent his assassination, however. He was shotgunned to death on March 21, 1980, as he sat in a car in front of his home. Bruno was 69 years old.

One of the top suspects in the killing was Bruno's consigliere (adviser) Antonio "Tony Bananas" Caponigro. It is believed Caponigro was impatient with Bruno, whom he regarded as a doddering old fool, unwilling to jump into the drug trade or take advantage of legal casino gambling in Atlantic City, New Jersey. Some speculation posits that Caponigro had delusions of grandeur and thought he might replace Bruno as top boss of the city.

Whatever the case, Bruno's death unleashed a wave of violence as Mafiosi fought for control. Before the end of 1980, Caponigro was dead, along with three other men suspected of involvement in the assassination. The butchery didn't stop with the quartet's demise. "In the 19 years immediately following Bruno's murder, there were 35 mob-related killings in Philadelphia," stated *Philadelphia Magazine*.[14]

Bruno was replaced by his underboss, Philip "the Chicken Man" Testa. Testa ruled the city for only a few short months before being blown to pieces by a remote-control explosive device at his home. Testa was replaced by the notorious Nicodemo "Little Nicky" Scarfo. "Little Nicky ran the Philadelphia Mafia from his apartment . . . in Atlantic City [New Jersey] during the 1980s, and set a gangland record for killing off, demoting and exiling members of his own crime family," stated an August, 15, 2007 article in the *Philadelphia City Paper*. "He was an arrogant, in-your-face Mafia don, the epitome of the egocentric 1980s, a matching mob bookend for New York's John Gotti," added Anastasia, in *The Goodfella Tapes*.[15]

Scarfo ruled—or, rather, misruled—from 1981 to 1987. In one notorious incident, Scarfo demoted Salvatore Merlino from underboss (i.e., second-in-command) to soldier (the lowest caste in the hierarchy of "made" Mafiosi). Needless to say, this caused bad blood within Scarfo's crime family.

Scarfo was arrested in 1987 and eventually convicted, in separate trials, for extortion and racketeering. The latter case centered around nine murders and four attempted members in which he allegedly had a hand. Scarfo was found guilty and given a steep sentence. He is currently scheduled for release in 2033. Given that he is in his 80s, it is doubtful Little Nicky will ever be a free man again.

With Scarfo behind bars, his enemies turned their attention to members of his biological family. On Halloween night 1989, Scarfo's son, Nicodemo Scarfo Jr., was eating in a South Philadelphia restaurant when a gunman wearing a Batman mask entered and shot him seven times at close range. Amazingly, Scarfo Jr. survived and left the hospital after only a week of convalescence. It is believed that Joseph

"Skinny Joey" Merlino (son of the underboss demoted by Little Nicky Scarfo) was responsible for the shooting. The motive: simple revenge against the flesh and blood of the man who wronged his father.

Scarfo was a paranoid case and a bad manager of Mafiosi talent. Instability at the top made the Philly mob more vulnerable to the forces of law and order.

Despite this chaos, the Philly Mafia plunged on. By the late 1980s, John Stanfa had stepped up as top don. He was convicted in 1995 on racketeering charges involving five murders and sentenced to life in prison. Stanfa was replaced by Ralph Natale, who had an alliance with Skinny Joey Merlino. In 1999, Natale was indicted for drug trafficking. He turned government witness and was given a 13-year sentence, served in protective custody in a federal penitentiary, as his reward for testifying against his peers. Natale was released from prison in 2011 and is said to be working on his memoirs.

Skinny Joey Merlino took over from Natale, following more factional fighting. Merlino proved to be an irresponsible ruler, more interested in a good time than in running a successful mob family. Skinny Joey's time at the top was brief. In 2001, he was slapped with a 14-year sentence for racketeering. That same year, Ligambi took over and instituted a reign of relative peace.

"Prevalent opinion holds that Joe Ligambi's crew is all about the things Joey Merlino never demonstrated: Restraint. Stealth. Discretion. Merlino allegedly did it all—theft, cocaine, murder—then hit the nightclubs on Delaware Avenue on weekends where he partied the night away and extorted money from the owners," stated *Philadelphia Magazine*.[16]

Ligambi was still high profile enough to attract the attention of authorities, however. On May 23, 2011, Ligambi and a handful of mob cronies were arrested by the FBI on gambling and loan sharking charges. In a press release, Assistant Attorney Lanny Breuer described the takedown as "the largest enforcement action in a decade against La Cosa Nostra in Philadelphia."[17]

Interestingly enough, the 50-count superseding indictment hinted that Ligambi's crew was coasting on their past image as barbarians. "According to the superseding indictment, the defendants promoted and furthered their illegal money-making activities through violence, actual and implied threats of violence and the cultivation and exploitation of the Philadelphia LCN family's long-standing reputation for violence."

In April 2012, the imprisoned Ligambi was hit with another indictment, charging him with theft from an employee benefit plan run by the Teamsters union. More specifically, Ligambi was accused of holding a "no-show" job with the Teamsters, for which he received a salary and health benefits. As the name implies, a no-show job is a position in a legitimate business occupied by a member of the Mafia, who never turns up for work but gets paid in full anyway.

Interestingly enough, prosecutors in Ligambi's trial have suggested he isn't the actual leader of the Philly Mafia. A memo issued by prosecutors in May 2012 indicated that Skinny Joey Merlino (who was released from jail in 2011 and moved to Florida, where he claimed to be semiretired) was still in charge of La Cosa Nostra in Philadelphia. The memo was based on information gleaned from wiretapped mob conversations from a gangster turned government witness. This document referred to Ligambi as the "acting boss" of the Philadelphia Mafia, but not de facto chief. If the memo is correct, Merlino would be in violation of his parole, which states he is not supposed to associate with organized crime figures or anyone who is a known felon.[18]

For now, attention is focused on Ligambi, whose trial opened in October 2012. While another acquittal is possible, the recent history of Philadelphia Mafia bosses is grim. Unless he bucks the historical trend, Ligambi stands a good chance of either being incarcerated for years or murdered by rivals.

Notes

1. Edward Whelan, "The Life and Hard Times of Cleveland's Mafia," *Cleveland Magazine*, August 1978.
2. Angelo Lonardo, testimony before the Permanent Subcommittee on Investigations of the Senate Committee on Government Affairs, April 4, 1988.
3. Federal Bureau of Investigation, "Investigative Programs: Organized Crime: Gamtax," http://www.fbi.gov/about-us/investigate/organizedcrime/cases/gamtax.
4. James Buccellato and Scott M. Burnstein, "Organized Crime in Detroit: Forgotten but Not Gone," CBS Detroit website, June 24, 2011, http://detroit.cbslocal.com/2011/06/24/organized-crime-in-detroit-forgotten-but-not-gone.

5. Los Angeles Police Department, "About the Vice Division," http://www.lapdonline.org/detective_bureau/content_basic_view/1987.
6. Paul Lieberman, "Crusaders in the Underworld: The LAPD Takes on Organized Crime," first of seven parts, *Los Angeles Times*, October 26, 2008.
7. Kim Murphy, "Not Entrenched Like Eastern Families: The L.A. Mob: Eking Out a Living Working Streets," *Los Angeles Times*, June 29, 1987.
8. Kim Murphy, "7 Alleged Southland Mafia Figures Enter Guilty Pleas," *Los Angeles Times*, March 30, 1988.
9. Tim White, "The History of New England's Mob Bosses: A Rhode Island Legacy of Mafia Dons," WPRI-12 website, published November 24, 2008, updated March 26, 2012, http://www.wpri.com/dpp/news/local_wpri_underworld_bosses_rhode_island_20081124.
10. Peter F. Neronha, United States Attorney, District of Rhode Island, U.S. Department of Justice, "Acting New England Crime Boss Pleads Guilty in Racketeering and Extortion Conspiracy," September 13, 2012.
11. Shelley Murphy, "A Contrite Salemme Sentenced to 11 Years," *Boston Globe*, February 24, 2000.
12. Steve Volk, "What Ever Happened to the South Philly Mob?" *Philadelphia Magazine*, August 2009.
13. George Anastasia, *The Goodfella Tapes* (New York: HarperCollins, 1998), 38–39.
14. Volk, "What Ever Happened to the South Philly Mob?"
15. Anastasia, *The Goodfella Tapes*, 15.
16. Volk, "What Ever Happened to the South Philly Mob?"
17. U.S. Department of Justice, "Leadership, Members and Associates of the Philadelphia La Cosa Nostra Family Charged with Racketeering Conspiracy and Related Crimes," May 23, 2011.
18. George Anastasia, "Merlino Still Runs Philly Mob, Court Document Says," *Philadelphia Inquirer*, May 4, 2012.

CHAPTER FIVE

Law and Order

New Orleans police chief David Hennessy was almost certainly the first American law officer murdered by the Mafia, or at least, an embryonic version of it. Chief Hennessy was gunned down by assailants on October 15, 1890, during an intense period of strife between Sicilian American gangs in the city.

While lurid New Orleans newspaper headlines blamed the assassination on "the Mafia," an organized American Mafia wouldn't actually emerge until decades later. The violence gripping the city was more of a case of Old World banditry applied to a New World setting. No matter; citizens of New Orleans panicked at the prospect of a new, foreign criminal organization in their midst. Mass hysteria ensued, followed by a mass lynching of suspected "Mafiosi."

Chief Hennessy's involvement with the Sicilian American underworld remains an open question. Some sources suggest the chief was corrupt and taking bribes from gang leaders, while other accounts peg him as an honest man determined to crush the mobsters in his midst.

If Chief Hennessy was ambivalent in his dealings with the underworld, the same cannot be said about New York police lieutenant Joseph Petrosino. At the turn of the twentieth century, Lieutenant

Detective lieutenant Joseph Petrosino heads the Italian Squad of the New York City police force (ca. 1908). The Italian Squad was a regular arm of the police department that did undercover work against the Black Hand (a forerunner of the American Mafia). All members were Italian with the exception of an Irish officer, who spoke Italian. (New York Daily News *Archive via Getty Images)*

Petrosino headed up an "Italian squad" that dealt with issues in that community. One of the biggest issues facing Sicilian and Italian American immigrants at the time was the presence of "the Black Hand." Another forerunner of the Mafia, the latter was a loose band of Italian Americans who used the (largely fictitious) specter of an underworld gang called "The Black Hand" to extort money from their countrymen. The fearless Petrosino made hundreds of Black Hand arrests and wasn't above beating up suspects in the street for added humiliation.

In March 1909, Petrosino traveled to Palermo, Sicily, to investigate Black Hand links with the Sicilian Mafia. On March 12, 1909, he was murdered, almost certainly by Mafia assassins. He remains the only New York City police officer killed while on assignment in another country. When his body was returned to the United States, an estimated 250,000 people viewed his coffin as it passed by on the streets of New York, mourning a brave cop.

The 1920s saw the advent of Prohibition, the U.S. government's ill-fated attempt to stamp out liquor by force of law. Aspiring gangsters who might have remained small-time thugs created a thriving black market in illegal alcohol and became rich in the process. In the early 1930s, some of these gangsters united in a structured, organized American Mafia. Bloated with cash derived from bootlegging, this new American menace was particularly virulent in Chicago and New York City.

The federal response to the advent of a homegrown Mafia was feeble at first. The Bureau of Prohibition (the agency charged with enforcing the national ban on alcohol) was riddled with corruption and incompetence. The Federal Bureau of Investigation (FBI), meanwhile, was weak, understaffed, and not particularly interested in fighting organized crime.

Founded in 1908, the FBI was a controversial agency from its birth. The agency's mission was to enforce federal laws. Southern politicians feared that the FBI would investigate civil rights abuses in Dixie. They were not eager to hand over resources and power to a national police force with the authority to combat segregation in the South. As a result, for decades after the FBI's birth, agents weren't even allowed to carry guns or make arrests. The FBI was a purely investigatory body.

These Southern politicians need not have worried. Longtime FBI director J. Edgar Hoover had no interest in enforcing civil rights. The agency wouldn't move on such matters until ordered to by President Lyndon Johnson.

Nor was Hoover terribly concerned with organized crime. When finally granted authority to carry firearms and make arrests in the mid-1930s, the FBI focused on gun-toting bandits such as Pretty Boy Floyd, the Barker family, John Dillinger, and Baby Face Nelson. Hoover flatly rejected the notion of a domestic, organized U.S. Mafia with a national reach.

There are many theories to explain Hoover's detached view, from the conspiratorial (the Mafia had compromising pictures of Hoover, a confirmed bachelor) to simply bureaucratic (it was easier to focus on arresting bank robbers and car thieves; investigations into organized crime might take years and produce scanty results at considerable expense). Hoover might have had practical considerations, too: investigating organized crime would have opened FBI agents to corruption. Hoover remembered Prohibition and how the agents in charge of enforcing the law were paid off to look the other way. It was safer to focus on common criminals who had neither the resources to bribe their way out of trouble nor friends in high places.

In stark contrast, Harry Anslinger, commissioner of the Federal Bureau of Narcotics (FBN), readily acknowledged the presence of an American Mafia. Like Hoover, Anslinger was a veteran bureaucrat who remained in office for decades. While he had a more realistic understanding of organized crime than Hoover, Anslinger believed the U.S. Mafia was controlled by kingpins in Sicily—which was completely untrue. While some early Mafia leaders such as Salvatore Maranzano emerged from the Sicilian Mafia, La Cosa Nostra (i.e., the American Mafia) has always been independent of foreign-based crime bosses. Given that Anslinger's men could act only when federal drug laws were violated, the FBN's impact on the Mafia was limited.

Some mobsters, such as Al Capone in Chicago, did face determined action from government officials. Authorities in the Internal Revenue Service (IRS) carefully built a tax evasion case against Capone, while flamboyant local policeman Eliot Ness raided his illegal businesses. In 1931, Capone was convicted of income tax evasion and sent to prison—a clear victory for the U.S. government.

Five years later, hard-driving special prosecutor Thomas Dewey targeted the operations of New York Mafia boss Charles "Lucky" Luciano. Luciano was found guilty of running a prostitution ring and sentenced to 30–50 years in jail. Luciano served only a few years, however. He was released after World War II for unspecified services rendered to the U.S. government.

Dewey went on to prosecute fellow New York crime boss Arthur Flegenheimer (aka "Dutch Schultz"—whose Jewish heritage precluded him from joining the Mafia) and to be elected state governor. Dewey ran unsuccessfully for president on the Republican ticket in

1944 and 1948 and is still viewed today as an icon of integrity and dogged persistence.

The postwar record of law enforcement against the Mafia is extremely mixed. Right up to the late 1950s, FBI director Hoover continued to insist there was no such thing as an American Mafia. Hoover's stance was a little hypocritical, given that FBI agents did in fact keep close watch on gangsters throughout the 1940s and 1950s. Their efforts, however, were primarily focused on surveillance, not making cases.

If Hoover was complacent, others weren't. In the early 1950s, Tennessee senator Estes Kefauver held televised hearings around the country into organized crime. In total contradiction to Hoover's stance, Kefauver acknowledged the existence of a domestic Mafia.

While authorities argued about whether a U.S. Mafia existed, the underworld continued to rumble. On October 25, 1957, Gambino crime family boss Albert Anastasia was murdered in a barber chair in Manhattan's Park-Sheraton Hotel. The assassination had been hatched by Vito Genovese and Carlo Gambino.

The same year Anastasia was killed, a group of Mafia bosses decided to get together for a conference in small-town Apalachin, New York. The conference was held in mid-November, 1957 on the bucolic estate of Joseph Barbara, president of the Canada Dry Bottling Company and longtime Mafia associate. It is believed the meeting was called at Genovese's behest. Genovese wanted to justify Anastasia's murder and was eager to put himself forward as "boss of bosses" in New York City.

Another topic of discussion was the Mafia's role in drug trafficking. Mafia leaders were squeamish about illegal drugs largely because penalties were so severe at the time.

It was a full agenda, but the 60–100 mobsters who descended on Barbara's estate never had a chance to discuss any of it. On November 13, 1957, a state trooper named Edgar Croswell became intrigued by the number of big, black limousines driving through the countryside. Croswell sought help from the local unit of the federal Bureau of Alcohol, Tobacco, and Firearms. Sergeant Croswell and another trooper, backed by two agents from the ATF, drove out to Barbara's house on November 14, 1957. The officers spotted about 30 vehicles parked at the residence. Prominent crime bosses present included Joseph Bonanno,

Joseph Profaci, Paul Castellano, Santo Trafficante, Sam Giancana, and a slew of others. The gangsters, who were getting ready to enjoy a nice barbecue, panicked at the sight of the police. Some mobsters took to the woods and tried to run through brush while clad in dress shoes and expensive overcoats.

Croswell called for reinforcements and police quickly established roadblocks. Authorities detained about 46 men who tried to get past the roadblocks in vehicles. They caught another dozen or so who were running around the forest. Police were astonished at the amount of money each mobster had on hand. Some of them carried thousands of dollars in cash. They were also amazed to discover the mobsters came from across the United States. Clearly, this was not just a local gathering of small-time criminals.

The gangsters were smart enough not to carry concealed weapons (which would have left them open to criminal charges), so the police let them go. It was obvious that the mob bosses were plotting criminal activities at Barbara's house, but police couldn't prove it.

Even though the attendees weren't charged with any crimes, the botched conference was extremely embarrassing for the underworld. The incident punctured the aura of secrecy that made the Mafia such a potent force (the names of all those detained were published in newspapers). Also, the image of mob bosses taking to the forest to flee a handful of cops was embarrassing in the extreme.

After Apalachin, it became much harder for Hoover to say the Mafia didn't exist. To save face, the FBI director fixed on the term "La Cosa Nostra" (an Italian expression meaning "our thing" and the term American Mafia members used to describe their organization) and claimed it was a brand new criminal group. According to Hoover, authorities everywhere had somehow missed out on the birth of this new, organized underworld.

Post-Apalachin, Hoover had his aides put together a special report on the Mafia. The study was completed in July 1958, and was top secret at the time. The authors of the study (which was officially called the "Mafia Monograph") were blunt in their assessments.

"The roundup of 61 Sicilian-Italian hoodlums at Apalachin, New York on November 14, 1957, once again focused the public spotlight on the Mafia in the United States," stated the report. "For years, there have been speculations as to the existence or nonexistence of such an organization in this country. Available evidence shows that beyond the shadow of a doubt, the Mafia does exist today in the United States, as well as in Sicily and Italy, as a vicious, evil and tyrannical form of organized criminality." The report added, for good measure, that "[t]he Mafia represents one of the most ruthless, pernicious and enduring forms of criminality ever to exist in the United States."

Authorities estimated the U.S. Mafia boasted 4,000–5,000 formal members (plus 10 times that number of associates) in 24 crime families across the country.

Shortly after Apalachin, the FBI introduced a "Top Hoodlum Program" (THP). Each FBI office was instructed to come up with a list of exactly 10 "top hoodlums" in their region. Once identified, these hoods would be subjected to greater FBI scrutiny. While at least a start, the THP had obvious flaws. FBI offices in New York and Chicago had hundreds of gangsters to choose from, but bureaus in rural locales and underpopulated states had difficulty filling their quota of hoods. THP was useful, however, in gathering information that was later put to good use in future crackdowns on the mob.

The late 1950s saw two other major developments. In 1957, the Select Committee of the U.S. Senate launched a probe into labor racketeering. The purpose of the probe was to determine if the Mafia and certain unions—particularly the Teamsters—were working in collusion. These hearings are primarily remembered today for the epic clash between Robert Kennedy, on the investigators' side, and Teamsters president Jimmy Hoffa. The probe did, however, alert the public to the dangerous inroads the Mafia had made into legitimate labor organizations.

Cracking the Mafia's tradition of secrecy had always been a source of frustration for law enforcement groups. The Mafia didn't hold public meetings at which they discussed their plans for the future. Meetings were private, plans were clandestine. To find out what the Mafia was talking about, police had to either slip an informer into the mob's ranks (difficult but not impossible), rely on the occasional traitor such as Joseph Valachi to come forward (a rare occurrence), or plant listening devices in underworld locales. The problem was that listening devices (better known as "bugs") were illegal to use.

Back in 1934, legislation was passed prohibiting "wiretapping"—that is, inserting a bug on a telephone to record conversations. The logic was, in order to plant a bug, you had to trespass on private property, and that was against the law. The same applied to bugs planted in walls, light fixtures, or elsewhere.

Prior to World War II, the U.S. attorney general said the FBI could plant wiretaps in cases involving national security. In 1954, Attorney General Herbert Brownell reaffirmed this ruling, and said it was fine to bug subversive groups if national security was at stake. The attorney general had the Communist Party in mind, but according to some accounts, FBI director Hoover took a broader view. He decided the ruling also applied to investigations of organized crime groups. The Top Hoodlum Program, for example, relied heavily on electronic surveillance. Despite the attorney general's assurances, evidence gathered through bugs still fell into a legal gray area and wasn't admissible in court.

Electronic surveillance was finally legalized in June 1968 with the passage of the Omnibus Crime Control and Safe Streets Act. The act permitted authorities to plant bugs and wiretaps, provided they got a court order first. Police and federal agencies now had a powerful weapon to use against the underworld. Words spoken in private by Mafia bosses could be surreptitiously recorded and used in court to secure convictions. Gambino family boss John Gotti, for example, was brought down in part by his habit of delivering voluble monologues about Mafia business that were recorded by police.

Protecting witnesses was another issue that law enforcement had long struggled with. In the past, authorities occasionally made informal arrangements to protect witnesses, such as Valachi.

The Organized Crime Control Act of 1970 established a formal witness protection program for people testifying against criminal organizations. Called the Witness Security Program, the initiative is run by the U.S. Marshals Service. In some cases, witnesses are simply guarded to ensure they make it to court. In other cases, witnesses and their families are given new identities, complete with phony identification and documentation, and relocated around the country. Housing and living expenses are paid for by the government. "The U.S. Marshals have protected, relocated and given new identities to more than 8,300 witnesses and 9,800 of their family members since the program began in 1971," reads a notice on the U.S. Marshals Service website.[1]

The existence of the Witness Security Program has proven a powerful lure to wavering witnesses fearing Mafia retaliation. Famous Mafiosi participants in the program include Henry Hill and Salvatore "Sammy the Bull" Gravano, Gotti's right-hand man. Both men were kicked out of the program for committing new criminal acts. For less unruly participants, the Witness Security Program has proven highly effective. "No Witness Security program participant, who followed security guidelines, has been harmed while under the active protection of the U.S. Marshals," boasts the agency's website.

The Organized Crime Control Act of 1970 also addressed another major issue that had long bedeviled law enforcement. The hierarchical structure of the American Mafia made it difficult to hold family "bosses" to account for crimes committed on their behalf. Since most bosses were smart enough to let low-echelon members handle the family's dirty work (bosses rarely participated in "hits," for example) gathering evidence against them was difficult. Even if authorities did successfully prosecute the odd Mafia boss (such as Luciano), another mobster simply took their place.

This situation was largely rectified by the advent of the Racketeer Influenced and Corrupt Organizations (RICO) Act. Included in the Organized Crime Control Act of 1970, RICO essentially criminalized the Mafia and groups like it. It no longer mattered if you didn't commit any crimes yourself; the issue was whether you belonged to an organization that broke the law. If you did, you could be put in jail.

"Under the statute, the leaders of any organization can be prosecuted when the group's members commit crimes that show a pattern of racketeering. Prosecutors do not have to prove that the leader personally committed the illegal acts, only that he supported the specific crime in some ways, such as approving them or sharing in any illegal profits," explained a March 4, 1985, story in *Time* magazine. Thanks to RICO, prosecutors could go after an entire Mafia family, not just individual members. The untouchable family bosses could finally be brought down.

RICO also attacked mobsters on the financial front, where they were extremely vulnerable. RICO allowed authorities to launch civil suits for damages and freeze suspects' assets even before they were convicted. Needless to say, this made mounting a defense quite a bit more difficult and lessened the possibility of bribed jurors and judges.

Unfortunately, RICO was complicated and burdensome and was largely ignored for years. Some prosecutors wondered whether it was even constitutional (it did, after all, make free association a crime).

Under President Ronald Reagan, the U.S. government's war on organized crime was drastically ramped up. New hard-driving prosecutors such as Rudolph Giuliani came to the fore. From 1983 to 1988, Giuliani served as U.S. attorney for the Southern District of New York. Giuliani was firmly committed to attacking the Mafia with every means at his disposal, including RICO.

As a U.S. attorney, Giuliani was a prime mover in the effort to incarcerate every New York Mafia Family boss. In February 1985, federal authorities indicted all five bosses on RICO charges involving labor racketeering, extortion, and murder. The indicted five consisted of Paul Castellano of the Gambino family, Carmine Persico of the Colombo (formerly Profaci) family, Anthony "Tony Ducks" Corallo of the Lucchese family, Philip "Rusty" Rastelli of the Bonanno clan, and Anthony "Fat Tony" Salerno of the Genovese family. The Family underbosses were indicted as well. This unprecedented sweep was designed to cripple "the Commission"—the Mafia board of directors set up by Lucky Luciano.

Not all the bosses who were indicted ended up in court. On December 16, 1985, Castellano and his underboss, Thomas Bilotti, were gunned down in front of the Sparks Steak House in Manhattan. Their murders had been carefully arranged by Gotti, who then seized control of the Gambino clan.

The so-called Commission trial began in September 1986. Rastelli was severed from the trial because he had charges pending elsewhere. A key government witness was FBI agent Joseph Pistone, who as "Donnie Brasco" had successfully infiltrated the Mafia in New York. In November 1986, all the defendants were found guilty and received huge sentences (in some cases, upward of 100 years in jail).

Under Giuliani's reign, hundreds of Mafiosi were imprisoned. His successors have continued the fight, using RICO as a legal bludgeon. "Finally realizing the full potential of the once slighted Racketeer Influenced and Corrupt Organizations Act, federal prosecutors are trying to destroy Mafia families by convincing juries that their very existence is a crime, that their leaders should be imprisoned for long terms and that, eventually, even their ill-gotten gains can be confiscated," stated a *Time* magazine article from June 24, 2001.

An article in the March 5, 2006, *New York Times* cited mob expert Jerry Capeci (author of several Mafia-related books) on RICO's impact: "The mob's biggest loss of sway and overall earning power, has not been the result of criminal prosecutions but of civil racketeering statutes. The Racketeer Influenced and Corrupt Organizations Act—RICO—has let authorities oust hundreds of mobsters and associates from unions with a long history of corrupt activities."

If RICO has proven a brutally effective tool of federal law enforcement, the Mafia has also been hounded by state authorities over the past few decades. "The combined federal and state campaigns (of the 1980s and 1990s) were arguably the most successful anti-crime expedition in American history. Over a span of two decades, 24 mob families, once the best organized and most affluent criminal associations in the nation, were virtually eliminated or seriously undermined," wrote crime author Selwyn Raab in his book, *Five Families*.[2]

Law enforcement continues to ratchet up gains against a weakened Mafia. On January 20, 2011, for example, 91 members and associates of seven Mafia families from New York, New Jersey, and New England were charged with a wide range of crimes, from loan sharking, murder, robbery, and arson, to labor racketeering and illegal gambling. Attorney General Eric Holder described the indictments as the "largest single day operation against La Cosa Nostra," in a Department of Justice press release.[3]

"Some believe organized crime is a thing of the past; unfortunately there are still people who extort, intimidate and victimize innocent Americans. The costs legitimate businesses are forced to pay are ultimately borne by American consumers nationwide," stated FBI director Robert S. Mueller III in the same press release.

As the FBI director acknowledged, no one in law enforcement thinks organized crime in general and the American Mafia in specific is going to disappear any time soon. The difference today, however, is that federal agencies such as the FBI are fully engaged against the Mafia and similar crime organizations. Equally important, prosecutors can now unleash an effective, well-tested arsenal of legal weapons, including RICO, witness protection, and electronic surveillance, whenever the Mafia makes its presence known.

Mafia Masquerade

Known as "Donnie Brasco," FBI agent Joseph Pistone managed to infiltrate the Mafia with spectacular results. His in-depth investigation resulted in major changes in the way the Mafia handled membership.

Sicilian by heritage, Pistone was born in 1939 and raised first in Pennsylvania, then in Paterson, New Jersey. His father worked in a silk mill and ran some bars. Pistone played high school sports and went to college on a basketball scholarship. He dropped out at age 20 to get married and spent a year doing construction and other kinds of physical labor.

Pistone harbored a yearning to become an FBI agent. He spent a few years with Naval Intelligence, assisting with military investigations, and then joined the Bureau. He was sworn in as a special agent on July 7, 1969, and underwent intensive training. After graduation, he was assigned to an FBI office in Florida.

By 1974, Pistone was working on a case, involving a ring of thieves who specialized in stealing 18-wheel trucks, bulldozers, and luxury cars along the East Coast. Thanks to the year he spent in construction, Pistone knew how to drive 18-wheelers and bulldozers. The FBI decided to launch an undercover operation, spearheaded by Pistone.

Pistone settled on a cover name ("Donnie Brasco") and assumed a fake identity complete with a phony ID. As Donnie Brasco, Pistone easily penetrated the theft ring and joined their ranks. Thanks to Pistone's efforts, 30 members of the ring were arrested by FBI and the Florida Highway Patrol in February 1976.

Pistone remained in undercover mode; the FBI wanted him to continue investigating other truck hijackings in New York City. Police intelligence suggested the Mafia might be involved in some of the thefts. If the Mafia wasn't actually stealing the vehicles, it was believed they might be "fencing" (i.e., purchasing and selling) stolen goods from the trucks.

The FBI in New York wanted to initiate a long-term undercover operation to infiltrate and arrest the "fences" who handled these stolen goods. Once again, Pistone was chosen for this mission. He had undercover experience, had a Sicilian background, and spoke fluent Italian. He was cool under pressure and had no reservations about tackling the Mafia.

Pistone spent months prepping for his new role. It was decided he would keep his previous pseudonym, Donnie Brasco. It was also decided that Donnie Brasco would be a jewel thief and a burglar, who usually worked alone, avoided violence, and varied his time between New York City, Miami, and California. Brasco would be a bachelor and an orphan, in the hope that this would take care of nosy questions about his family. The FBI gave the operation a six-month time span.

In September 1976, Pistone went undercover as Donnie Brasco. He couldn't tell friends, coworkers (outside his immediate FBI circle), or relatives about his mission. For them, it was as if Pistone had disappeared. His own wife and children (by this point, Pistone had three daughters) knew only the barest details about his mission.

The FBI set up some "hello phones"—i.e., numbers Mafia members could call for character references. The people answering the phones were either FBI agents or informants who had been prompted to say good things about Brasco if anyone called. Pistone opened a checking account, leased an appropriate gangster car (a 1976 yellow Cadillac Coupe de Ville with Florida tags), and got a one-bedroom apartment in Manhattan.

The FBI had a list of bars, nightclubs, and restaurants patronized by gangsters and "fences." Pistone started to frequent these places, dining or drinking alone, just to get his face known in underworld circles. Among other locales, Pistone frequented a Manhattan restaurant called Carmello's that was owned by members of the Genovese Mafia family.

Pistone noticed many of the gangsters at Carmello's liked to play backgammon for money. Pistone sensed an opening. One day, he challenged the winner of a backgammon match to a new game. He introduced himself for the first time (as "Don") and chatted up the patrons. He later befriended the barkeep and tried to interest him in some allegedly stolen jewelry to establish his criminal credentials.

Pistone continued to ingratiate himself with underworld figures. In early 1977, he was introduced to members of the Colombo Mafia family. He became chummy with a Mafiosi named Jilly whose "crew" hung out at a store in Bensonhurst, Brooklyn. Pistone started spending time there, observing various low-echelon Mafiosi in action.

FBI protocol meant Pistone couldn't take part in any burglaries, hijackings, or violent crimes with Jilly's crew. He made himself useful, however, by helping unload stolen goods from trucks that pulled up to the store. Sometimes, Pistone brought in "swag" (stolen jewels or other items from FBI storage) to impress his peers.

In March 1977, Pistone met Anthony Mirra, a "made" (i.e., formal member) of the Mafia. Through Mirra, Pistone was introduced to Benjamin "Lefty Guns" Ruggiero. Both Mirra and Ruggiero were "soldiers" in the Bonanno crime family. A lean, chatty hit man in his early 50s, Lefty ran a Little Italy social club that served as a meeting place for Bonanno family members and associates.

Pistone began to follow a routine. At around 10:00 a.m., he would go to Ruggiero's club, drink coffee, and read the papers. He did his best to listen in conversations, without seeming obvious about it. In the afternoon, Pistone would go to Brooklyn and hang out at Jilly's store. In the evening, he would connect with Anthony Mirra, who struck him as extremely unstable and deadly.

Among other hustles, Ruggiero handled bookmaking operations for Nicky Marangello, underboss of the Bonanno family. In this capacity, Ruggiero was bringing in $20,000–$25,000 every weekend. Pistone discovered the Mafia earned most of their revenue from gambling, particularly sports betting and "numbers" (i.e., illegal lotteries). Ironically, many Mafiosi also loved to gamble. Ruggiero himself was a heavy gambler, constantly hustling to pay off his debts.

Ruggiero started taking Pistone with him as he drove around town, picking up money from bettors. Eventually, Ruggiero grew so comfortable with Pistone, he had him report to Marangello and provide updates on the bookmaking business.

Ruggiero began to mentor Pistone in the way of the mob. Ruggiero instructed Pistone to dress sharply, shave his mustache, and always show deference to made men. Always take a wiseguy's side, even if he's wrong, explained Ruggiero. As a mob "associate," Pistone was expected to keep in constant contact with Ruggiero. If Pistone needed to leave town or wanted to pull a hustle, it had to be cleared with Ruggiero first.

Like most Mafiosi he encountered, Ruggiero still lived in the same neighborhood near Little Italy where he had grown up. Ruggiero was fond of fish and had several tanks of them in his apartment.

Working with Ruggiero could be a challenge. In one incident, while driving along Third Avenue in New York, Ruggiero became enraged after a taxi cut him off twice. After the second occasion, the two cars stopped at a light. Ruggiero stepped out of his vehicle, grabbed a tire iron from the trunk, and proceeded to smash the cabbie's window. Pistone couldn't intervene, for fear of blowing his cover.

Ruggiero was divorced, with four grown children. His son Tommy was a junkie, a condition Ruggiero constantly fretted over. Ruggiero at one point married his girlfriend. He asked Pistone to be his best man.

By midsummer 1977, Pistone was making solid inroads in the underworld. Every few days, Pistone phoned his FBI contact agent to give him a rundown of his activities. Once or twice a month, he met the agent in person, to receive money for living expenses. Pistone got to see his family only every two or three weeks, if that often.

The undercover operation was starting to take on a new dimension. While Pistone hadn't become particularly close to any mob "fences," the FBI was delighted with how deep he was getting with the Bonanno and Colombo clans. The Bureau decided to extend, and alter, Pistone's mission. His new assignment was to gather evidence against the New York Mafia.

Occasionally, Pistone took part in underworld operations, albeit in a peripheral role. One time he pretended to sell some guns that one of Jilly's men had picked up in a robbery. Pistone handed the weapons over to the FBI as well as the cash he made on the sale.

In July 1979, Bonanno boss Carmine Galante was murdered, triggering a bitter inner-family struggle for succession. Ruggiero was allied with rising Bonanno star Dominick "Sonny Black" Napolitano, who in turn was allies of Philip "Rusty" Rastelli. Rastelli had been Bonanno boss but stepped down to let Galante rule after he was released from prison in the late 1970s. Rastelli still aspired to the top position, however, and was one of the prime movers in the plot to kill Galante. After Galante was killed, Rastelli took control of the Bonanno family once again. Napolitano was made a captain and became Ruggiero's immediate commander. Napolitano was a swarthy man with jet-black dyed hair (hence the nickname). Pistone worked his charm on the new mob boss and soon was on friendly terms with him.

Pistone continued to accompany Ruggiero on various operations. He journeyed to Milwaukee, where he met local Mafia boss Frank Balistrieri. In Florida, Pistone was introduced to Santo Trafficante, a big-time Mafia leader.

By mid-1981, Pistone was close to becoming a "made" Mafiosi. Sonny Black Napolitano was willing to recommend "Donnie Brasco" for official entry into the ranks of the Mafia. His induction could take place as early as that December. No FBI agent had ever been "made" before. It would be a tremendous coup for law enforcement. There was only one catch: in order to be "made," Napolitano wanted Pistone to murder a mobster named Anthony "Bruno" Indelicato.

Indelicato was a member of the Mafia faction opposed to Rastelli's rule. As part of the struggle, Indelicato's father, Alphonse "Sonny Red" Indelicato (who was also in the mob), had been murdered, along with Philip "Philly Lucky" Giaccone and Dominick "Big Trin" Trinchera. The three men were summoned to a meeting and then killed on Rastelli's command.

Bruno Indelicato was supposed to have been at the same meeting, but he ducked out of it. Now, Napolitano wanted to tie up loose ends and have the man "whacked." And Pistone seemed to be the perfect candidate to carry out the hit.

Pistone and his FBI handlers debated the issue. Pistone was eager to stay undercover and try to become "made" without murdering anyone. The Bureau thought it was too risky. "Donnie Brasco" would be put under tremendous pressure to kill Bruno Indelicato in order to advance up the Mafia hierarchy. To Pistone's disappointment, the six-year undercover operation was terminated on July 26, 1981.

Shortly after Pistone's undercover role ended, FBI agents approached Napolitano and informed him who "Donnie Brasco" really was. Napolitano told his crew. There was disbelief. It was suspected that the FBI was merely playing mind games.

For a few days, Napolitano and his men sat on this information, as they desperately tried to track Pistone down. In this, they failed. Pistone had completely withdrawn from the underworld and was busy giving information to the FBI and being reunited with his family. Feeling he had no choice, Napolitano broke the news about "Donnie Brasco" to his superiors.

Seventeen days after Pistone's mission ended, Napolitano was ordered to attend a mob meeting in New Jersey. He headed off to the meeting, and no one saw him again.

A few months later, Anthony Mirra was shot dead in the parking garage of an apartment in Manhattan. His assailants didn't bother taking the thousands of dollars in currency he had on him. This was a deliberate message, that robbery wasn't the motive for the murder. Ruggiero was also targeted for murder by the mob, but FBI agents tracked him down and arrested him before he could be killed. Pistone and his family, meanwhile, were put under 24-hour FBI protection.

On August 2, 1982, Pistone began testifying against his former colleagues in federal court. Ten days later, a body was recovered from a creek on Staten Island. The body bore bullet wounds and the hands were cut off. This was a Mafia indication that the victim had violated mob secrecy. Through dental records, the body was determined to be Sonny Black Napolitano. "I was sorry it was Sonny. I was glad it wasn't me," wrote Pistone.

Pistone spent much of the 1980s testifying in court. He ended up testifying at 10 trials and many more grand juries. His testimony led to 200 indictments and 100 convictions of members of the Mafia, including Ruggiero.

Pistone didn't feel much guilt in "betraying" his comrades: "I felt close to Sonny Black. I felt a kind of kinship with him. But I didn't feel any guilt of betrayal because I'd always maintained in my own mind and heart the separation of our worlds," he would write.[4] "I knew that both Lefty and Sonny loved me in their own ways. Either would have killed me in a minute," he added.

Indeed, following Napolitano's murder, the FBI heard through the underworld grapevine that a $500,000 "open contract" had been put on Pistone's life. Usually, the Mafia avoids murdering policemen and federal agents (for fear of massive retaliation). They apparently were willing to make an exception for Pistone.

Pistone left the FBI in 1986. One year later, his book, *Donnie Brasco: My Undercover Life in the Mafia*, was released. This was turned into a successful movie in 1997, with Johnny Depp as Pistone and Al Pacino as Ruggiero. Pistone lent his expertise to other police forces and helped Scotland Yard in the UK with an investigation into Asian

Triad crime gangs. As part of the investigation, Pistone pretended to be a Mafiosi from New York.

It is believed that the contract against Pistone was eventually lifted. Nonetheless, Pistone continued to travel incognito under a fake name. He was also licensed to carry a gun. Pistone avoided going to Atlantic City, New Jersey, or any other place where the Mafia were known to congregate.

In testimony before a U.S. Senate subcommittee in 1988, Pistone discussed steps that the Mafia had taken steps to prevent any future infiltration from FBI or police agents: "I understand that the New York families have instituted new rules to thwart further undercover penetrations. They have reinstituted the requirement that before someone is made a soldier, he will have to 'make his bones,' that is, he will have to kill someone. In addition, they are now requiring two 'wiseguys' to vouch with their own lives for the new member, rather than as before, when only one did so."[5]

As for any residual personal feelings he might have had about his six-year mission, Pistone offering the following rationalization: "I knew that no matter what I did, I was not going to reform anybody, they were going to lie, steal, cheat, murder and kill, whether Joe Pistone [or] Donnie Brasco was there or not. So my main goal was to gather information for later prosecutions. I was not a social worker nor a reformer and that is the mindset I had, and I also maintained that if they found out who I was, they would kill me just as soon as they have killed their best friends."

Notes

1. U.S. Marshals Service website, http://www.usmarshals.gov.
2. Selwyn Raab, *Five Families: The Rise, Decline, and Resurgence of America's Most Powerful Mafia Empires* (New York: St. Martin's Press, 2005), 689.
3. U.S. Department of Justice, "91 Leaders, Members and Associates of La Cosa Nostra Families in Four Districts Charged with Racketeering and Related Crimes, Including Murder and Extortion," January 20, 2011.
4. Joseph Pistone and Richard Woodley, *Donnie Brasco: My Undercover Life in the Mafia* (New American Library, 1987), 397.
5. Joseph Pistone, testimony before the U.S. Senate Permanent Subcommittee on Investigations, 1988.

CHAPTER SIX

Twenty-first-Century Mafia

Digital Dons

In May 2012, 13 alleged members of the Genovese Mafia family in New York State and New Jersey were arrested on racketeering and conspiracy charges in relation to sports betting. While the Mafia has run gambling operations for decades, this particular scheme was unique in that it was conducted online from websites based in Costa Rica.

"The use of Internet gambling and offshore locales demonstrates an evolution and increased sophistication," on the part of the Mafia, stated Michael Ward, head of the FBI's Newark, New Jersey, office in the *Philadelphia Inquirer*.[1] The article pointed to an unpleasant reality: "[T]he mob has discovered the Internet."

While the Mafia is still heavily invested in traditional moneymaking activities such as drug trafficking, gambling, prostitution, loan sharking, and extortion, the underworld has expanded into new ventures. These include online gambling, health insurance fraud, and even phone fraud. "Today's gangster—like any good venture capitalist—has adapted to the times," noted online magazine *Slate*, in a piece posted in January 2011.[2]

The Mafia has set up shop in Central and South American countries where sports betting isn't a crime. From such lush locales, the Mafia operates websites that process illicit bets made on sporting events taking place in the United States. "The Costa Rican computer servers effectively operated as digital wire rooms, keeping track of stateside betting accounts while bouncing data through different server nodes to evade U.S. law enforcement detection," explained *Slate*.

Four years previously, federal authorities in Queens County, New York City, issued a multiple-count indictment against 26 people, including alleged members of the Gambino family, for Internet-related gambling offenses. "In keeping up with modern technology, the illegal gambling enterprise in this case is alleged to have gone on-line, supplementing the traditional wire room and street corner bookie who penciled in wagers in a little black book with off-shored based internet websites—designed for sports betting and casino-style gambling—and toll-free telephone numbers through which they were able to manage numerous gambling accounts, out of which criminal proceeds were collected and distributed throughout the New York City–metropolitan area," stated Queens County district attorney Richard Brown in a press release.[3]

From the Mafia's perspective, computers and websites have been a boon: "[C]omputerized wire rooms operate around the clock and can handle a large volume of bettors at any one time, thus allowing the organizers to increase their illicit profits without having to bother with the time-consuming record-keeping aspects of a more traditional, paper-based bookmaking operation," noted DA Brown.

Even the most cutting-edge criminal schemes still contain elements of old-school thuggery, however. Gambino family members arrested in Queens County were also charged with lending cash at exorbitant rates (200 percent or thereabouts) to patrons of their online gaming services.

The Mafia has utilized the Internet for other ends, besides gambling. On April 20, 2010, the U.S. attorney for the Southern District of New York charged 14 Gambino family members and associates with racketeering, murder, sex trafficking, and other offenses. Among those charged were Daniel Marino, "a long-time member [of the Mafia] and currently a boss of the Gambino family," according to a press release from the U.S. attorney's office.[4] "Marino has over 200 fully-inducted or 'made' Mafia members under this command, as well as hundreds of associates who commit crimes with and for the Mafia," added the release. The sex trafficking charges stemmed from ads placed on Craigslist and other popular websites.

The modern Mafia has also proven capable of finding new ways to extract money from old technology. In February 2004, for example, federal authorities in New York State arrested two Gambino family members and various associates for racketeering and money laundering in connection with phone fraud. According to the U.S. government, the Gambino Mafiosi worked with corrupt telephone executives on a scam that generated phony charges on phone bills. In a five-year period, the scam pulled in an estimated $200 million.

Cindy Ferrebee sits at the kitchen table in her Elyria, Ohio, home with a photo of her daughter, Army National Guard sergeant Christina Ferrebee, July 2006. Cindy has no idea how her daughter's name, Social Security number, and birth date ended up with a voicemail provider. Neither woman fed information to the provider, she said. Ferrebee is one of more than 100 phone customers who may have have been victims of "cramming." (AP Photo/Mark Duncan)

The scheme marked "the first time organized crime figures have been charged with using the billing fraud known as 'cramming' to fill mob coffers ... [Cramming] is the common term for larding a telephone bill with unauthorized charges," stated the *New York Times* on February 11, 2004.

"The nationwide scheme was sophisticated, officials said, but the idea was simple: callers responding to advertisements for free samples of services like psychic phone lines, telephone dating services and adult chat lines were unknowingly charged up to $40 a month on their phone bills for services they never requested and never used," noted the *Times*.

Just before the turn of the millennium, the Mafia extended its reach again, with a foray into health care. This scam involved Tri-Con Associates, a New Jersey company that "arranged group medical, dental and optical programs for employees and unions with networks of health-care providers," according to the *New York Times*.[5]

Starting in 1994, it was alleged that a Mafia crew led by Genovese family members essentially took Tri-Con over. The company began inflating fees and pocketing the difference. If insurance administrators balked at the higher costs, they were threatened with violence.

The scam came to light in August 1996. "We are alleging for the first time the involvement of organized crime in the health-care industry ... we hope it's not a national trend, but we cannot dismiss that possibility," said Peter Verniero, attorney general of New Jersey, in the *New York Times*. Given the massive size of the U.S. medical system, it's a legitimate concern, especially considering the Mafia's enthusiasm for finding new sources of plunder.

Notes

1. George Anastasia, "13 Alleged Mob Members Arrested for Running N. J. Online Gambling Ring," *Philadelphia Inquirer*, May 23, 2012.
2. Stayton Bonner, "Modern Mafiosi: How Does the Mob Make a Living These Days?" Slate.com, January 21, 2011, http://www.slate.com/articles/news_and _politics/explainer/2011/01/modern_mafiosi.html.
3. Richard Brown, District Attorney, Queens County, "Twenty Six Charged in $10 Million Gambino Organized Crime Family Gambling, Loan Sharking and Prostitution Operation," February 7, 2008.

4. U.S. Attorney's Office, Southern District of New York, "Manhattan U.S. Attorney Charges 14 Gambino Crime Family Associates with Racketeering, Murder, Sex Trafficking and Other Crimes," April 20, 2010.

5. Selwyn Raab, "New Jersey Officials Say Mafia Infiltrated Health-Care Industry," *New York Times*, August 21, 1996.

Conclusion

While the Mafia has learned some new high-tech tricks, the organization as a whole is in bad shape. Indeed, when Mafia boss Joseph Massino went to trial in 2004, the media referred to him as "the last Don"—a reflection of his status as an old-school, traditional mob boss.[1]

Arrests and civil actions from law enforcement have drastically reduced the Mafia's underworld scope and presence. La Cosa Nostra also faces stiff competition from Asian and Russian mobsters, African American street gangs, outlaw motorcycle clubs, and Mexican criminal organizations. A 2009 report by the National Drug Intelligence Center of the U.S. Department of Justice cited Mexican "drug trafficking organizations" (DTOs)—not the Mafia—as the biggest organized crime threat facing the United States.

"Today the old mobs are but a show of what they once were," stated crime writer Thomas Reppetto, in his book, *American Mafia*.[2] It's premature, however, to say the Mafia is completely spent.

The same year Massino went on trial, the State of New Jersey Commission of Investigation released a report called "The Changing Face of Organized Crime in New Jersey." Despite its title, the report took a broad view, examining La Cosa Nostra activity throughout

Joseph "Big Joey" Massino, the head of the Bonanno crime family for 14 years, is seen in this undated file photo released by the U.S. Attorney's Office. Massino became the first boss from the Five Families in New York City ever to turn cooperating witness. These days, mob membership in key cities is dwindling while the number of mob turncoats is soaring. (AP Photo/U.S. Attorney's Office File)

the Eastern Seaboard. The study focused on "top LCN groups" in the New York/New Jersey/Philadelphia region—namely, the Gambino, Genovese, Lucchese, Bonanno, Colombo, DeCavalcante, and Bruno families. Of all these gangs, the Genovese clan is strongest, said the report. "In the battered underworld of traditional organized crime, the New York–based Genovese organization is considered the most formidable element in a field of out-of-shape contenders, having surpassed the once-dominant Gambino LCN family in both strength and numbers over the past decades," read the report.[3]

At the time of the study, the Genovese family boasted 250–300 "made" members and over 1,000 associates. Entrenched in New York City, the Genovese clan also has business interests in New England, Florida, California, and Nevada. The Genovese family dominates bookmaking and loan sharking operations in New York/New Jersey and generates income from extortion, kickbacks, illegal gambling, labor racketeering, and illegal drugs. With an eye to the future, the Genovese family has embraced health-care and Internet scams and has shown a willingness to work with criminals outside the Mafia.

The once-dominant Gambino family had 150–200 core members and between 1,500 and 2,000 associates at the time of the report. The family is based in Brooklyn but has operations throughout New York State, New Jersey, New England, Pennsylvania, Florida, Nevada, and California. The Gambino clan was the preserve of Mafia superstar John Gotti, who rose to prominence in the 1980s only to die behind bars following a decisive takedown. Gotti's mercurial leadership led to a sharp decline in the Gambino family's fortunes.

The Lucchese family has also been hurt hard by law enforcement: "[V]irtually the entire top leadership ranks have been decimated by successful prosecutions and at least 20 members including a number of top players in the New Jersey/New York region have become government informants and/or cooperating witnesses since 1990," stated the report. Lucchese membership was pegged at 110–140 "made" members and about 1,100 associates, active primarily in New Jersey and New York.

While the study didn't cite the size of the Bonanno family, it noted the clan historically has been among the smaller Mafia gangs in the New York/New Jersey region. The Bonanno family suffered a major humiliation in the 1980s when it was revealed that FBI agent Joseph Pistone had successfully infiltrated its ranks, under the guise of faux gangster Donnie Brasco.

The Colombo (formerly Profaci) family was estimated at 112 members and 500 associates. The report said infighting and arrests had weakened the family, though it was still active in traditional LCN rackets. The Colombo family has also branched out into new scams such as motor-fuel tax evasion and securities fraud.

The DeCavalcante family, based in New Jersey, continued to function despite the intense efforts of law enforcement. This organization is relatively small, with about 40 core members and 50 associates, noted the study.

The Bruno family, which once dominated Philadelphia, was depicted as floundering. The organization "has been decimated by factional violence, internal treachery, and a succession of wide-ranging state and federal prosecutions," stated the report. At the time of the study, the Bruno clan had 50 "made" members (half of whom were in jail) and about 270 associates.

Since the Commission of Investigation report was released, the Mafia has continued to be battered by law enforcement. On January 20, 2011, the FBI and other police personnel arrested nearly 130 members of the Mafia in New York City and elsewhere. Those arrested included Luigi Manocchio, 83, former boss of the New England LCN; Andrew Russo, 76, street boss of the Colombo family; Benjamin Castellazzo, 73, acting underboss of the Colombo family; Richard Fusco, 74, consigliere of the Colombo family; Bartolomeo Vernace, 61, a member of the Gambino family; and Joseph Corozzo, 69, a consigliere with the Gambinos.

Charges against the men included murder, arson, drug trafficking, loan sharking, illegal gambling, labor racketeering, and witness tampering.

"The Mafia—also known as La Cosa Nostra (LCN)—may have taken on a diminished criminal role in some areas of the country, but in New York, the Five Families are still extremely strong and viable" said Dave Shafer, an assistant special agent in charge who supervises FBI organized crime investigations in New York, in an FBI press release.[4] Asked by the *New York Times* what remained of the "old Italian-American mob families," Mafia expert Jerry Capeci offered the following: "They're beleaguered, battered and bruised but they are far from wiped out. They have been hurt by nearly three decades of prosecutions, mostly by federal authorities. But the five families in New York and those in other metropolitan areas, notably Chicago and its suburbs, remain viable criminal networks. Without resorting to as much outward violence, they are doing their best—most people would say worst—to make money and maintain themselves and their status."[5]

"The Mafia is not dead. It is alive and kicking. Modern mobsters may be less colorful, less flamboyant, and less glamorous than some of their predecessors but they are still terrorizing businesses, using baseball bats and putting people in the hospital," echoed Manhattan U.S. attorney Preet Bharara in a 2010 press release.[6]

Notes

1. Richard Corliss and Simon Crittle, "The Last Don," *Time*, March 22, 2004.
2. Thomas Reppetto, *American Mafia: A History of Its Rise to Power* (New York: Henry Holt and Company, 2004), 275.
3. State of New Jersey Commission of Investigation, "The Changing Face of Organized Crime in New Jersey: A Status Report," May 2004.
4. Federal Bureau of Investigation, "Mafia Takedown Largest Coordinated Arrest in FBI History," January 20, 2011.
5. Mary Jo Murphy, "Will the Real Mob Please Stand Up," *New York Times*, March 5, 2006.
6. U.S. Attorney's Office, Southern District of New York, "Manhattan U.S. Attorney Charges 14 Gambino Crime Family Associates with Racketeering, Murder, Sex Trafficking and Other Crimes," April 20, 2010.

Biographical Sketches

Mafia Leaders

Charles "Lucky" Luciano: The Visionary

(1897–1962)

Time magazine called him "Horatio Alger with a gun, an ice pick and a dark vision of Big Business." The FBI credited him with "making the American (Mafia) what it is today." He was jailed for vice crimes but escaped punishment for murder. On his rise to the top, he killed two mob bosses and seized their empires.[1]

Salvatore Lucania was born in 1897 in Lercara Friddi, a village near Palermo, Sicily. In 1907, his family joined the Sicilian exodus to the United States, settling in a mixed Italian-Jewish neighborhood in New York's Lower East Side.

Salvatore was an ugly child, with a pockmarked face due to bad acne. While proud of his heritage, he was eager to be seen as American. Like a lot of sons and daughters of first-generation immigrants, he changed his name. Lucania became the easier-to-pronounce "Luciano." Salvatore was dropped for the more American "Charlie" or just plain "Charles." The "Lucky" tag would come in later years.

Little Charlie grew up wild and tough. He was part of a gang of Sicilian American urchins who terrorized their neighborhood. Among other activities, the gang liked to swarm individual Jews (whom they perceived as cowardly), beat them, and take their money. This was allegedly how Luciano came to meet fellow criminal-in-training Meyer Lansky.

According to mob legend, Luciano and his snarling horde confronted Lansky on the street, and demanded money. Lansky was a wispy, frail Jewish boy, but he didn't lack for confidence. He told Luciano off and wouldn't back down. Far from being angered, Luciano was impressed by Lansky's courage and befriended the boy.

In another tale, Luciano came across a girl having sex with a young Jewish run-around named Benjamin "Bugsy" Siegel. The girl was apparently from Luciano's stable; he was her pimp, and he was outraged that Siegel was getting the benefit of her charms for free. Luciano stormed up and attacked the couple with his fists. Lansky interrupted, breaking up the fight by smacking Luciano on the head with a wrench.

Whatever the actual truth of their first encounter was, Luciano became lifelong pals and business associates with Siegel and Lansky. Such cross-ethnic friendships were unusual in an era that was much more parochial than today, especially in new immigrant communities.

Luciano dropped out of school at age 14 and took a factory job, which he hated. He started hanging around poolrooms and continued to hustle on the side. An enterprising lad, Luciano at one point purchased a supply of opium, which he proceeded to dole out to local addicts for a price. He was caught and served six months in a reformatory as punishment.

Like a lot of delinquents, Luciano would have most likely remained a petty criminal were it not for Prohibition. Luciano, Lansky, and Siegel rejoiced when alcohol became a banned commodity in early 1920. As the underworld realized (even if the federal government didn't), the public wasn't about to change their drinking habits just because alcohol was criminalized. If citizens couldn't buy liquor from legitimate sources, they would get it from gangsters, who were more than happy for the business.

Working with Lansky, Luciano became a major bootlegger. The two young mobsters sold liquor to speakeasies (illegal bars and nightclubs) throughout the city. This booze was brought into New York by sea. A mother ship containing a large cargo of liquor (purchased from Canada or Europe, where it was legal to manufacture spirits) would drop anchor a few miles off the coast. Smaller, faster boats would rendezvous and then bring the precious cargo to shore.

Luciano's life as a budding gangster was not without a few scrapes with the law. In 1923, federal agents caught him selling cocaine and opium to a police informer. To avoid arrest, Luciano sheepishly led authorities to a larger stash of drugs, setting up another dealer for arrest. Luciano was greatly embarrassed when this sleazy incident was revealed in court years later. Under the code of the streets, arrested criminals were expected to stay mute, not turn in their peers.

During this formative period, Luciano made the acquaintance of several rising mobsters, including Jack "Legs" Diamond and Arnold Rothstein. Rothstein was a major underworld player who preferred to fund other people's criminal operations instead of running rackets himself. Rothstein was more financier than gang leader. He convinced Luciano to tone down his flashy wardrobe and to wear sober, conservative men's suits.

The most influential mobster Luciano met as a young man was Giuseppe "Joe the Boss" Masseria, who commanded a vast criminal organization. In 1927, Masseria asked Luciano to join his growing empire as a lieutenant. The highly ambitious gangster jumped at the chance. Masseria put his new hire in charge of criminal activities in lower Manhattan.

As Luciano soon discovered, Masseria had some major shortcomings. He was Sicilian born, like Luciano, but the similarity ended there. Masseria was clannish and narrow-minded. He behaved like an old-world Mafia chief, demanding fealty and tribute from his minions while obsessing on points of honor. Masseria wouldn't do business with non-Italians. By contrast, Luciano would work with anyone who could make him money.

Masseria's main enemy was another Sicilian American mobster named Salvatore Maranzano. One year after Luciano joined the Masseria mob, his boss went to war with Maranzano. Gunmen representing each boss fought it out on the streets or wrecked each other's businesses. At stake was who was going to lead the Italian American underworld in New York.

It was around this time that Luciano acquired the nickname, "Lucky." As Luciano told it, he was standing idly by on a sidewalk in midtown Manhattan in October 1929 when a car pulled up. Three armed men forced Luciano into the vehicle and slapped tape over his lips. The trio took Luciano to a deserted beach on Staten Island and proceeded to hang him by his fingers from a tree while torturing him with lit cigarettes among other painful implements. Luciano was burned, beaten, and slashed. In the middle of this brutal punishment, he passed out and was left for dead.

While terribly injured, Luciano was still alive. After coming to, around 2:00 a.m., he staggered around the beach and almost ran into a policeman on patrol. The officer took the bloodied gangster to a hospital. While Luciano survived, his face retained scars from the incident. His left eye acquired a permanent droop. Nonetheless, this was a small price to pay for the extremely rare feat of being "taken for a ride" and surviving.

It was unclear who Luciano's attackers were. Some historians point to a rival gang boss, who wanted Luciano to reveal where he had hidden some drugs. Other sources suggest he was tortured by Masseria's enemies in order to take out one of Joe the Boss's top men. His assailants could have even been police officers, who put Luciano through a rather harsh interrogation in the hope he would reveal mob secrets.

Luciano didn't have time to dwell on the identity of his shadowy attackers. Masseria was still caught up in his vendetta with Maranzano. The press called it "the Castellammarese War" after the small Sicilian town both men came from. By the early 1930s, the Castellammarese War had taken dozens of lives with no end in sight. Luciano found the whole thing utterly pointless. He wanted to get rich, not settle scores.

Luciano had a lot of ideas. He wanted to modernize the mob, to elevate it above simple clannish thuggery. Luciano saw no reason why Italian and Jewish gangs couldn't work together. Raised in New York, Luciano thought of himself as an American, not a transplanted Sicilian (this despite never taking out U.S. citizenship). He contemptuously dismissed old-style Mafia chiefs like Masseria as "Moustache Pete's."

On his own initiative, Luciano went behind Masseria's back and struck a deal with Maranzano. Luciano would arrange for Masseria to be killed. In exchange, Maranzano promised to bring the Castellammarese War to a close.

Masseria remained oblivious to these machinations. When Luciano asked if he felt like a meal at a Coney Island restaurant on April 15, 1931, Joe the Boss readily agreed. The two men, plus Masseria's three bodyguards, repaired to a restaurant called Nuovo Villa Tammaro (some accounts say they met at a place called Scarpato's). Once the sumptuous meal was over, Luciano suggested a card game was in order. Feeling mellow and sedated from the vast quantities of food, Masseria happily played cards with his top lieutenant.

At some point, Luciano excused himself to use the bathroom. Masseria's bodyguards suddenly disappeared and a death squad of four men came rushing into the restaurant. The squad (whose members included Ben Siegel and Albert Anastasia, a rising underworld sadist) shot Masseria to death at close range. When police arrived, Luciano expressed complete shock. He said he hadn't witnessed the shooting, being in the bathroom at the time, and had no idea who or why anyone would shoot Masseria.

Maranzano quickly took over Masseria's rackets and took command of his gang members. He kept his end of the bargain and ended the Castellammarese War.

Maranzano had a grand vision of organizing crime in New York City, which Luciano heartily endorsed. Maranzano wanted to divide the main Italian gangs into five families, each with a boss, underboss, capos, soldiers, and associates.

At a mass meeting of mobsters shortly after Masseria's death, Maranzano outlined his vision. The five families would be led by Luciano, Joe Bonanno, Joseph Profaci, Vincent Mangano, and Thomas Gagliano. Luciano would take over what used to be Masseria's gang.

Luciano might have gone along with the plan, except Maranzano added a twist. He wanted to be supreme leader (*capo di tutti capi*, or "boss of the bosses"). His word would be law, and all other gangsters would be expected to obey him unconditionally. Luciano didn't care for this idea, and he began plotting against his new boss.

As capo di tutti capi, Maranzano proved to be extremely paranoid. He arranged for the mentally unstable Vincent "Mad Dog" Coll (who acquired his nickname after shooting a bunch of children during a botched "hit") to murder his rebellious underlings. Maranzano drew up a death list, and Luciano's name was featured prominently on it.

Through contacts, Luciano caught wind of the plot and decided to launch a counterattack. On September 10, 1931, a group of gunmen disguised as U.S. Treasury agents burst into Maranzano's Park Avenue headquarters. They held up Maranzano's guards and then stabbed and shot the gang leader to death.

In a little under half a year, Luciano had arranged the assassination of the two biggest mob bosses in New York City. To smooth things over with his peers, Luciano put out the word that Maranzano was power-mad and was preparing to murder a slew of gangsters. Killing Maranzano in other words, had been an act of self-defense. New York gangsters could appreciate this kind of logic and thus they didn't try to avenge Maranzano's death.

Luciano retained Maranzano's concept of an underworld made up of crime families each with their own specific territories, rackets, and hierarchy. Luciano's refinement was to create the position of "consigliere" (adviser) to the bosses. He also added a top level called "the Commission." The Commission would act as a board of directors, settling disputes between families and sanctioning high-level hits. To sit on the Commission, you had to be a top-ranking boss.

The Commission's purview would extend beyond New York City. Essentially, it would oversee Mafia rackets throughout the United States. All five New York families had representation on the Commission. Luciano also made sure there was room reserved for families from other cities, especially Chicago (dominated by Al Capone at the time).

The Commission has been depicted as an underworld nerve center, with a cabal of mob bosses plotting schemes of national importance. This image is false. The Commission largely dealt with territorial disputes (i.e., which branch of the underworld would handle a particular vice in a given area) and had far less power than the media credited it with.

Luciano wanted organized crime to work like a corporation, not a village clan. To this end, he placed great stress on cooperation, negotiation, and amassing of political power. While Luciano didn't hesitate to use violence to eliminate anyone in his way, he didn't kill out of spite or sadism. To further distance himself from Masseria and

Maranzano, Luciano eliminated the "boss of bosses" position and refused to accept cash tributes from fellow mob leaders.

That said, Luciano's modesty was a bit of a facade. While there was no single supreme leader of the U.S. Mafia any more, Luciano was treated as the de facto boss of bosses throughout his career.

Luciano's own crime family consisted of roughly 500 frontline soldiers ready to do his bidding on the streets. His men ran rackets in New York Harbor and the Fulton Fish Market in Manhattan. Luciano ally Tommy Lucchese (aka "Three Finger Brown") controlled the huge kosher poultry sector, while another ally, Louis Buchalter, ran the garment district in New York.

For all of Luciano's innovations, the American Mafia remained a fluid entity, with a constant churn of new members, new alliances, and new deals. It had an amorphous quality in which secrecy, guile, and deceit were inherent. The Mafia was never simply the mirror image of General Motors or any other huge U.S. corporation. The underworld created by Luciano did not issue annual reports or hold public stockholder meetings to discuss expansion plans. Unlike legitimate companies, the Mafia avoided all publicity and did not actively solicit new members.

While Luciano refused to accept the "boss of bosses" title, he had no problem living in luxury. He had a private plane at his disposal and a suite at the extremely swanky Waldorf-Astoria. His apartment cost $7,600 a year in rent (roughly equivalent to $100,000 in contemporary figures). To avoid any hassles with hotel management, Luciano registered under the name "Charlie Ross."

Even as he moved into the top tier of organized crime, Luciano retained his old street smarts. He was very circumspect about talking on the phone (for fear it was tapped) and didn't keep a paper trail (he maintained details of deals in his head). He was also canny enough to operate his business in the shadows. He didn't rub his position in the public's face, as John Gotti did decades later. If anyone asked, Luciano claimed he earned his keep through sports gambling, craps, and bookmaking (i.e., taking wagers).

Luciano was always on the prowl for new money-making opportunities. With the repeal of Prohibition in 1933, all gangsters had to find new rackets. Luciano expanded his operations in bookmaking, prostitution, drugs, loan sharking, robbery, and labor racketeering, among others.

In June 1935, New York governor Herbert Lehman appointed vigorous, straight-arrow attorney Thomas Dewey as a special prosecutor with a view to cleaning up organized crime in the Big Apple. At first, Dewey and his office were mainly concerned with industry and labor racketeering and mob control of the "numbers" racket. As almost a side issue, Dewey launched what he thought would be a limited probe into corruption and case-fixing at New York's Women's Court. What his investigators found was evidence of a massive prostitution ring, allegedly run by none other than Lucky Luciano.

Wiretaps in brothels revealed that an outfit called "the Combine" or "the Combination" controlled prostitution in New York City. The Combination managed about 300 brothels (some of which were tiny one- or two-woman operations) and 2,000 prostitutes. Dewey's investigators estimated that the organized sex trade in New York brought in about $12 million a year in revenue. Dewey's team discovered that Dave "Little Davie" Betillo was the mob's overseer of prostitution. Betillo happened to be one of Luciano's trusted lieutenants.

In January 1936, Dewey's agents raided 80 brothels simultaneously across New York City. While this mission was supposed to be top secret, roughly half of the brothels were empty when investigators stormed inside, indicating that someone had tipped off management. Nonetheless, authorities arrested hundreds of working girls, madams, and brothel managers (called "bookers").

Ordinarily, a prostitute who worked for the Combination followed a set script when arrested. They would inevitably give police a sob story about being from out of town and visiting a friend in an apartment, which through some terrible coincidence happened to be a brothel. Bail would be set at around $300, which a bail bondsman (who worked for the Combination) would pay. When the case came to court, prostitutes were usually given a small fine or told to get out of town.

Dewey took a considerably tougher tack. He had bail set at $10,000 for each arrested girl and threatened to keep them in pretrial custody for a lengthy period of time. His staff could also play nice, taking some of the arrested women to movies or buying them treats such as ice cream. The "good cop–bad cop" routine worked, and soon some of the suspects were talking. They told Dewey they knew Luciano was directly involved in prostitution.

Feeling the noose tightening, Luciano fled New York for Hot Springs, Arkansas, a very corrupt town that was something of a resort/hideout for gangsters. Dewey obtained an extradition order to force Luciano back to New York City. He was poised to charge the mob boss with 90 counts of aiding and abetting compulsory prostitution. At first, it looked like Luciano wouldn't have to worry about facing Dewey's wrath. He was let out of jail on only $5,000 bail (extremely low for a major mobster wanted in connection with a top-level investigation) after only spending a few hours in lockup. New York authorities took this as another indication of the level of municipal corruption in Hot Springs.

Dewey decided more drastic measures were necessary to bring Luciano to justice. Convinced that Luciano's lawyers would keep him in Hot Springs forever, Dewey sent agents down south to fetch him. Working with state troopers, these agents more or less kidnapped Luciano and hustled him back to New York.

The trial of Luciano and 12 of his underlings began in May 1936. About 68 witnesses testified, most of them prostitutes, pimps, bookers, or madams. On the stand, they freely admitted they had been promised more lenient sentencing in return for their testimony. Only a handful (three) of witnesses offered any evidence directly linking Luciano to the sex trade. One of these witnesses was a heroin addict with the intriguing nickname Cokey Flo Brown. Ms. Brown claimed to have been present at meetings between Luciano and her pimp, during which time the gang boss talked business. Another prostitute spoke of being sent to the Waldorf-Astoria to have sex with Luciano himself. After the sex was over, the prostitute allegedly overheard the mob boss discussing the prostitution racket with his colleagues. In damning testimony, staff at the Waldorf-Astoria said they had seen the witness (and other prostitutes) in Luciano's company.

The trial revealed the degree of organization Luciano had imposed on the prostitution racket. Jurors were told that the prostitutes working for the Combination typically put in a 12-hour shift per day, with one day off a week. The average working girl made $300 a week (not a bad salary for the time). Of this, $150 went to her madam (plus an additional $30 for meals and medical care), leaving each woman with a bit over $100. This would be divided between the girl and her pimp.

Mob lawyers typically discourage their clients from testifying on their own behalf. Gangsters on the stand have a tendency to unnerve juries. Plus, if they lie (which was more or less a given), they opened themselves to charges of perjury. In a brave move, Luciano decided to take the stand. In response to softball questions from his lawyer, Luciano insisted that he earned his keep through gambling and bookmaking. He denied meeting any of the witnesses who said they had been with him.

When the cross-examination took place, Luciano's confidence collapsed. Dewey quickly had him sweaty and squirming. Luciano became evasive, claiming vaguely that he couldn't remember certain details about his business dealings. Luciano's case was not helped when Dewey introduced phone records, indicating a series of calls from the Waldorf-Astoria to a parade of known gangsters, including Al Capone. Dewey also introduced Luciano's tax records from 1929 to 1935. The records pegged Luciano's highest annual income at a mere $22,500 (ridiculously low considering his extravagant lifestyle). When pressed, Luciano was unable to come up with a convincing explanation as to how he managed to live like a tycoon on this income.

Luciano and all his codefendants were found guilty. Ironically, the mob boss might have beaten the charge if he hadn't testified. The evidence against him was shaky at best and not terribly substantial (with only three witnesses claiming direct knowledge of Luciano's involvement in prostitution). In truth, Luciano was probably not directly involved in the sex trade. Smart mob bosses like Luciano knew it would be folly to micromanage 300 separate brothels.

Emboldened by his conviction of Luciano, Dewey became a national hero. He was eventually elected governor of New York state and ran unsuccessfully for president, on the Republican ticket, in 1944 and 1948.

Convicted on 62 counts, Luciano received a sentence of 30–50 years in jail. He was imprisoned in Clinton Penitentiary, a maximum-security state facility in Dannemora, New York. Luciano did not serve hard time. He used his position, as well as bribes of food and money, to get fellow prisoners to look after him by cleaning his cell, taking on his work duties, and cooking his meals in a special kitchen. The guards largely left Luciano alone.

Luciano might have remained in jail for the rest of his life, were it not for the advent of World War II. When the U.S. jumped into the fray in late 1941, following the bombing of Pearl Harbor, the federal government became extremely worried about infiltration and sabotage along the unguarded East Coast. German submarines, called U-boats, began sinking dozens of American ships, giving rise to fears that fascist sympathizers on shore were revealing nautical secrets to the enemy. This sense of paranoia reached new heights in February 1942, when the French liner *Normandie*, which was being refitted as a troop ship, caught fire and sank in the Hudson River in New York City. The fire was later determined to be accidental, but for the moment, authorities were convinced the ship had been sunk by sabotage.

Feeding paranoia in Washington, D.C., was the fact many Italian Americans worked as longshoremen, dock laborers, and fishermen along the East Coast. Would these new immigrants remain loyal to the United States, or would their sympathies lie with the fascist powers, Italy being an ally of Nazi Germany? U.S. government agents tried to penetrate this mysterious world of Italian American docksiders but failed miserably. Italian Americans had little interest in talking to nosy government officials.

In despair, the Office of Naval Intelligence settled on an unconventional plan. Naval Intelligence approached Luciano's friend Meyer Lansky with an eye to helping the government. Lansky was induced to visit Luciano in jail and explain the situation to him. Luciano did not have direct command of all waterfront activities—in New York or anywhere else. He did, however, have plenty of contacts and a reputation as a well-respected mob boss. Through Lansky, Luciano agreed to spread the word among his contacts that it was all right to speak freely to U.S. intelligence agents. Luciano encouraged his countrymen to report any suspicious activity on the coast. In June 1942, when Nazi Germany landed eight spies on American soil via U-boat, the FBI caught them quickly, thanks in part from tips from the public.

It's important not to overestimate Luciano's wartime role. The *Normandie* aside, there were no incidents of sabotage along the East Coast during the Second World War. Most Italian Americans remained loyal to the United States and did nothing to encourage the Axis powers.

This wasn't the only connection between organized crime and the U.S. government during the war. In 1943, the U.S. Army helped liberate Sicily. Invading American forces encountered Mafiosi who had been languishing in jail since the 1920s, when Fascist authorities launched a brutal crackdown. Since they had been imprisoned by the Fascists (with whom the United States was now at war), the military decided these Mafiosi were actually political prisoners and released them. In this manner, the Sicilian Mafia quickly reasserted itself after decades of dormancy.

Luciano's efforts were deemed sufficient to set him free. In January 1946, Dewey (now governor of New York State) approved Luciano's release from jail on the condition that he be deported back to Italy.

On February 10, 1946, a ship containing Luciano left the dock in Brooklyn. He was taken across the ocean to his native village of Lercara Friddi in Sicily. While Luciano was given a hero's welcome, he didn't care to hang around his hometown. He departed, first for Palermo, then for Naples. By the late 1940s, Luciano was living in a luxury apartment in Rome, with a blonde mistress in her late 20s. He ran a small bakery as a front business and got involved in drug operations.

Luciano lived well in Italy but was quite homesick. *Time* magazine quoted him as saying, "I'm a city boy. Italy's dead—nice, but dead. I love movement. Business opportunities here are no good. All small-time stuff."[2]

In early 1947, Luciano traveled to Cuba in a failed attempt to run his U.S. crime interests offshore. The U.S. government found out and applied pressure until Cuba kicked their unwanted guest out.

In the fall of 1950, Meyer Lansky testified before the Kefauver Commission that was looking into organized crime. The commission was led by Senator Estes Kefauver of Tennessee. Lansky didn't answer many questions, though he did happily discuss Luciano's work during World War II.

Luciano spent the rest of his life in genteel exile. He helped set up some drug rings, but mostly he just strolled about, sat in cafes, read the paper, and ate in good restaurants. He talked about writing his memoirs or having a feature film made about his life. He even allowed reporters to interview him.

The proposed memoir and feature film never got off the ground. Luciano died of a heart attack on January 26, 1962, in Italy, a country he disdained compared to his adopted homeland in the United States.

Notes

1. Edna Buchanan, "Criminal Mastermind," *Time*, December 7, 1998.
2. "City Boy," *Time*, July 25, 1949.

John Gotti: The Celebrity

(1940–2002)

He was called the "Dapper Don" for his taste in expensive clothes and the "Teflon Don" for his ability to duck convictions. The best-known gangster in the United States since Al Capone, John Gotti was also thoroughly incompetent. His high media profile and demands for regal deference made it easier for authorities to eventually convict him.

Gotti was born on October 27, 1940, in the South Bronx, the 5th of 13 children. His parents, John and Fannie Gotti, hailed from the Naples region of Italy. Gotti grew up poor and somewhat resentful (his father seemed incapable of keeping even the most basic of jobs, from construction to factory work). The Gotti family moved around quite a bit. By the time he was 12, Gotti family had settled in Brooklyn.

A tough kid, Gotti routinely got into fistfights with other youths in his neighborhood. While still in his youth, Gotti began working for local mobster Carmine Fatico, a capo in what would eventually become the Gambino family. Gotti ran errands and did other small chores for Fatico.

As a teenager, Gotti worked as a car thief, mugger, and small-time burglar. He was relatively bright but had a desultory school record, often getting into trouble for mouthing off to teachers and fighting students. Gotti's undistinguished academic record came to an end at age 16.

The high school dropout worked a series of low-end jobs, including pants presser in a garment factory. He also took up another, more steady vocation, as an enforcer for Fatico. After the notorious Albert Anastasia was murdered in 1957, the crew Fatico belonged to became part of the Gambino crime family.

John Gotti was the most visible organized crime figure of the late twentieth century. Within the mob, Gotti controlled New York's Gambino crime family after the 1985 assassination of Paul Castellano. He was convicted on federal racketeering and murder charges in 1992 and died in prison in 2002. (AP Photo/Daniel Sheehan)

Gotti admired the thugs who lounged at Fatico's club, who seemed to have plenty of cash (in sharp contrast to his ne'er-do-well father). Gotti noted how the "wiseguys" at Fatico's place had the respect of everyone in the neighborhood. He set his sights on becoming a mobster.

In March 1962, when Gotti was 22 years old, he married Victoria DiGiorgio, a half-Jewish 19-year-old with whom he already had a daughter named Angela. It was not a smooth relationship, and in the early years, Gotti wasn't bringing in much money as a fledgling mobster and blue-collar worker. Victoria had to take him to court a few times for nonsupport of his child. The two eventually reconciled, and their family expanded to include three sons and two daughters. The Gotti clan moved into an apartment in Howard Beach, a middle-class neighborhood in the borough of Queens.

Gotti continued to commit robberies, steal cars, and fistfight on the street with assorted miscreants. Under Fatico's tutelage, Gotti also hijacked cargo trucks leaving nearby Kennedy Airport. On these jobs, he often worked with Angelo Ruggiero, a rotund young man who hung out at Fatico's clubhouse and, like Gotti, dreamed of entering the underworld big leagues.

At the time, Kennedy Airport handled $200 million in freight each year and employed thousands of workers. For a gangster like Fatico, the airport presented vast opportunities for theft, not to mention loan sharking and bookmaking with staff.

Gotti's progress up the Mafia's hierarchy was slow and interrupted by arrests. On the last day of March 1965, a policeman caught him in the act of using a crowbar to break into a tavern. Gotti ended up serving two-and-a-half years for the offense.

By the time Gotti was released, his patron Fatico had moved his headquarters from Brooklyn to Ozone Park in the borough of Queens. The mobster wanted to be nearer to Kennedy Airport and further away from the black and Hispanic families moving into his old neighborhood. Fatico established a base of operations on 101st Street and took over some storefronts to create a hooligan hangout dubbed the Bergin Hunt and Fish Club. Gotti resumed his chores for Fatico, stealing cargo from Kennedy Airport. He sometimes worked with Ruggiero or Gene Gotti, his younger brother.

In 1968, the FBI arrested Gotti for stealing airport cargo. He was also slapped with hijacking charges from some capers in New Jersey. Gotti was incarcerated at Lewisburg federal penitentiary in Pennsylvania, where he attracted the notice of imprisoned Mafiosi Carmine Galante.

A member of the Bonanno family, Galante was the top Mafia leader at Lewisburg. At some point, Gotti approached Galante with a complaint. In jail, Galante kept his crew supplied with contraband steak and whiskey. Although Gotti wasn't a "made" man, he complained about not getting his fair share of liquor and meat. Far from being offended, Galante was impressed by the upstart's moxie. He invited Gotti to join the Bonanno family when he was released. Gotti appreciated the offer but decided to rejoin Fatico instead.

Gotti was released from Lewisburg in 1972, after serving three years. When Fatico began to experience legal woes, Gotti was appointed acting capo, with the firm endorsement of Aniello Dellacroce, a well-placed Gambino family member. Gotti got along well with Dellacroce. Both men enjoyed gambling and had no qualms about using violence to get their way. Dellacroce would become underboss of the Gambino family, second only to Carlo Gambino. Dellacroce used a locale called the Ravenite Social Club, located in Manhattan's Little Italy, as a headquarters and hangout.

Roughly a year after Gotti got out of Lewisburg, Manny Gambino—nephew of Carlo—was kidnapped. His abductors demanded $100,000, which Carlo Gambino paid up. His nephew was murdered anyway and buried in a dump in New Jersey. The FBI had two suspects in the case, who they took into custody. A third suspect, a career criminal named James McBratney, remained at large. Carlo Gambino put a contract on his life, which Gotti decided to collect.

On May 22, 1973, Gotti, Ruggiero, and a third man named Ralph Galione barged into a Staten Island bar that McBratney patronized. Claiming to be policemen, they said they were there to arrest McBratney. McBratney didn't believe the trio were cops, however, and fought back with his fists. The bar patrons began cheering McBratney as he struggled with the three intruders.

In frustration, Galione produced a pistol and shot McBratney dead. Shortly after, Galione himself was murdered, most likely as punishment for the fumbled hit. Gotti laid low for a year after the botched assassination but was eventually picked up by the FBI.

For his part, Carlo Gambino was delighted that his nephew's death had been avenged. To show his appreciation, Gambino hired notorious lawyer Roy Cohn to represent Gotti and Ruggiero (who had also been picked up). A courtroom deal was cut. Gotti pled guilty to attempted manslaughter and got four years. Gotti stayed at the Green Haven Correctional Facility in upstate New York, where he received privileged prisoner status.

By the mid-1970s, Gambino was in ill health. It was widely assumed the family boss would appoint Dellacroce as his successor. Instead, Gambino chose Paul Castellano as his replacement. The choice almost certainly reflected family favoritism; Gambino was married to Castellano's sister Katherine. Gambino himself died of cancer in 1976, and Castellano took the family over.

"Big Paul" Castellano was seen as weak and ineffectual, more concerned with personal wealth than extending the Gambinos' power. Gotti disliked Castellano, and the feeling was mutual. The two managed to put their differences aside for the sake of business. Castellano even presided over Gotti's induction ceremony as a "made man" once he got out of prison.

As an official Mafia chieftain, Gotti earned a reputation for ruthlessness that was startling even by underworld standards. He threatened minions with instant death unless they obeyed his every command. Gotti's crew engaged in typical mob money-making pursuits such as loan sharking, theft, and gambling but also dealt drugs, which was frowned upon in some Mafia circles. Gotti didn't care, as long as his men cut him in on their drug profits.

Gotti's violence spilled over into his personal life. In March 1980, for example, Gotti's 12-year-old son Frank rode his bicycle into the path of a car driven by neighbor John Favara and was killed. Frank's death was a tragic accident, but Gotti and his wife didn't see it that way. Favara, a quiet family man with no mob connections, started to receive threatening phone calls. The word "murderer" was spray-painted on his car. Favara put up his house for sale and planned to flee. In July 1980, as he left his shift as a service manager at a furniture plant, Favara was forced into a car. He disappeared and his body was never found. John and Victoria Gotti made sure they were in Florida at the time. They insisted they knew nothing about Favara's disappearance.

Frank's death remained an open wound in Gotti's life. He regularly visited the crypt where his son was buried. Each year on the boy's birthday, Gotti ran an In Memoriam ad in the *New York Daily News*.

In 1981, authorities managed to tap two phones in the office of the Bergin Hunt club. Later that same year, the FBI got a court order permitting them to bug Ruggiero's home phone. Ruggiero had a tendency to gossip about mob business, a trait that earned him the less-than-flattering nickname "Quack Quack" from his peers.

Ruggiero thought he was safe from electronic eavesdropping because he used his daughter's pink Princess phone (which was on a separate line from his home phone). The court order extended to this phone as well, however, and the FBI gleefully recorded all his conversations. When Ruggiero moved to Cedarhurst, Long Island, federal authorities planted listening devices in his new home. A microphone was placed in the dinette. As luck would have it, this was the precise location where Ruggiero liked to confer with fellow gangsters.

Once a week, Ruggiero had a face-to-face meeting with Big Paul at the latter's regal Staten Island mansion. After returning home, Ruggiero would immediately call Gotti and relay what Castellano had told him.

On the basis of information gathered from the Ruggiero bug, the FBI got court permission to plant listening devices in Castellano's and Dellacroce's residences. Among other details, they discovered that Ruggiero served as Gotti's unofficial valet. Like many gangsters, Gotti was a night owl, spending late evenings eating, drinking, partying, and meeting with his fellow gangsters. Ruggiero would call on Gotti around noon at his home, to wake the groggy don up.

On May 6, 1982, Ruggiero's brother, Salvatore, died in a jet plane crash off the coast of Georgia. Salvatore was a major heroin trafficker. Via wiretaps, the FBI determined that Ruggiero inherited his brother's drug connections. The same bugs also revealed that Gotti's brother Gene was deeply implicated in drug deals.

In August 1983, the U.S. district attorney indicted Ruggiero, Gene Gotti, and a third man named John Carneglia on drug charges. The indictments infuriated Castellano, who had pretensions of being accepted as a legitimate businessman. Ruggiero's lawyer had FBI transcripts of his client's bugged conversations. Castellano demanded to see the transcripts. He threatened to demote Gotti to the rank of soldier, disband his crew, and transfer his men to other crews if he wasn't obeyed.

Ruggiero and Gotti had good reason not to give up the transcripts. The bugs revealed that Ruggiero and other Gambino family members disliked their boss and called him names behind his back. These mid-level mobsters were also angry that Castellano banned them from selling narcotics but apparently had no problem accepting cash from drug dealers.

Throughout the spring of 1985, Gotti continued to stonewall, refusing to hand over the transcripts. Gotti sought advice from Dellacroce (who was chronically ill with cancer). His old mentor urged Gotti to surrender the incriminating documents.

Gotti had other plans. He began scheming against Castellano. He drew a select crew of rebels to his side, who were equally displeased with Castellano's rule. These rebels included Salvatore Gravano, nicknamed "Sammy the Bull"—a violent, low-profile Gambino thug.

As Gotti plotted, the pressure on Castellano increased. In February 1985, Big Paul and all other New York Mafia bosses were indicted on racketeering charges. Dellacroce was indicted as well, but Gotti was solely focused on Castellano. Given that he was dying of cancer and had a reputation for toughness, it was unlikely Dellacroce would cut a deal for lenient treatment. Mobsters were less sure about Castellano, who was a senior citizen and perceived as soft. It wasn't clear if Castellano could uphold the tradition of Omerta and keep his mouth shut.

At this juncture, Castellano proceeded to make some questionable staffing decisions. He boosted his pal, Thomas Bilotti, to the position of capo, which made him Gotti's equal. Mob gossip suggested Bilotti would be promoted to underboss once Dellacroce died. Then, if Castellano had to serve time, Bilotti would become acting family boss. Gotti would be left out in the cold, a mid-level capo with no chance of further advancement.

Other mid-level mobsters had issues with Castellano. He was perceived as greedy, someone who made a huge amount of money but wouldn't share it with his lieutenants. The circle of rebels united against Castellano began to grow. Among others, a capo named Frankie DeCicco gravitated to Gotti's side.

On December 2, 1985, Dellacroce died of cancer. Castellano did not attend the funeral—being under indictment, he didn't want to be seen in public with known mobsters. It was a good legal move, but bad Mafia politics. Not attending the funeral was seen as a shocking breech of underworld etiquette. In the eyes of his Mafia family, Castellano had again proven to be a distant, cowardly leader. A tougher mob boss would have used Dellacroce's death as an occasion to clean house and eliminate annoying subordinates such as John Gotti. Castellano did no such thing, however.

In mid-December 1985, Gotti informed his fellow conspirators, who now numbered around a dozen, that they were going to take part in a major hit. Gotti was vague about the target. DeCicco meanwhile, arranged a meeting with Castellano and Bilotti at Sparks Steak House in Manhattan, on December 16, at 5:00 p.m.

Shortly before this meeting, Gotti gathered his team together. He informed them their target was Castellano and then got his men in place. Gotti and Gravano got into a car and drove to Sparks.

On December 16, 1985, at around 5:25 p.m., Bilotti steered a car through heavy Manhattan traffic toward the scheduled rendezvous with DeCicco. His only passenger in the vehicle was Castellano. Streets swarmed with holiday shoppers. Both Bilotti and Castellano were unarmed.

Bilotti steered the vehicle to the sidewalk and stepped out, along with Castellano. As the two mob bosses exited their car, four assassins wearing identical white trench coats and fur hats (to confuse witnesses) stepped forward and opened fire with semiautomatic pistols. Another team of killers lurked nearby, in case the gunmen screwed up. The second team was unnecessary; Castellano and Bilotti were repeatedly shot and collapsed on the street. Gotti and Gravano cruised by the murder scene to make sure both men were dead, then drove off. The fur-hatted assassins slipped out of the area on foot.

Following this killing—the most spectacular takedown of a mob boss since Albert Anastasia's murder—Gotti took over the Gambino family. Gotti feigned shock and promised to lead an internal investigation into Castellano's death. In mid-January 1986, Gotti held a meeting with 20 Gambino capos (all of whom probably had a good idea who murdered Castellano). The capos unanimously selected him as the next Gambino boss. Gotti made Frank DeCicco underboss and Gravano a captain. Gotti began hanging out at the Ravenite Social Club, which had been Dellacroce's domain.

The hit on Castellano propelled Gotti from mid-level mobster to the most famous gangster in New York City. His visage began regularly turning up on the front page. Unlike most mob bosses who never spoke to the press, Gotti was happy to chat with reporters. He seemed eager to flaunt his Mafiosi pedigree, dressing in attention-grabbing double-breasted silk suits and expensive accessories.

Some of Gotti's peers weren't impressed by his rapid rise. Vincent "the Chin" Gigante, head of the Genovese mob family, was annoyed that Gotti hadn't asked for permission to kill Castellano. According to long-standing Mafia protocol, hits against a family boss had to be approved in advance by the Commission, the mob's quasi-administrative head. Gigante worked with the Lucchese family to come up with a suitable plan of revenge. On April 13, 1986, Gambino underboss DeCicco opened the door to his parked car and was blown to pieces by a bomb. At the moment of his death, DeCicco had been standing next to a mobster who resembled John Gotti. The bomb had been remotely activated, which suggested the real target was Gotti himself.

Gotti was alarmed by this close call, but not unduly worried. He was more focused on the fabulous wealth that suddenly came his way as family boss. To his surprise, he discovered the Gambinos were involved in several white-collar rackets, from pornography to a gas excise tax scam. As boss, Gotti was entitled to a cut of the proceeds.

Gotti held to a regular schedule. He slept in late each morning, then got picked up in a chauffeur-driven Mercedes-Benz that took him to the Bergin Club for lunch. After lunch, he chummed around with his cronies and looked after his appearance. A backroom at the Bergin was turned into a grooming station for Gotti. A stylist came in every day to wash, cut, and blow-dry his silvery pompadour. Gotti also did daily sun lap treatments to maintain an even tan. In addition to hair care products, Gotti kept a vast collection of expensive suits, shirts, ties, shoes, and underwear at the club. He would select an appropriate outfit, then at around 5:00 p.m., would head over to the Ravenite Club. Dinner would be conducted in a high-profile restaurant. Afterward, Gotti would go clubbing. He drank expensive brandy and champagne and had regular sexual encounters with women drawn to his gangster celebrity.

Once a week, all high-ranking Gambino members had to report to the Ravenite Club to update the boss on their activities. Gotti would frequently conduct "walk-talks" with his men. In a walk-talk, gangsters discussed business while briskly strolling on the sidewalk, to foil any attempt at police eavesdropping.

Even though he was now boss of a rich Mafia family, Gotti remained in his old Howard Beach home. Every July 4, he acted as benevolent neighborhood patron and arranged a huge party for area residents, complete with free carnival rides, card games, music, and food. These parties would climax with a thundering fireworks display. Gotti never bothered to get a permit for his pyrotechnics. Police typically stood around and gawked at the festivities.

Needless to say, Gotti was a popular figure in his clannish, blue-collar neighborhood. His neighbors were pleased to see someone from their own ranks become rich and powerful, even if it was through organized crime. Ironically, Gotti was frequently broke, despite earning millions a year. An obsessive but losing gambler, Gotti lost much of what he made in bad bets. In 1982 alone, Gotti blew $90,000 in losing bets on college football games.

In the spring of 1986, Gotti was hit with federal racketeering charges. The trial started in Brooklyn, in August 1986, and lasted until March 1987. Gotti and a handful of codefendants were prosecuted by Diane Giacalone, assistant U.S. attorney in the federal Eastern District. Giacalone lacked experience with Mafia cases, and her case was further weakened by a lack of cooperation among authorities.

Gotti and his codefendants were charged with three murder conspiracies, among other racketeering offenses. The prosecution had 30 hours of evidence gleaned from listening devices and 90 witnesses, but the case was still weak. Several of these witnesses were former gangsters themselves, who left a bad impression on the jury. Gotti was represented by Bruce Cutler, a bald, abrasive former high school wrestling champion and college football star. In his opening statement, Cutler lambasted the whole trial, denied the existence of the Mafia, and tossed the indictment into a wastepaper basket, saying it made him sick. He also tore apart the prosecution's witnesses on the stand. These dramatics worked and the jury found Gotti and company not guilty.

During the late 1980s, Gotti and Gravano became close. Gravano was heavily involved in the construction trade and prided himself on his technical knowledge of the field. Gravano found himself elevated to the position of family consigliere (adviser).

Gotti continued to be a media celebrity. The press called him the "Dapper Don"—after his extensive wardrobe—or the "Teflon Don"—a reflection of the seeming inability of authorities to successfully convict him.[1] The FBI, however, methodically built a case against Gotti. The FBI established a secret viewing post near the Ravenite Club, where Gotti had more or less established his permanent headquarters. Every time a Mafia leader came by to pay homage to Gotti, they were photographed by FBI agents.

In the spring of 1988, the FBI planted bugs at the Ravenite Club, but sound problems rendered them useless. A year later, the FBI caught a lucky break. In late 1989, federal authorities discovered that Gotti used an apartment above the Ravenite for meetings. The apartment belonged to Nettie Cirelli, former wife of a dead Gambino soldier. While wary of potential bugs in the Ravenite itself, Gotti apparently thought it was safe to talk business in Cirelli's apartment. Whenever Gotti felt like holding a meeting, Cirelli would go out shopping for a few hours, and her residence became a temporary Gambino family nerve center.

On November 19, 1989, an FBI surveillance team spotted Cirelli leaving her apartment with a suitcase, almost certainly departing for a Thanksgiving vacation. Seeing their chance, the FBI cautiously broke into Cirelli's residence and planted bugs. To their delight, the bugs picked up crystal-clear conversations featuring a chatty Gotti and his underlings. Gotti completely let his guard down in Cirelli's residence, and openly talked about murder, Mafia intrigue, and problems with employees. He frequently criticized Gravano for allegedly building up his own power base and for murdering anyone he had business problems with. On the surface, however, Gotti remained on good terms with Gravano, promoting him to underboss in early 1990.

Gotti began the 1990s on a high note. On February 9, 1990, he was found not guilty in a trial stemming from the assault on John O'Connor. A crowd of 1,000 people greeted Gotti as he walked out of the courthouse like a conquering hero. To celebrate Gotti's win, residents in South Ozone Park festooned the area with balloons and banners.

The government wasn't through, however. The listening device in Cirelli's apartment was picking up extremely valuable information. Federal authorities carefully put together another slate of charges against Gotti and his top leadership. On December 11, 1990, the FBI struck. They burst into the Ravenite, as Gotti presided over a meeting with Gravano and 30 other associates, soldiers, and capos. Gotti, Gravano, and a third man named Frank Locascio were arrested and taken to FBI headquarters in downtown Manhattan.

One day after the raid, the trio heard the charges against them. They were indicted as leaders of a criminal association. They were slapped with 13 counts under the RICO (Racketeer Influenced and Corrupt Organizations) Act. These counts included murder, conspiracy, illegal gambling, income tax evasion, loan sharking, and obstruction of justice. Gotti was also indicted for taking part in the murders of Castellano and Bilotti.

Ten days before Christmas, Gotti received a shock. To prevent the judge from granting bail, prosecutors played snippets of the Cirelli tapes in court. For the first time, Gotti realized some of his most private conversations had been recorded by the FBI. Federal District Court judge Leo Glasser listened to the tapes, then denied bail.

Gotti faced setbacks on another front. Federal prosecutors managed to get four lawyers working for Gotti and Gravano disqualified. Their ranks included the pugnacious Bruce Cutler. The attorneys had been picked up on bugs giving advice to Gotti. As a result of these recorded conversations, the lawyers might be called as witnesses. This would create an impossible conflict of interest for the attorneys, so they were disqualified.

In court, the Cirelli tapes proved devastating. Gravano was shocked to hear his boss put him down, complaining about Gravano not giving him a fair share of his proceeds from construction operations. Prior to their arrest, Gravano had been feeding Gotti $2 million a year, but this wasn't enough to satisfy the greedy don. The tapes also revealed that Gotti seemed somewhat jealous of Gravano.

Gravano became rapidly disenchanted. He was annoyed by Gotti's constant self-aggrandizing in court. Despite Gotti's constant reassurances, Gravano began to suspect his boss was setting him up, trying to make him the fall guy for Gambino family violence. Realizing he faced at best, a life sentence behind bars, Gravano did the unthinkable. In early fall 1991, he turned traitor and decided to reveal what he knew about the Gotti organization to authorities.

In January 1992, jury selection began in what was now a case against Gotti and Locascio. It was a case the federal government absolutely had to win. Were they to lose again, Gotti would gain a reputation as untouchable. Gotti put up a defiant front in court, stage-whispering insults about the judge and prosecutors that reporters overheard. Judge Glasser was no pushover, however, and ordered Gotti to stop the outbursts.

Instead of the steadfast Bruce Cutler, Gotti was defended by Albert Krieger, an able but less blustery trial attorney from Florida. The jury, meanwhile, was sequestered and billeted under guard at hotels, to prevent bribery or intimidation. As a further precaution, the identities of the jurors were kept secret.

The courtroom atmosphere verged on circus-like at times. Fans and family of Gotti routinely showed up to show their support. Sometimes, groups of pro-Gotti demonstrators picketed outside the courthouse. Celebrities such as Mickey Rourke and Anthony Quinn dropped by to watch the proceedings.

The prosecution continued to play the damning tapes from the Cirelli bug. To underline Gotti's importance, the prosecution displayed blown-up photographs of Mafia leaders coming and going to the Ravenite.

The tapes alone might not have been enough to convict Gotti. Combined with Sammy the Bull's testimony, however, Gotti had no chance. Gravano spent nine days giving extremely detailed testimony. Gravano's testimony, combined with the wiretap evidence, proved devastating for Gotti.

On April 2, 1992, the Teflon Don was found guilty on all 13 RICO counts. His codefendant Frank Locascio (who was almost entirely overlooked by the media in the proceedings) was also convicted of most charges.

Two months later, a smirking Gotti appeared before Judge Glasser for sentencing. To no one's surprise, Gotti received life in jail without parole. Locascio got the same. When the verdict was announced, a crowd of several hundred people outside the courthouse began a small riot. Cars were overturned and angry voices raised. Members of this support group were from the Bergin Hunt and Fish Club or from Gotti's old neighborhood.

Gotti arrived in shackles at the federal penitentiary in Marion, Illinois, on June 24, 1992. After being processed, Gotti was placed in a tiny cell, where he was kept 22 hours a day. Meal trays were slid into his cell through a slit in the door. The only visitors allowed were lawyers and relatives, and they were separated by a glass wall and had to communicate via telephone. For entertainment, Gotti was allowed a small black-and-white television set in his cell. For exercise, he was periodically allowed to walk the tier outside his cell, in shackles.

At first, Gotti believed he could still run the family from behind bars. He put members of his kin—brother Peter and eldest son John Gotti Jr.—in charge of family business.

Thanks to his father, John Gotti Jr. had enjoyed a spectacular rise up the Mafia hierarchy. That he was even in the mob was contrary to longstanding Mafia tradition, in which family bosses tried to steer their sons into legitimate professions. Exceptions were continually made for John Jr.; he became a "made man" at age 24, despite not having a pure Italian lineage, due to his mother being partly Jewish.

Officially, John Jr. was a businessman who owned successful trucking and real estate firms. Unofficially, he was made acting boss of the Gambinos by his imprisoned father. John Jr. would be assisted in day-to-day operations by three capos, whose ranks included Peter Gotti.

John Jr. was not well liked by the Mafia rank and file. They resented his fast promotion and the obvious nepotism that put him at the front of the family. Mafiosi doubted his leadership abilities and disliked his perceived arrogance and inept handling of business. The Genovese family outright refused to negotiate with John Jr., regarding him as a joke.

Authorities were determined to make John Jr.'s ascension to family boss as trying as possible. In 1998, he was slapped with a RICO indictment. John Jr. was accused of running gambling, loan-sharking, and extortion rackets. Among evidence seized by police was a list, found in John Jr.'s office, of soldiers who had been inducted into the New York Mafia from 1991 to 1992. Such information was never supposed to be written down, for the very reason that authorities might use it against the mob. The discovery of this piece of evidence further diminished John Jr.'s reputation. Eventually, the Mafia son copped a plea and, in September 1999, was sentenced to six years and five months' imprisonment plus a fine of $750,000.

The Ravenite Club, meanwhile, was seized by the government, on the grounds that it was a major center for illegal racketeering. The building was auctioned off by authorities and purchased by a new landlord who turned it into a store for women's accessories.

Back in Marion, John Gotti remained in virtual isolation, cut off from the family he had led. In the late 1990s, he was diagnosed with neck and head cancer. In June 2002, the cancer killed him. Gotti had an appropriately splashy, $200,000 funeral. His bronze casket was coated in gold and transported through Queens with 22 limos in its wake and hundreds of private cars. Some 19 vehicles alone were needed just to transport flowers.

The elaborate funeral could not cover up the fact that Gotti's reign had been disastrous. He had taken over the biggest, most powerful Mafia family in the United States, and left it a wreck. Gotti ignored the fact that the mob's very strength depended on secrecy and stealth. Keeping out of the spotlight was a major Mafia tenet, then and now.

Gotti violated other Mafia commandments, such as the unwritten rule that mob bosses are chosen on the basis of merit, not family connections. Making his son the boss of the Gambinos merely confounded Gotti's mistakes. If Gotti Sr. was a weak leader, his son was outright incompetent and widely disliked.

In 2004, as John Jr. was about to leave prison, he was hit with new RICO charges. After three trials, John Jr. was set free, only to be arrested again in August 2009 on conspiracy charges in Florida. The charges related to large-scale cocaine trafficking and the murder of three men in New York City. This fourth court battle took place in New York City and ended in yet another mistrial. When asked by reporters, jurors from the fourth trial explained that they didn't find the witnesses (mostly mob informants) or the case against John Jr. to be credible. It was a sentiment shared by jury members in the first three trials.

While out of jail for the moment, it's unclear if John Jr.'s legal woes are over yet. If he is brought to trial yet again, the court fight would take place against the backdrop of a new Hollywood film about the Gotti family. Barry Levinson is said to be directing, with Al Pacino as Neil Dellacroce and Ben Foster as John Jr. The Teflon Don himself is being played by superstar John Travolta—a bit of casting Gotti Sr. certainly would have approved of.

Note

1. Selwyn Raab, "John Gotti Dies in Prison at 61; Mafia Boss Relished the Spotlight," *New York Times*, June 11, 2002.

Joseph Colombo Sr.: The Crusader

(1922–1978)

Joseph Colombo Sr.'s career arc in the Mafia began in a fairly traditional fashion, only to take a bizarre turn when he decided to become a civil rights crusader for Italian Americans.

Colombo himself was a second-generation hood. His father, Anthony Colombo, "was a successful Brooklyn mobster until he was garroted one night in 1938 in the back seat of his car, along with his girlfriend," noted *Time* magazine.[1]

Joseph was 16 when his father died and used his death as an excuse to drop out of high school. He worked in a printing plant and did other jobs to support his mother and sister. During the Second World War, Colombo joined the Coast Guard but didn't fare well. He was eventually discharged from the Coast Guard with a medical diagnosis of "psychoneurosis." It's unclear if the diagnosis was based on real symptoms or if Colombo was merely playing at being mentally ill to get out of the service.

Discharge in hand, Colombo returned to Brooklyn. He began committing petty crimes and doing a variety of thuggish tasks, from being an enforcer on the piers to running rigged dice games. Colombo impressed his elders and was selected to join an assassination team controlled by Mafia boss Joe Profaci. Two other members of the team were Larry and "Crazy Joe" Gallo.

The five-man death squad performed well, killing around 15 people by the end of the 1950s. In 1959, however, the crew was hit with a crisis of conscience after being ordered to kill one of its own members. This "hit" was carried out, but then the remaining assassins had sober second thoughts. If Profaci could order the death of one of their own, what was stopping him from murdering the rest of the squad?

In a violent break with Mafia mores, which demand total obsequiousness on the part of low-ranking members, the Gallo brothers abducted some Profaci men. Instead of a ransom, Larry and Joe Gallo demanded that Profaci give them a greater share of the proceeds of crime. While the kidnapped men were eventually released, this action triggered a bitter gang war. Said war lasted three years and saw the death of nine mobsters and the disappearance of three others.

Colombo somehow managed to stay aloof from the fray. He remained loyal to Profaci but (ironically, in light of his later activities) kept an extremely low profile. For all that, the Gallo brothers did attempt to kill him. The hit was set for July 4, 1963, as Colombo journeyed home from the country club where he liked to play golf. Colombo discovered the plot and took a different route home.

By remaining more or less on the sidelines, Colombo was in a good position to arrange a truce between warring mob factions intent on exterminating each other. In this manner, Colombo stumbled into a second underworld war. Two bosses, Joe Bonanno and Joe Magliocco, ordered Colombo to kill three other Mafia leaders, Carlo Gambino and Thomas Lucchese of New York City and Stefano Magaddino from Buffalo. Colombo decided not to carry out the contract and informed the intended targets of the plan. The end result was the "Bananas War" (Bonanno's Mafia nickname was "Joe Bananas"), which saw the death of seven mobsters. Once again, Colombo emerged unscathed.

In 1963, Colombo took over the Profaci family. He was only 40 years old, quite young by Mafia boss standards. He was also very little known. While Colombo had an extensive rap sheet (12 arrests and three convictions, of a fairly minor nature) he had almost no profile in the media.

The Profaci family was renamed the Colombo family, after their new leader. As a family boss, Colombo's money-making rackets included gambling operations in Brooklyn and Nassau County, loan sharking in Manhattan, and stealing freight at Kennedy Airport.

Colombo was obsessed with his family's public image. He demanded that his Mafia minions hold legitimate jobs in addition to their underworld duties. Needless to say, this caused no end of grumbling, given that one of the attractions of being a criminal is the ability to avoid the drudgery of the 9-to-5 lifestyle. Colombo himself dressed conservatively and claimed to be a successful real estate salesman. He lived in an inconspicuous split-level home in Brooklyn with his wife and three kids. Allegedly, he also had a more posh pad in Orange County, New York, complete with swimming pool, tennis courts, and a track for horse racing.

Colombo briefly went to prison in 1966 when he refused to tell a grand jury what he knew about Mafia involvement in legitimate companies. In doing so, he upheld the Mafia tradition of "Omerta"—silence in the face of legal threats.

In the early 1970s, however, Colombo suddenly took on a new role as a civil rights crusader. Colombo was irked by Mario Puzo's bestselling novel, *The Godfather*, and other media depictions associating Italian Americans with the Mafia. He was further outraged by what he perceived as "harassment" by the FBI, who had the temerity to follow him around and question his friends and family. The last straw was the arrest of his son, Joseph Colombo Jr. in April 1970. Colombo Jr. was accused of melting coins to make silver ingots (he was acquitted when the case came to court).

In the spring of 1970, Colombo launched the Italian-American Civil Rights League. Among other activities, the League picketed FBI offices in New York City. Colombo's newfound activism struck a nerve in many Italian Americans, who were tired of being seen as shifty Mafiosi. On June 29, 1970, the Italian-American Civil Rights League held a huge rally at Columbus Circle in New York City. The rally, supposedly celebrating "Italian-American Unity Day" attracted 50,000 people, including prominent politicians. New York State governor Nelson Rockefeller, for one, requested—and was granted—honorary membership in the League.

In addition to pickets and rallies, the League held fund-raising dinners. At one such affair, held at Madison Square Garden, Frank Sinatra provided the entertainment. A total of $500,000 was raised for Colombo's organization at this event.

Colombo became the most visible face of the Italian-American Civil Rights League. Here was a true case of chutzpah: a known mob boss complaining about unflattering media depictions of Italians and harassment from government agencies.

Other underworld leaders recoiled at Colombo's oddball crusade. Mafia bosses were supposed to lie low and operate from the shadows. Colombo by contrast, gave interviews to the press, aired his grievances on TV, and made speeches at public gatherings. Like J. Edgar Hoover before him, Colombo steadfastly denied there even was such a thing as an American Mafia. The Italian-American Civil Rights League began to attract some unusual allies, including black, Jewish entertainer Sammy Davis Jr.; and Rabbi Meir Kahane, fiery leader of the militant Jewish Defense League.

In addition to drawing unwanted publicity to the underworld, Mafia bosses fretted that Colombo wasn't keeping his mind on mob business. The bosses were also annoyed that Colombo was raising millions through the League but wasn't sharing any of this largesse with his peers.

Spring 1971 brought a new focus to Colombo's activism. Paramount studios started filming a movie version of *The Godfather* in New York City. Colombo was deeply offended. He allegedly met with studio bosses and convinced them not to use the words "Mafia" or "La Cosa Nostra" in the film.

On June 28, 1971, Colombo organized a second Italian American unity day rally in Columbus Circle. Among the thousands in attendance was a young African American named Jerome Johnson, who touted a camera and claimed to be a photojournalist. At some point during the rally, Johnson produced a gun, approached Colombo, and managed to shoot him at point-blank range, despite the presence of hulking bodyguards. Johnson was quickly gunned down in turn by assailants unknown.

A group called the Black Revolutionary Attack Team claimed credit for the attack, but this was probably a ruse. Johnson had no history of political involvement. He did, however, have a reputation as a minor-league criminal and hustler. It was speculated by the press that Johnson had been set up—offered a huge payout for shooting Colombo. Instead of whisking him to safety as promised, Johnson's employers likely shot him dead.

While it's never been conclusively proven that the Mafia was behind Colombo's death, it had the most to gain from his assassination. Virtually no one believed Johnson acted on his own, much less a dubious band of black radicals.

Colombo wasn't actually killed at the rally, but badly wounded. He was rushed to the hospital but did not recover. Colombo remained in a vegetative state for years, finally dying on May 22, 1978, at St. Luke's Hospital in Newburgh, New York.

Without Colombo's energetic leadership, the Italian-American Civil Rights League quickly fell apart. The very threat that the League dismissed as a media fiction had made its point. As *Time* magazine succinctly put it, "The Mafia that [Colombo] insists is nonexistent almost surely tried to kill [him]."[2]

Notes

1. "The Capo Who Went Public," *Time*, July 12, 1971.
2. "The Mafia: Back to the Bad Old Days?" *Time*, July 12, 1971.

Vincent "The Chin" Gigante: The Oddfather

(1928–2005)

They called him "The Oddfather"—a disheveled, shambling wreck of a man in a ratty bathrobe, who wandered aimlessly on the streets of Greenwich Village, muttering incoherently to himself.[1] At least, that was his public image. In reality, Vincent Gigante was in full control of his senses and was merely playacting "crazy" to avoid being put in jail. That he could successfully pull off this charade for decades gives credit to his acting abilities and craftiness. It's not every Mafia don who is willing to humiliate themselves in public to stay out of prison.

Gigante was born in March 1928 and grew up in the same Greenwich Village area of New York City, where he would later base his

Vincent L. Gigante, 29, looks out from behind bars at police headquarters in New York City on August 20, 1957. (AP/Wide World Photo)

criminal fiefdom. Gigante's father was a watchmaker, his mother a seamstress. Both originally hailed from Naples, Italy. In addition to Gigante, the family had four other boys. As a child, Gigante acquired the lifelong nickname "the Chin" for his prominent lower jaw.

A poor student, Gigante managed to get through Public School 3 in Greenwich Village but dropped out of high school in ninth grade. As a teenager, he caught the eye of powerful Mafia leader Vito Genovese, who headed a mob family of the same name. The Genovese family had been founded in the early 1930s and was once led by legendary gangster Charles "Lucky" Luciano.

As a young man, Gigante was arrested several times, on charges ranging from possession of an unlicensed handgun, to auto theft, arson, bookmaking, and receiving stolen goods. He was not punished too harshly for these misdeeds. A two-month sentence for gambling crimes was the stiffest sentence he served as a budding Mafiosi.

While trying his hand at various crimes and misdemeanors, Gigante also boxed in the light heavyweight category. He proved his worth in the ring, with a career record of 21 wins against four losses.

During the 1950s, Gigante used his pugnacious talents to become an enforcer. In 1957, Gigante was tapped to be an assassin. The target was Frank Costello, head of a New York Mafia family that the Genovese clan was eager to take over. In the foyer of a Central Park West apartment building, someone fired a shot at Costello but missed. In the ensuing trial, the gunman was identified as Gigante. Costello refused to "finger" Gigante as the gunman, however, and "the Chin" was acquitted on charges of attempted murder. Allegedly, Gigante thanked Costello, as the latter departed the courtroom, for not "ratting" him out.

Gigante proved less successful at evading conviction in 1959, when he found himself up on federal charges of heroin trafficking. In the dock with him was his former mentor Vito Genovese. The trial was held in Manhattan, and Gigante was found guilty. He was sentenced to seven years in prison, but he served only five. Upon release, Gigante received a Mafia promotion from "soldier" (the lowest rank in the Mafia hierarchy) to "capo." This meant he was in now in charge of a "crew" of Mafia soldiers and "associates" (mob helpmates).

Gigante's base of operations was his childhood neighborhood of Greenwich Village. He made a home, however, in Old Tappan, New Jersey. There, he lived with his wife, three daughters, and two sons.

In 1969, Gigante found himself charged with conspiring to bribe all five members of the Old Tappan police department. He was accused of paying off these peace officers to alert him to surveillance efforts by more honest police forces.

It was during this trial that Gigante first tried out the act that later made him infamous. In court, Gigante's lawyers argued that their client was mentally ill. Clearly, a man with a severe psychiatric disorder couldn't be responsible for his actions, claimed the attorneys. The judge and jury bought it, and Gigante found himself acquitted.

Behind the scenes, Gigante remained a clever, ambitious Mafiosi. He took over the Genovese family in the early 1980s, in an unusually peaceful transfer of power. The former family head, Philip Lombardo, left the post due to ill health.

As a Mafia boss, Gigante proved to be obsessed with secrecy and security. Genovese family members weren't even supposed to use his name or nickname when holding conversations or making phone calls. The general accepted form of communication when someone needed to refer to Gigante was to point to your chin or make the letter "C." Gigante himself did not rant and rave about Mafia business, over the phone or in his hideouts as some bosses were apt to do. He was determined not to give any information away that could be easily picked up by surveillance "bugs" planted by police.

In public, however, Gigante proved more than willing to attract attention to himself. Throughout the 1980s and 1990s, he became a familiar sight in Greenwich Village, wandering aimlessly in what appeared to be a stupefied daze. He would often wear dirty pajamas and a robe during these excursions. The fact Gigante was always trailed by a bodyguard during his ramblings was a hint as to the real state of his mental faculties. Truly psychotic people aren't concerned with personal safety.

Gigante followed a particular routine. In the evening, he would wander from his mother's apartment on Sullivan Street in Greenwich Village, dressed in his shabby attire. He would stumble his way to the Triangle Civic Improvement Association (a front organization for his Mafia headquarters). Once inside the association's storefront offices, he would play cards and whisper commands to his cronies. Around midnight, Gigante might go to the Park Avenue townhouse owned by his mistress. There, he would change into dressier clothes and network with various Mafiosi and business clients. Around 9:00 or 10:00 a.m., the grubby pajamas and bathrobe came back on, and he would be driven back to Sullivan Street or some other locale to sleep.

When not playing insane, Gigante rose to the pinnacle of Mafia power. He became a force on "the Commission" (the loosely organized, administrative head of the New York City Mafia, charged with adjudicating disputes and plotting underworld strategy).

Under Gigante's rule, the Genovese family was a well-organized, disciplined machine that became the most powerful Mafia clan in the city. Authorities estimated that the family had 200 "made" members and five times that number of associates. Annual proceeds in the early 1990s topped $100 million. The Genovese family was involved in the usual rackets such as gambling, loan sharking, extortion, and union shakedowns. The Genovese clan also had a hand in private garbage collection and ripping off trucking and shipping companies in New Jersey and Florida (firms paid the Genovese family to ensure labor peace).

As cautious as he was in private and "crazy" as he was in public, Gigante couldn't completely evade the attention of authorities. In 1990, Gigante and 14 others were hit with federal racketeering charges in Brooklyn. Prosecutors accused Gigante and his peers of rigging bids and soliciting payoffs from contractors working for the New York City Housing Authority.

When it came time to appear in court, Gigante fell back on his usual charade, dressing in shabby clothes and acting deranged. Gigante's case was severed from the others and ground on for seven years, as lawyers and psychiatrists debated whether he was mentally competent to stand trial.

In 1993, Gigante was slapped with a superseding indictment—that is, an indictment that takes the place of a previous charge. Gigante was accused of running the Genovese family and approving the murder of six gangsters and planned assassination of three others. The latter targets included John Gotti of the Gambino family. Gigante was highly displeased by Gotti's rise to power in the 1980s, which came about after the flamboyant mobster orchestrated the murder of mob family chief Paul Castellano. Gigante had worked with Castellano, but it wasn't sentimentality that spurred him. Gotti had broken a major Mafia tenet, which required all "hits" against mob bosses to be okayed by the Commission. Gotti hadn't bothered getting permission before arranging Castellano's murder. To Gigante, such effrontery marked Gotti for death.

In March 1996, sanity hearings were held to determine if Gigante was fit to stand trial on the counts of racketeering. Gambino family defector Sammy "the Bull" Gravano offered devastating testimony in which he recalled secret meetings with Gigante, who seemed perfectly sane. On the stand, Gravano offered a revealing anecdote. He spoke of a meeting in the late 1980s at which Gotti boasted that his son, John Jr., had become a "made" member of the Mafia. Gigante was not impressed and said he was sorry to hear this, that none of his boys were involved in the Mafia. It was a telling story—if Gigante was clear-headed enough to keep his kin out of the underworld, it was hard to believe he wasn't in control of his senses.

Gigante's lawyers, however, insisted their client was insane, suffering from everything from depression to psychosis and schizophrenia. Authorities weren't buying it. In August 1996, a judge in Federal District Court in Brooklyn ruled that Gigante was sane enough to stand trial. Gigante promptly pled not guilty.

The ensuring trial in 1997 proved a bizarre spectacle. Gigante was eased into the Brooklyn court in a wheelchair, looking utterly bewildered and spaced out. Gigante did not take the stand in his own defense, allegedly because he was too addled to testify.

Time magazine caught the spirit of the occasion, describing the court proceedings as "the most gloriously twisted show in New York City." The cast of the show included "a muttering, reputed Mafia don in his wheelchair" and Gigante's loyal brother, who happened to be a Catholic priest and former prison inmate.[2]

In July 1997, the jury decided that Gigante was faking his symptoms. They found him guilty of running various rackets and conspiring to kill Gotti. Five months later, Judge Jack B. Weinstein in federal court sentenced Gigante to 12 years in jail, on racketeering and murder-conspiracy charges. Judge Weinstein took note of how low Gigante had sunk. "He is a shadow of his former self, an old man finally brought to bay in his declining years after decades of vicious criminal tyranny," the judge told reporters, as quoted in the *New York Times*.[3]

Gigante was fined $1.25 million in addition to his jail sentence. Even at this late juncture, Gigante was still pulling his "crazy" act, supporting himself on tables and desks as he stepped into court, looking utterly lost and confused during sentencing procedures.

By this point, few people were fooled. In 2001, for example, the *New York Daily News* ran a story, citing new information from an FBI probe that showed Gigante in his real light. "[F]ederal investigators say 73 year-old Vincent (Chin) Gigante has replaced ailing Gambino crime boss John Gotti . . . as the most powerful gangster in America."[4] Gotti, at this point, was incarcerated and dying of cancer.

When he appeared in Federal District Court in Brooklyn on April 7, 2003, Gigante was no longer playacting crazy. By this point, Gigante was 75 years old, elderly by any standards but absolutely ancient in Mafia circles, where lives have a tendency of being abruptly cut short. Already serving time for racketeering, Gigante was faced with the prospect of another trial, for heading the Genovese crime family from jail. He decided to take a plea instead. In return for not being prosecuted, he admitted his madman demeanor had all been a ruse to delay his racketeering trial in the 1990s. Gigante spoke coherently in court, politely referring to federal Judge I. Leo Glasser (the same justice who had presided over John Gotti's final trial) as "your honor" in response to questions from the bench. Gigante drew an additional three years in jail but avoided having to go through yet another lengthy trial. "The jig is up. Vincent Gigante was a cunning faker and those of us in law enforcement always knew that this was an act," stated Roslynn Mauskopf, U.S. attorney for eastern district of New York, outside the courtroom according to the *New York Times*.[5]

Gigante didn't have long to live after "coming out," so to speak. He died on December 19, 2005, in the United States Medical Center for Federal Prisoners, based in Springfield, Missouri. He was 77 years old. Interestingly enough, Gigante died in the same prison hospital where Gotti expired three years earlier.

Unlike most mob bosses before him, Gigante did not have a garish, over-the-top funeral with dozens of cars carrying floral bouquets. Instead, his still-loyal priest brother gave a funeral mass to friends and family at a church near the very tenement apartment in Greenwich Village where Gigante had grown up.

Looking back, it seemed obvious from the start that Gigante was only playing at being a lunatic. *The Sopranos* aside, it would be very unlikely that a Mafia boss who was actually mentally ill would be allowed to remain on top. Most likely they would be eliminated by either their own family or their peers, for fear they might disclose Mafia secrets.

"Genuine insanity would be dangerous for someone in Gigante's reputed line of work. A Mafia gambling czar named Willie Moretti was shot to death in 1951 because he had become mentally ill and was talking too much," noted a perceptive *Time* magazine article, published in September 1990.[6]

Notes

1. Greg Smith, "Genovese Family Keeps Its Chin Up," *New York Daily News*, August 12, 2001.
2. Steve Lopez, "In the Land of the Gigantes," *Time*, July 21, 1997.
3. Joseph Fried, "Gigante Sentenced to 12 Years and Is Fined $1.25 Million," *New York Times*, December 19, 1997.
4. Smith, "Genovese Family Keeps Its Chin Up."
5. Andy Newman, "Mob Boss Admits Insanity an Act, Pleads Guilty: Mafia 'Oddfather' Gets 3 More Years," *New York Times*, April 8, 2003.
6. Richard Behar, "Is the Godfather Insane, or Crazy Like a Fox?" *Time*, September 3, 1990.

Informers

Joe Valachi

(1904–1971)

Joseph Valachi was the first full member of the American Mafia to go public with the organization's secrets. Some critics have suggested Valachi merely mouthed information police already had on file, for the benefit of the press. Still, Valachi remains a fascinating figure, the man who depicted the inner workings of a secret crime society.

Valachi was born on September 22, 1904, in the then thriving Italian community of East Harlem, New York City. Valachi's father was an alcoholic pushcart peddler and wife beater. A school truant, Valachi became a petty criminal when he was still a boy. From 1919 to 1923, he was the getaway driver for a burglary gang that committed hundreds of crimes. Throughout the 1920s, Valachi alternated between burglary sprees and stints in jail. His activities drew the attention of more established criminals in the city.

In 1930, the vicious Castellammarese War erupted between Sicilian American gang leaders Salvatore Maranzano and Joe "the Boss" Masseria. Both gangsters were eager to bolster their ranks, which is how Valachi was formally inducted into Maranzano's gang.

Valachi's initial duties with the Mafia were anything but glamorous. Among other chores, he served as a bodyguard and chauffeur for higher-ranking mobsters. During his whole criminal career, Valachi never rose above the level of "soldier"—the lowest rank in the Mafia hierarchy.

Valachi was called to perform his first "hit" as a Mafia member in late November 1932. The target was a man named Michael Reggione (aka "Little Apples"), whom Valachi didn't know. Valachi carried out the hit and, over the next three decades, committed roughly 30 additional murders (he wasn't sure of the exact total). Valachi also engaged in a variety of other rackets, including loan sharking, gambling, and slot machines. During World War II, he dealt in black-market ration and gasoline stamps. After the war, he got into jukeboxes in a big way. He "earned a living" in mob lingo, but wasn't particularly affluent and certainly was no powerhouse in the Mafia leadership.

Valachi also dealt narcotics. In early 1956, he was arrested on drug charges. Found guilty, he was given five years in jail. Valachi got out on bail pending an appeal, then his conviction was reversed. Following this close call, Valachi plunged back into the drug trade and was arrested again, in November 1959. This time, he jumped bail and hid out. Learning that his Mafia masters were displeased with him, Valachi decided to take his chances at trial. He turned himself in and promptly drew a 15-year sentence, to be served at the federal penitentiary in Atlanta.

In August 1961, Valachi went through a new drug trial in New York, for which he received another 20 years, to be served concurrently with his first sentence. Upon returning to Atlanta, Valachi was unnerved to find himself ostracized by imprisoned Mafia boss Vito Genovese. Genovese, who had a lot of power over other incarcerated Mafiosi, suspected Valachi was going to turn informer. Valachi caught wind of this and began to fear for his life. While Valachi had loyally served the underworld for decades, he was certain he was going to be murdered.

On June 22, 1962, at 7:30 a.m., Valachi was approached by a fellow convict named John Saupp. Saupp meant no harm, but Valachi mistook him for a Mafia assassin. In rage and terror, Valachi grabbed an iron pipe from a jailyard construction site. Wielding the pipe like a club, he attacked Saupp and viciously beat him. The shocked convict didn't have a chance to fight back. Saupp lingered for a couple days in hospital but eventually succumbed to his injuries.

Following this assault, Valachi was transported to Westchester County Jail, north of New York City. It was there he began to tell authorities what he knew about organized crime. It's unclear why Valachi broke Omerta. Valachi himself claimed he wanted to warn the public about the menace posed by the Mafia. This seems rather unlikely, in light of Valachi's lengthy career as a criminal. A more likely explanation is that Valachi hoped that by talking, he could avoid a death sentence for killing Saupp. Coming forward also gave Valachi a feeling of being important. After a lifetime spent toiling in the Mafia's lower ranks, Valachi was treated as a criminal superstar by the federal government.

In September–October 1963, Valachi testified before a U.S. Senate subcommittee chaired by Senator John McClellan that was investigating organized crime. Valachi was guarded by scores of federal marshals, to prevent anyone from collecting the $100,000 "contract" the Mafia had put on his head.

Valachi described the Mafia's structure to the subcommittee, how it was divided into "families" run by "capos" or bosses, assisted by "subcapos" or underbosses. As a soldier, Valachi was one of several thugs that made up a Mafia "crew" or regime. This crew carried out the mob's dirty work, under the supervision of a "caporegime" or lieutenant.

Some of the information Valachi gave was erroneous. He repeated the myth of the "Night of the Sicilian Vespers" (a supposed nationwide purge of old-time Mafia members that followed Maranzano's murder) and was known to get names and other details wrong.

The biggest question around Valachi, however, was how a lowly soldier could know so much about upper-level Mafia management. It has been suggested that federal authorities used Valachi as a "mouthpiece." According to this theory, Valachi simply echoed information that had been given to him by government sources.

In June 1964, the Department of Justice encouraged Valachi to write a personal biography of his life in crime. Valachi diligently spent the next 13 months scribbling away, eventually churning out 300,000 words. Journalist Peter Maas edited this text down to size and used it as the basis for a book called, *The Valachi Papers.*

Despite the huge bounty on him, Valachi wasn't brought down by Mafia bullets. He died of a heart attack at federal prison in El Paso, Texas, in April 1971.

Henry Hill

(1943–2012)

Henry Hill was fascinated by gangsters as a boy. Born in 1943, Hill grew up in the working class Brownsville East section of Brooklyn. His father was Irish American, his mother Sicilian American. He had seven brothers and sisters and little interest in leading an ordinary, respectable life, like his electrician father.

Hill was drawn to a cabstand near his parents' apartment where mobsters ("wiseguys" in Mafia lingo) congregated. The stand was owned by Paul Vario, a capo in the Lucchese crime family. As a young boy, Henry started doing odd jobs for Vario. In 1955, he dropped out of school for good, to hang out full time at the cab stand and rub shoulders with gangsters.

Besides admiring their clothes, money, and attitude, Hill had one other reason for liking gangsters so much—they treated him decently, unlike his father, who beat him after discovering his son was consorting with criminals.

Ironically, Hill was ineligible to join the very organization he so admired. His half-Irish ancestry precluded him from ever being formally inducted into the Mafia as a "made" man. He was welcome, however, to hang around as a mob "associate."

After serving a stint in the army in the early 1960s, Hill returned to New York City, where he began working with fellow Irish American Mafia associate Jimmy Burke and the violent, unstable

Tommy DeSimone. In concert with other associates and Mafiosi, the trio pursued various felonies, including loan sharking, bookmaking, and selling stolen goods. Burke's specialty was hijacking cargo-laden trucks as they left John F. Kennedy Airport. Burke typically gave drivers $50 for their trouble, a gesture that earned him the nickname "Jimmy the Gent."

By the mid-1960s, Hill had acquired a cover job (he had a union card with a local bricklayers' association) and a Jewish American girlfriend named Karen. Karen was impressed with Hill's bon vivant lifestyle, which included top tables at leading nightclubs, expensive restaurant meals, and premium liquor. Shortly after she met Henry, Karen went for a drive with a boy from her Long Island neighborhood. The boy tried to grope her, Karen slapped him, and the boy ditched

Henry Hill cuts a tray of pizza in the kitchen of the Firefly restaurant where he cooks in North Platte, Nebraska, 2005. The exploits of Hill, who sought refuge in the witness protection program after agreeing to testify against his former mob bosses from New York, were the basis for the book Wiseguy *by Nicholas Pileggi, which was later turned into the 1990 film* Goodfellas *directed by Martin Scorsese. (AP Photo/Nati Harnik)*

her miles from home. Karen called Hill, who stormed over to the boy's house, pistol-whipped him, and then asked Karen to hide his soiled gun.

Such macho displays didn't turn Karen off, and she and Hill were married on August 29, 1965. They briefly lived with Karen's parents (to the chagrin of her mother, who referred to her new son-in-law as "that gangster"). Eventually, the newlyweds moved to an apartment in Island Park, New York. They quickly produced two children, Gregg and Gina.

In addition to hijacking trucks, Hill took part in an infamous 1967 robbery at Kennedy Airport, in which nearly half a million dollars was stolen from an Air France storage room. He continued to work with Burke. At one point, the duo traveled to Florida to collect a debt from a gambler by beating him up. Burke and Hill were slapped with federal extortion charges for crossing a state line to commit the assault. Hill received a 10-year sentence. He served six years, dealing drugs in prison and befriending fellow jailed Mafia members and associates. Hill was paroled on July 12, 1978, after Vario promised authorities to give him a job at a nightclub he owned. This position was in fact a "no-show" job like Hill's membership in the bricklayer's union.

Two days after he was paroled, Hill bribed an official at his halfway house in New York and flew to Pittsburgh (in violation of his parole conditions). In Pittsburgh, he met with a man named Paul Mazzei, who owned him money. In lieu of cash, Mazzei gave Hill two suitcases filled with marijuana to sell. Too wary to bring this luggage on a plane, Hill took a bus back to New York and started selling pot.

In becoming a drug dealer, Hill managed to violate the tenets of both the parole board and the Mafia. Vario had a standing rule that no members or associates of his family were allowed to deal drugs. He feared that the harsh sentences handed down for drug crimes could induce his underlings to cut deals and reveal family secrets if they were ever arrested.

Hill wasn't hemmed in by such strictures. He established a big drug operation covering several states. He dealt marijuana, cocaine, heroin, and Quaaludes and dipped frequently into his own supply. Soon, Hill was snorting three to four grams of cocaine a day, on top of Quaaludes (to take the edge off the cocaine) and copious amounts of alcohol.

The infamous Lufthansa heist at Kennedy Airport was Hill's most notable criminal achievement. On December 11, 1978, six or seven men wearing masks and toting guns broke into the Lufthansa cargo building at the airport, tied up the guards, and absconded with $5.8 million in cash and jewels. At the time, it was one of the largest robberies in U.S. history.

Hill helped set up the heist. A cargo agent (who happened to be an avid gambler) had heard that the Lufthansa warehouse would be easy to rob. The cargo agent told a bookie, who introduced the agent to underworld associate Marty Krugman. Krugman talked to Hill, who passed the information on to Jimmy Burke. Burke met with Krugman, then arranged the robbery. Hill didn't participate in the actual theft.

Shortly after the Lufthansa heist, Burke began killing all the partners who helped him pull it off, to cover his tracks. In January 1979, Krugman disappeared, likely murdered by Burke. By the spring of 1979, six people with connections to the Lufthansa robbery had been murdered or disappeared.

Around the same time Krugman vanished, Tommy DeSimone dropped out of sight. It is believed DeSimone was lured into a house by mobsters under the pretense of being formally inducted into the Mafia. Instead, he was shot and killed, Mafia payback for DeSimone's previous murder of made Gambino member Billy Batts. In the Mafia, made members are only supposed to be killed with the sanction of family bosses.

In the late 1970s, Hill cooked up a point-shaving scam with Mazzei, involving the Boston College basketball team. Hill and Mazzei bribed a couple of Boston College players to miss a few easy baskets in order to alter the score. Hill found bookies who could handle large bets and served as background coordinator of the whole scheme.

On April 27, 1980, Hill was arrested in Nassau County, New York for drug trafficking. He made bail, only to be arrested again as a material witness for the Lufthansa heist. Hill began to suspect that his former colleagues were planning on murdering him. Vario and Burke both had reason to: for breaking the no-drugs rule, and to maintain silence about the Lufthansa heist, respectively. Hill was spending his days in a stoned or drunk haze, which exacerbated his paranoia. He decided to make a deal with authorities.

Three weeks after his arrest, Hill, his wife Karen, and their two kids entered the U.S. Marshals' Witness Protection Program. In return for testifying against former business partners, Hill would be relocated somewhere in the United States and given a monthly fee, a new name, and a clean criminal record. His family was included in the deal.

Hill testified in several trials that resulted in dozens of convictions. In early 1982, Burke received 20 years for his involvement in the point shaving scam. Two years later, Burke got a life sentence for murder. He died in jail at age 69, on April 13, 1996.

Hill also helped convict his old mentor Vario. The Lucchese capo received four years for lying to federal authorities about the "no-show" job that helped win Hill's parole. He also got 10 years for extorting air freight companies at Kennedy Airport. Vario died behind bars at age 73, on May 3, 1988.

In between court appearances, Hill continued to drink and take huge amounts of drugs. His family was moved around from Nebraska to Kentucky, finally ending up in Washington State. Even while receiving a state stipend, Hill ran scams, sold drugs, and generally burned through any money he had. Hill also seemed incapable of keeping a low profile. He gave interviews to *Sports Illustrated* magazine about the Boston College point-shaving scandal. In September 1981, Hill signed a book deal. He worked with a crime writer to put together a memoir that was eventually published under the title *Wiseguy*.

Hill racked up several new arrests in Washington State for drunk driving and burglary (he tried to break into a deli, while drunk, to steal a pack of cigarettes) among other offenses. In 1984, Hill was dropped from witness protection due to his inability to remain out of trouble and out of sight. During this same period, Hill began using heroin, on top of other drugs and alcohol. More arrests, on drug charges, followed. In the late 1980s, Hill and Karen divorced. Hill's children were extremely displeased with his career trajectory: "My father was a cheating, wife-beating, drug-dealing, thieving, gambling, alcoholic ex-con drug addict. I had nothing to rebel against. My only rebellion was to behave," wrote Gregg Hill.[1] Gina Hill was a little more forgiving, at least, at least until her drunken father tried to run her over with a car, then beat her up.

Even if his personal and professional life was a mess, Hill found himself becoming famous. *Wiseguy* was published in December 1985 and became a bestseller. Director Martin Scorsese turned the book into the well-received 1990 movie, *Goodfellas*, which offered a brutal depiction of low-ranking Mafiosi and associates. The book and the movie turned Hill into a mob celebrity.

As a senior, Hill took up art and sold his amateur paintings on eBay, peddled a pasta sauce he created, and worked as a chef. Hill became a regular guest on the *Howard Stern Show* and continued to run into problems with the law. He got arrested twice for public intoxication in May 2008. He acquired a fiancée named Lisa Caserta and lived in Southern California.

On June 12, 2012, at age 69, Hill died in a Los Angeles hospital of heart complications.

Note

1. Gregg Hill and Gina Hill, *On the Run: A Mafia Childhood* (New York: Time Warner Book Group, 2004), 2005.

Salvatore Gravano ("Sammy the Bull")

(1945–)

Salvatore "Sammy the Bull" Gravano admitted to killing 19 people during his Mafia tenure, but he is best known for turning against two different mob bosses.

Gravano acquired his nickname because of his short, squat physique. Born to Sicilian American parents in 1945, Gravano grew up in Brooklyn. He gravitated to crime at a young age, eventually joining the Colombo Mafia family. Gravano soon earned a reputation for extreme violence. He killed his first man at age 25 and proceeded to murder several others while in the mob.

Gravano marched to the beat of his own drummer. At one point, he transferred his allegiance from the Colombo family to the Gambino family. Gravano had his boss's permission to switch families, but his lateral move—highly unusual in Mafia circles—still raised eyebrows. Idiosyncrasies aside, Gravano established himself as a major player in New York City's Mafia-dominated construction racket.

As a member of the Gambino family, Gravano became acquainted with rising Mafia star John Gotti. In the mid-1980s, Gotti began plotting against Gambino family boss Paul Castellano, who was widely regarded as distant and weak.

Gotti arranged for Castellano and underboss Thomas Bilotti to be assassinated on December 16, 1985, as they prepared to attend a mob meeting in Manhattan. Gravano was with Gotti as the double murder unfolded, watching from a waiting car.

Initially, Gravano benefitted from this coup. He was made a capo of the Gambino family, then promoted again to family consigliere (adviser). Unlike his boss, Gravano shunned the spotlight. He dressed down, in blue jeans, and wouldn't accompany Gotti on his nightly partying rounds. In spite of his exalted position with the Gambino family, Gravano occasionally carried out murders himself. This was a huge departure from Mafia tradition, in which top leaders let underlings do their dirty work.

Gotti and Gravano did not enjoy their moment at the top for long. On December 11, 1990, the FBI raided a Gotti hangout, arresting him, Gravano, and a third man named Frank Locascio. The trio was charged with murder, conspiracy, illegal gambling, loan sharking, and other crimes under the RICO statute.

In court, Gravano was shocked when wiretap evidence revealed that Gotti held him in low regard. Surveillance recordings caught Gotti bad-mouthing Gravano. Among other things, Gotti complained that his underboss was stingy with the profits from his various rackets. Gravano soon had enough. Gotti's flamboyant courtroom manner annoyed him and suspected his boss was going to try to deflect blame onto him. In early fall 1991, Gravano turned against Gotti and agreed to testify for the prosecution.

On November 8, 1991, Gravano was removed from the prison where he was staying with Gotti and transferred to protective custody in a secret locale. Gravano was then taken to the FBI training academy in Quantico, Virginia, where he was questioned extensively. Gravano revealed the inner workings of the Gambino family, including the plot to murder Castellano and Bilotti. Gravano also confessed to 19 murders.

As Gotti's trial got underway, prosecutors continued to play the damning tapes they had made of his supposedly private conversations with Mafia minions. The tapes alone might not have been enough to convict Gotti. Combined with Sammy the Bull's testimony, however, Gotti had no chance.

Gravano testified under tight security. He spent a total of nine days on the stand, offering minute details of the Gotti organization. As part of the deal he made with the prosecution, Gotti had to reveal his full criminal history to the court. This was a small concession on Gravano's part, given that he had been promised a 20-year sentence in return for cooperating.

Sammy the Bull was one of the most significant Mafia turncoats ever. He was much higher placed than Joe Valachi. While most of his testimony centered on murder plots and felonies, Gravano also took the time to explain arcane Mafia slang and gestures and detail day-to-day life as a mobster.

The longer Gravano testified, the more unnerved Gotti became. He was dismayed both by his lawyer's inability to shake Gravano's composure and by Gravano's comprehensive memory of Gambino family business.

On April 2, 1992, Gotti and codefendant Locascio were both found guilty on most charges. They each received life in jail without parole at sentencing. Gravano himself served only five years in jail (which, the media pointed out, amounted to roughly three months for each of the 19 murders to which he admitted). After release, he was placed in witness protection and ended up in Arizona, where he tried to start a business installing swimming pools.

Like a lot of ex-Mafiosi, Gravano found life as a legitimate citizen boring. He was soon trafficking Ecstasy with a gang that included his son, wife, and daughter and assorted felons. At their peak, Gravano's crew sold over 20,000 pills per week. Such entrepreneurship attracted the attention of authorities. Some members of the drug ring were arrested and, like Gravano before them, told police all they knew. Gravano and some of his remaining crew were arrested in February 2000. Charges were laid in Brooklyn because Sammy the Bull had purchased 40,000 Ecstasy tablets from a New York supplier.

Gravano and his son were put on trial in the same federal courthouse where Gotti had been successfully prosecuted. Looking "tired and sallow," in the words of the *New York Times*, Gravano pled guilty in May 2001. On September 6, 2002, Gravano received a 20-year sentence for his crimes.[1]

Gravano is currently serving time in Arizona. Should he ever be released, Gravano will likely face the prospect of being on parole for the remainder of his life.

Note

1. Alan Feuer, "Gravano and Son Plead Guilty to Running Ecstasy Drug Ring," *New York Times*, May 26, 2001.

Appendix A: Secrets and Rituals

In late 1930, street thug Joseph Valachi was formally inducted into the Mafia's ranks. Valachi was taken to a private house in New York City, where he found himself in a room with 40 other gangsters sitting around a rectangular table. Valachi recognized Salvatore Maranzano (father of the U.S. Mafia) and other rising mobsters such as Thomas Lucchese, Joe Bonanno, and Joe Profaci.

Valachi was seated. On the table in front of him rested a .38-caliber pistol and a knife. As everyone stood at attention, Maranzano began the induction ritual. Speaking in Italian, he told Valachi that the weapons "represent that you live by the gun and the knife and you die by the gun and knife." Valachi was instructed to put his fingers together to form a cup. A piece of paper was placed in his hands and set alight. As it flickered, Valachi was required to say, "This is the way I will burn if I betray the secret of this Cosa Nostra" in Italian.[1]

Cosa Nostra—Italian for "our thing"—was the name Maranzano's mobsters used to describe their organization. Valachi was told to value Cosa Nostra over family, friends, religion, and country. He was also expected to live by the code of Omerta—silence. If caught by authorities, he was supposed to reveal nothing and not help the police in any way. In addition, Valachi was instructed not to sleep around with other member's wives, on pain of death.

Maranzano announced that Bonanno would serve as Valachi's "godfather"—i.e., someone who would watch out for him. Bonanno pricked Valachi's trigger finger, drawing blood, as Maranzano intoned, "This blood means that we are now one family." Many of these elaborate rituals were devised by Maranzano, who in turn borrowed them from organized crime groups in Italy.

According to Valachi, the whole ceremony took about 10 minutes. When all the rituals were over, food was brought in and the men feasted. This marked another important Mafia tradition—the ceremonial dinner, to draw members closer together. It's a ritual still followed today. Mafia members have traditionally spent hours eating or preparing elaborate meals, consumed with gusto in an all-male milieu.

In the unwritten rules of the Mafia, Valachi was now a made man—a formal member of the criminal tribe.

Made men, Valachi later told a U.S. Senate subcommittee, received no salary. Membership in the Mafia was considered remuneration enough. Made men were expected to generate their own income and give a cut of the proceeds to the mobster above them. In return, made men could count on the support of policemen, lawyers, politicians, and judges in their family's pay. Made men could also rely on countless associates in their employ.

When infiltrating the New York Mafia in the 1970s, undercover FBI agent Joseph Pistone once asked his mentor, Benjamin "Lefty Guns" Ruggiero, what the advantages were of being a "made man." "Lefty looks at me like I'm the world's biggest moron. He gets excited and jumps out of his chair and starts yelling and waving his arms. 'What are you, fucking crazy?' he says. 'Are you fucking nuts? When you're a wiseguy, you can steal, you can cheat, you can lie, you can kill people—and it's all legitimate,'" wrote Pistone, after leaving the Mafia.[2]

Ruggiero wasn't trying to be witty: "The wiseguy does not see himself as a criminal or even a bad person; he sees himself as a businessman, a shrewd hustler, one step ahead of ordinary suckers," added Pistone.

In Senate subcommittee testimony, Pistone revealed how frustrating his investigation was in the face of mob secrecy. Mafia members and associates were inevitably introduced to him by first name or a nickname. It was taboo to ask someone for their last name. Doing so would instantly peg you as an undercover cop or an informer.

"No one asked about what other members were doing or even who they were. There were people I worked with closely for six years who never told me their last names, only their nicknames," Pistone told the subcommittee.[3]

Mobsters were equally wary about sharing the spoils of their various schemes. There was good reason for this, Pistone discovered. Mafia soldiers and associates were expected to give a percentage of their proceeds to whoever ranked above them. There was no set fee, however, which meant greedy bosses could demand as much as they wanted. The end result was that "wiseguys" were forever lying about their earnings. A soldier who earned $200,000 from a "score" might tell his boss he only made $150,000, in the hope his superior took less of his loot, Pistone told the Senate subcommittee. Ironically, "holding out" in this fashion could be grounds for execution, along with the unforgiveable sin of revealing Mafia secrets.

Notes

1. Peter Maas, *The Valachi Papers* (New York: HarperCollins Publishers, 1968), 73–77.
2. Joseph Pistone, *The Way of the Wiseguy* (Philadelphia: Running Press, 2004), 9.
3. Joseph Pistone, testimony before the U.S. Senate Permanent Subcommittee on Investigations, 1988.

Appendix B: The Mafia in Popular Culture

The early 1930s saw the advent of an organized American Mafia. It also marked the emergence of what was to become a Hollywood staple: the Italian American movie mobster. "Sicilian and other Italian crime groups began to operate in America at the turn of the past century, but their pop culture incarnations didn't burst on the scene until the 1930s in gangland dramas like *Scarface* and *Little Caesar*," reads *An Offer We Can't Refuse*, a book that examines pop culture portrayals of the Mafia.[1]

Little Caesar featured Edward G. Robinson as brutish gangster Cesare Rico Bandello. Robinson himself was Jewish and hailed from Romania, but audiences didn't seem to care. They were transfixed by his powerhouse performance as a grasping, violent Italian American thug who makes it rich only to face the inevitable slide to the bottom.

At the end of the movie, the Bandello character is machine-gunned by police. Dying, he offers the celebrated movie line: "Mother of Mercy! Is this the end of Rico?"[2] It has long been rumored, but never confirmed, that the federal Racketeer Influenced and Corrupt Organizations (RICO) Act was named after Robinson's character. The film was hugely influential in other ways as well. "*Little Caesar* not only created the anti-rags-to-riches, dark side of the American dream motif of the gangster genre, but also introduced a whole new language to American cinema. This was the film that popularized such now clichéd gangster-speak as 'gats' (guns), 'molls' (girls) and 'bulls' (cops)," reads the book, *101 Gangster Movies You Must See Before You Die*.[3]

Scarface, meanwhile, featured Yiddish actor Paul Muni as Tony "Scarface" Camonte. While the filmmakers denied it, the character was clearly based on "Scarface" Al Capone, whose visage bore several slashes from a knife attack in his youth. Like *Little Caesar*, the film focuses on Camonte's ruthless rise and was considered extremely violent by the standards of the day.

The popularity of gangster films in the Depression is not too hard to discern. Audiences beaten down by the Depression were delighted to see vivid, violent characters "fighting back" against "the system" and becoming wealthy in the process. The fact that most the gangsters depicted on screen ended up either dead or in jail didn't bother film-goers. It was the mobster's pluck that they admired, even when that pluck was smashed by the forces of law and order.

The Italian American gangster archetype soon fell out of fashion, however. By the mid-1930s, the Motion Picture Production Code, a set of strict industry standards, began to be enforced. Among other things, the Code frowned on sympathetic portrayals of criminals, which limited filmmakers' scope when it came to depicting organized crime. By the early 1940s, with World War II raging in Europe, evil Nazis began to replace evil Italian American gangsters as the villains of choice in Hollywood movies.

The stereotypical Italian American Mafia mobster villain didn't really come back into fashion until the 1950s and 1960s, with TV shows such as *The Untouchables*. The latter portrayed the (exaggerated) exploits of Chicago lawman Eliot Ness fighting Al Capone during Prohibition. In real life, Ness was more of a nuisance to Capone than a nemesis. While Ness raided distilleries and seized Capone-owned trucks and vehicles with abandon, it was bureaucrats in the Internal Revenue Service (IRS) who actually put Capone behind bars.

The 1950s and 1960s also marked the first televised congressional hearings into Mafia operations. During hearings led by U.S. senator Estes Kefauver in 1951, mob boss Frank Costello demanded that his face not be shown during the proceedings. TV crews obliged and focused on his hands, which he kept on top of a table, as he testified. Viewers were fascinated by Costello's fidgety digits as the mob boss stumbled through a withering examination. That the camera never panned to the mobster's face made him seem all the more sinister and mysterious.

During the same era, Mafia turncoat Joseph Valachi became a household name. Valachi was a low-ranking Mafia soldier who was arrested and turned government witness. In front of Congressional committees, he offered a plethora of details about daily Mafia life, infamous crimes, and secret rituals (such as the elaborate induction ceremony for "made" members). His outpouring was used as the basis for the 1968 book *The Valachi Papers*. One year later, Mario Puzo's epochal tome, *The Godfather*, was released. The book depicts the murderous workings and clan dynamics of the rich and powerful Corleone Mafia family in New York City. While hardly first-rate prose, the book was a hit and stayed on bestseller lists for over a year. The book follows the transfer of power between aging mob boss Don Vito Corleone (modeled after real-life mobster Carlo Gambino) and his earnest son, Michael.

Interestingly enough, Puzo admitted he had no firsthand knowledge of the Mafia. Many of the incidents and details in the book were gleaned from media accounts of the Mafia and transcripts of congressional investigations.

Naturally, Hollywood studios were interested in making a film version of the book. Their interest did not come without controversy, however. In 1970, the Italian-American Civil Rights League (a rather bizarre organization put together by mobster Joseph Colombo Sr. to safeguard the public image of Italian Americans) held a rally at Madison Square Garden to protest Paramount studio's plan to film *The Godfather*. Like FBI director J. Edgar Hoover before him, Colombo denied there even was such an organization as the Mafia. His oddball crusade came to an abrupt end in 1971 when he was shot and badly wounded at a Civil Rights League rally in New York. The following year, Paramount's *The Godfather* was released.

As directed by Francis Ford Coppola, *The Godfather* movie is far superior to the pulp fiction book on which it's based. Beautifully filmed, featuring a dramatic score and excellent performances by Marlon Brando (as Don Corleone), Al Pacino, James Caan, Robert Duvall, and others, the movie was a smash with public and critics alike.

The Godfather contains images and dialogue that have become cultural touchstones: an uncooperative film director wakes to find a horse's head in his bed, a baby's baptism is intercut with scenes of mob bosses being gunned down, a police captain and Mafia thug are assassinated at close range in a restaurant, etc. The line, uttered by Don Corleone, "I'm gonna make him an offer he can't refuse" has gone down in cinematic lore.[4]

The Godfather grossed $134 million at the U.S. box office, at a time when hit films generally earned a fraction of this total. It picked up several Academy Awards, including Best Picture and Best Actor (an honor that the recipient, Marlon Brando, turned down to protest the plight of American Indians). Three other actors—Duvall, Caan, and Pacino—were nominated in the "Best Supporting Actor" category.

There are many theories as to why *The Godfather* film was such a sensation. Most obviously, it tells a compelling story in powerful fashion, with top-caliber acting. Another, more cerebral theory, points to the era in which it was released. The late 1960s and early 1970s were a tumultuous time, filled with conflict and generational strife. New notions about sex, drugs, and familial arrangements challenged traditional values. By contrast, *The Godfather* seemed like a flashback to simpler times, with a powerful patriarch, dutiful sons, and a celebration of traditional values (the film opens at the wedding of Don Corleone's only daughter).

The Godfather was followed by a celebrated sequel, *The Godfather Part II*, which made a star of Robert De Niro. *Part II* followed the early life of Don Corleone and the path led by his successor son Michael. It too was a hit, earning roughly $57 million in domestic box office, as well as Oscars for Best Picture, Best Actor in a Supporting Role (De Niro), and Best Director. A second sequel, *The Godfather Part III*, was widely panned and dismissed as greatly inferior to its predecessors.

"The Mafia gangster truly became a mythic figure in the late 1960s with the publication of Mario Puzo's novel, *The Godfather* and in the early 1970s with the release of the first two Godfather films ... *The Godfather*, in both its literary and cinematic incarnations, sold the public the fiction of a vast, centralized and enormously powerful criminal organization run by Sicilians and their American-born offspring," reads *An Offer We Can't Refuse*.[5]

In real life, the American Mafia is highly decentralized, with no central command. In contrast to Don Corleone, mob bosses aren't particularly eloquent or sophisticated. Aside from a tiny elite at the top, Mafiosi aren't generally rich. "Most real-life mobsters and associates lead hand-to-mouth, day-to-day lives. And when they make a score, after they pay off their loan shark debts and buy their wives and/or girlfriends a fur coat or piece of jewelry, they're borrowing more money while they scheme to make their next payday," stated mob expert Jerry Capeci, author of several Mafia-related books, in a *New York Times* interview.[6]

Fortunes are made, then quickly squandered. Mobsters can't make investments in their real names, lest authorities confiscate their assets—something that puts a huge crimp on long-term wealth building.

If the *Godfather* movies depicted life at the top of the Mafia hierarchy, Martin Scorsese's 1990 film, *Goodfellas*, showed what it was like to be an underworld bottom-feeder. The movie is based on the book *Wiseguy* by Nick Pileggi, which in turn was about Henry Hill, a half-Irish Mafia associate turned government witness.

Goodfellas offers a stark contrast to *The Godfather* saga. The gangsters in the film are violent boors who rip each other off and don't hesitate to murder close friends. *Goodfellas* depicts a considerably more blue-collar, foul-mouthed version of the Mafia than Coppola did. It too contains unforgettable scenes; at one point, the main characters nearly kick a "made" Mafiosi to death, then dump him in the trunk of a car. One of the attackers still lives with his mom. When they go to her house in the middle of the night to borrow a knife, she greets them and offers an impromptu meal. Satiated, the men drive off, murder the Mafiosi in the trunk, and then bury him by the road.

Like *The Godfather* movies, *Goodfellas* shows how claustrophobic Mafia life can be. One of the main characters notes that her entire social life revolves around her husband's mob buddies and their spouses.

Goodfellas was successful at the box office and also appealed to movie critics. It was nominated for six Academy Awards (including Best Picture and Best Director) and picked up a win for Joe Pesci in the Best Actor in a Supporting Role category. "No finer film has ever been made about organized crime—not even *The Godfather*—although the two works are not really comparable," wrote movie critic Roger Ebert in 1990.[7]

The book and subsequent 1997 film *Donnie Brasco* further "deglamorized" the Mafia. The book and movie followed FBI agent Joseph Pistone's adventures posing as a Mafia associate in New York City. The mobsters Pistone befriends spend much of their time playing cards, planning scores, and boasting about previous exploits. If *Goodfellas* depicted a smothering, all-encompassing Mafia lifestyle, *Donnie Brasco* shows how tedious mob existence can be. The film features Johnny Depp in the title role and the ubiquitous Al Pacino as Brasco's hapless mentor, Benjamin "Lefty Guns" Ruggiero.

The 1980s and 1990s saw a slew of other Mafia-related films including *Casino* (Scorsese's quasi-sequel to *Goodfellas*), *Married to the Mob* (Michelle Pfeiffer as a fetching mob widow) and *Prizzi's Honor* (Kathleen Turner and Jack Nicholson as underworld assassins who fall in love). Well-known books from this period include the previously mentioned *Donnie Brasco: My Undercover Life in the Mafia* written by agent Pistone, and *Underboss: Sammy "the Bull" Gravano's Story of Life in the Mob*, by Peter Maas. Mafia figures and storylines also came up regularly on TV shows such as *Oz* and *Law and Order*.

The Untouchables, directed by Brian De Palma and released in 1987, was a big screen adaption of the story covered by the 1950s TV show of the same name. Highlights included a brutish performance by Robert De Niro as Al Capone and various scenes of gun mayhem. The plotline was less than accurate—the plan to charge Capone with income tax evasion was not dreamed up by members of Eliot Ness's team. In one scene, Capone interrupts a fancy underworld dinner to beat a traitorous accomplice to death with a baseball bat. This was based on a true incident, except in real life Capone battered three victims, not one.

The year 1999 marked the debut of the cable TV series *The Sopranos*. Created by David Chase, this offbeat show moved the Mafia from its usual urban stomping ground to the well-manicured lawns of suburban New Jersey. Lead character Tony Soprano—a Mafia capo or captain—starts to see a psychiatrist because he's having panic attacks.

Tony Soprano (well played by the late James Gandolfini) has a mob princess of a wife named Carmela; two spoiled children, A. J. and Meadow; a harridan mother named Livia; and a bitter, aging relative and fellow Mafiosi, Corrado "Junior" Soprano. The psychiatrist, Dr. Jennifer Melfi, is played by Lorraine Bracco, who was Henry Hill's mob moll of a wife in *Goodfellas*. Tony Soprano's official line of work is garbage hauling. He describes himself as a "waste management consultant."

A running joke on *The Sopranos* is how much these mobsters are influenced by *The Godfather* movies. Characters are constantly referencing lines and scenes from the movie and measuring themselves against its cinematic glories.

The Sopranos makes it clear that the best years of the American Mafia are long past. Tony Soprano's crew mostly carries out low-level scams. Unlike the Corleone family, Tony Soprano can't count any U.S. senators or other high-ranking politicians as allies. The show doesn't make the mistake of turning the characters lovable, either. Every few episodes, Tony and his crew eliminate someone in cold blood. One repulsive mob boss, Ralph Cifaretto, beats his pregnant, teenage stripper girlfriend to death with his fists (an act so gratuitously sadistic even his mobster peers are appalled).

"The reel-life gangsters, while conducting their criminal business and in dealings with their relatives and 'comares' have a real feel to them. They're violent, fly off the handle quickly and are duplicitous double dealers with little or no honor. The dialogue rings true," stated Jerry Capeci in the *New York Times*, about *The Sopranos*.[8] According to Capeci, the most accurate detail of the show is the excessive profanity: "For example, in a videotaped conversation at Marion federal penitentiary, John Gotti . . . uttered nine obscenities in the first 40 seconds of a discussion he had about a love child fathered with a daughter of a mob superior," he told the *Times*.

For all that, *The Sopranos* isn't completely realistic. A real mob capo who started showing signs of mental illness (as opposed to putting on a "crazy" act, as Vincent "the Chin" Gigante did for decades in New York City) would likely be murdered, for fear they would reveal Mafia secrets. The series also has Tony Soprano having a direct hand in committing murders and other felonies. In reality, mob bosses try to insulate themselves from such activities through a rigid chain of command in which legions of low-ranking members carry out orders from the top.

Despite these flaws, *The Sopranos* has been praised as one of the best crime shows ever put on television. It lasted six seasons, won a slew of Emmy Awards, and topped several critics' polls. In a poll of the "35 Best Shows On TV—Ever" by writers at the *New York Post*, *The Sopranos* was ranked number one.[9] Likewise, TV critics at the UK newspaper *The Guardian* selected *The Sopranos* as the top television drama of all time.[10]

Certainly the same could not be said about *Growing Up Gotti*, a supposedly unscripted reality show about the travails of Victoria Gotti (daughter of infamous, flamboyant Gambino family boss John Gotti) and her three bratty sons. This series launched in 2004 and was widely panned. "Victoria Gotti has the warmth of an ice pick and her sons the charm of, well, thugs," noted Film.com writer Shirleen Holt.[11] Fortunately, *Growing Up Gotti* only lasted one year before being mercifully canceled.

There is apparently a movie in the works about John Gotti himself. If true, this film can be compared to the two TV miniseries that have already appeared about the ill-fated Mafia boss not to mention countless books.

A new, highly innovative cable TV series called *Boardwalk Empire*, launched in 2010, follows in the footsteps of *The Sopranos*. The show looks at the closely related underworld and upper crust of Atlantic City during Prohibition. Hailed by critics, *Boardwalk Empire* features several budding Mafia leaders, including Charles "Lucky" Luciano, Al Capone, and Johnny Torrio. The main protagonist is Nucky Thompson, a fictionalized political wheeler and dealer in uber-corrupt Atlantic City who socializes and plots with gangsters. Thompson is played by character actor Steve Buscemi. The debut episode of the series was directed by Scorsese. The show has received critical kudos and several Emmy Awards. *USA Today* described *Boardwalk Empire* as "extravagantly produced, shockingly violent and cold and hard as ice" populated by "an inspired array of top-level talent."[12] "This is, quite simply, television at its finest ... an expensive, explicit, character-driven program, tackling material no broadcast network or movie studio would dare touch," echoed *Variety*.[13]

The Mafia myth continues to endure. The American Film Institute's list of "Top 10 gangster movies" slots *The Godfather* at number one and *The Godfather Part II* at number three. *Goodfellas* took second, while the original *Scarface* was number six. *Little Caesar* and the 1983 remake of *Scarface* (which featured Al Pacino as a Cuban American crime boss) occupied 9th and 10th place.[14]

"Since the 1970s, the Mafia myth has saturated the entertainment media, spawning numerous spin-offs even parodies. Mediterranean mobsters not only appear in movies and television series, but also crop up in animated feature films and children's cartoon shows, in TV commercials, video games and on websites. Mafia imagery and themes influence other pop-culture genres, including rap performers who strike 'gangsta' poses and rhyme about criminal exploits, real and imaginary ... the seemingly endless stream of mob movies attests to the continuing fascination of filmmakers and movie-goers with Italian-American crime stories," notes *An Offer We Can't Refuse*.[15]

Notes

1. George De Stefano, *An Offer We Can't Refuse* (New York: Faber and Faber, 2006), 344.
2. Ibid., 72.
3. Steven Jay Schneider, *101 Gangster Movies You Must See Before You Die* (Hauppauge, NY: Barron's, 2009), 29.
4. De Stefano, *An Offer We Can't Refuse*, 18.
5. Ibid., 344
6. Mary Jo Murphy, "Will the Real Mob Please Stand Up" *New York Times*, March 5, 2006.
7. Roger Ebert, "Goodfellas," *Chicago Sun-Times*, September 2, 1990.
8. Murphy, "Will the Real Mob Please Stand Up"
9. Robert Rorke and Stephen Lynch, "The 35 Best Shows on TV—Ever," *New York Post*, May 1, 2008.
10. Tim Lusher, "The Guardian's Top 50 Television Dramas of All Time," *The Guardian*, posted January 12, 2010.
11. Shirleen Holt, "And the Amy Award Goes To ...," Film.com, posted July 18, 2008, http://www.film.com/tv/and-the-amy-award-goes-to.
12. Robert Bianco, "HBO Builds a Mighty, Brutal 'Boardwalk Empire,'" *USA Today*, September 17, 2010.
13. Brian Lowry, "Boardwalk Empire: There's So Much to Savor About 'Boardwalk Empire' It's Hard to Know Where to Begin," *Variety*, September 12, 2010.
14. "Top 10 Gangster," American Film Institute, http://www.afi.com/10top10/gangster.html.
15. De Stefano, *An Offer We Can't Refuse*, 345.

Glossary

Associate: Someone who works with the Mafia but isn't officially a member

Black Hand: The name of a fictitious organized crime society; also the name of an extortion scam

Bookmaking: Taking bets (also making book, or just book)

Citizen: Mafia term for someone who isn't in the Mafia

Consigliere: An adviser to a Mafia boss

Degenerate gambler: A gambling addict

Gat: A gun

Hit: An assassination

La Cosa Nostra: Literally, "our thing"; another name for the U.S. Mafia

Loan shark: Someone who provides loans at an exorbitant rate of interest

Made man: A formal member of the Mafia

Moustache Pete: An old-time Mafia boss

No-show job: A job, typically in construction or unions, in which a Mafia member receives full pay for no work

Numbers: An illegal lottery

Omerta: Mafia term meaning silence to authorities in the case of arrest

Open the books: To induct a new member of the Mafia

Piece: A gun

Racket: A scheme, scam, or service, usually illegal, that brings in money

RICO: Racketeer Influenced and Corrupt Organizations Act, a piece of legislation that adds additional criminal and civil penalties for offences committed on behalf of a criminal enterprise

Shylock: A loan shark

Sit down: Mafia term for a meeting

Skimming: The practice of diverting casino profits before they are taxed (also: skim)

Straightened out: The process of becoming a made man

Taken for a Ride: Specifically, the act of kidnapping someone in a vehicle, driving to an isolated locale, and murdering them; more generally, a slang term for murder

Vigorish: The rate of interest on a shylock loan (also "vig")

Whacked: Killed

Wiseguy: The term Mafia members use to describe themselves

Primary Documents

Coming on the heels of a police raid at a major Mafia conference in Apala-chin, New York, in November 1957, the Mafia Monograph *was the FBI's attempt at playing catch-up. For decades, FBI director J. Edgar Hoover had stubbornly insisted that there was no such thing as an American Mafia. Released post-Apalachin, the* Mafia Monograph *is surprisingly blunt in its assessments and lurid in style.*

The term Mafia as used here includes the transplanting to American soil from Sicily, Italy, the shared criminal traditions, customs and methods of a particular class of lawless Sicilians. It includes the contin-uance of essential blood ties, cultural similarities, intermarriages, racial cohesiveness and operational clannishness. All this takes on certain organizational forms ending in organized criminality. The result is the formation of a special criminal clique or caste composed primarily of individuals of Sicilian origin or descent who comprise a distinct but related segment of the whole of organized crime; a segment which takes on the characteristics of a lawless brotherhood.

The Mafia persists in Sicily as the most vicious and extensive racket ever to be foisted and imposed upon the public. To law enforce-ment, the Mafia presents the most deeply entrenched and monstrous challenge ever to have crept forth from the underworld. This challenge extends to law enforcement in the United States.

Source: Excerpted from *Mafia Monograph* (Washington, DC: Federal Bureau of Investigation, 1958).

In spite of its title, The Changing Face of Organized Crime in New Jersey: A Status Report *actually offers an insider's view on Mafia activities throughout the Eastern Seaboard. The report was released in May 2004 by the State of New Jersey Commission of Investigation. The* Changing Face *document notes that the Mafia has embraced computers and technology but also points to challenges facing La Cosa Nostra: arrests, long jail terms for key members, internal fighting, and rising competition from non-Italian gangs.*

Faced with internecine violence and unrelenting efforts by federal and state law enforcement authorities using tough anti-racketeering laws and effective investigative tools, the traditional organized crime families of the so-called *La Cosa Nostra* (LCN) have had to struggle to retain their accustomed power and wealth. Though each group to varying extents maintains a well-defined hierarchy consisting of a boss, underboss, consigliere (top advisor or counselor), caporegimes (capos, or captains/crew leaders), street soldiers and associates, many have been severely weakened by internal strife and successful prosecutions. However, elements of the LCN still dominate certain criminal activities and any slackening of law enforcement vigilance would permit them to revitalize their operations to become as large a threat to society as ever.

[The Mafia] has become more involved in and skilled at fraud, including identity theft, health-care fraud, computer crime, motor-fuel tax evasion and securities manipulation, as well as money laundering and new forms of gambling. Meanwhile, labor racketeering including pension and benefit fund schemes, such as kickbacks, self-serving investments and padding of costs, numbers running, illegal sports betting, loan sharking, extortion, narcotics trafficking and prostitution continue, occasionally disrupted but generally unabated.

Source: Excerpted from *The Changing Face of Organized Crime in New Jersey: A Status Report*, State of New Jersey, Commission of Investigation, May 2004.

In 1950, U.S. senator Estes Kefauver launched a series of nationwide hearings into organized crime. The U.S. Senate Special Committee to Investigate Organized Crime in Interstate Commerce cited Mafia figures by name and accused them of dominating the illegal drug trade in its final report, published August 1951.

Experienced enforcement officers believe that the present influx of heroin from abroad is managed by the Mafia with Charles "Lucky" Luciano, notorious gangster, vice-king, racketeer [and] deported convict, now resident in Italy, as the operating head ... world-wide in scope, the Mafia is believed to derive the major source of its income from the distribution and smuggling of narcotics. An undercover agent of the Treasury Department's Bureau of Narcotics testified at length before the committee just after his return from an extended assignment in Italy. Asked whether Luciano is the kingpin of the Mafia, the agent responded that if "Lucky" isn't the kingpin, "he is one of the royal family," that he receives large sums of money from American gangsters and that he certainly wields influence in Mafia policy matters. To the question, "Is Lucky Luciano the kingpin of the narcotics traffic in the United States?" he answered, "The United States and Italy."

Source: Kefauver Committee Final Report, U.S. Senate Special Committee to Investigate Organized Crime in Interstate Commerce, August 1951.

Angelo Lonardo was a top-ranking member of the Cleveland Mafia family. Arrested on drug charges, Lonardo was handed down a 103-year prison term in April 1983. Faced with the prospect of spending the rest of his natural life in jail, Lonardo decided to cooperate with authorities. He testified at various trials and, on April 4, 1988, spoke before the Permanent Subcommittee on Investigations of the Senate Committee on Government Affairs.

In the 1930s, my cousin, John Demarco and I murdered Dr. Romano, the former boss of Cleveland, because Romano had a role in the death of my father and we believed that he killed our cousin on the operating table. At the time, I was not a member of LCN, but Demarco was. As a result of the Romano murder, Demarco was condemned to death by the Commission for killing a boss without okaying it with the Commission. I was excused for my part in the murder, since I was not an LCN member and did not know the rules. Later, I attended a meeting with Al Polizzi, the boss of Cleveland, in Miami, Florida. It turned out that this was a Commission meeting and that Polizzi was defending Demarco's murder of Romano. I did not sit in on the meeting but afterwards Polizzi told me that he had 'straightened out' Demarco's problem with the Commission.

Source: Testimony from Angelo Lonardo before the Permanent Subcommittee on Investigations of the Senate Committee on Government Affairs, April 4, 1988.

If J. Edgar Hoover of the FBI insisted there was no such thing as an organized, U.S.-based Mafia, agents at the Bureau of Narcotics thought otherwise. Throughout the 1940s and 1950s, they kept detailed files on hundreds of suspected Mafia members and associates, regardless of whether they had any connection to the drug trade or not. These profiles were compiled in a 2007 book called simply MAFIA. *A sample profile*:

NAME:	Joseph Gallo
ALIASES:	Joe-the-Blonde
DESCRIPTION:	Born 4-6-29 Brooklyn, NY, 5'6", 145 lbs, slim build, brown hair, blue eyes.
LOCALITIES FREQUENTED:	Resides 639 E 4th St, B'klyn, NY. Frequents 108 Beverly Rd & various sections of Flatbush, Brooklyn.
FAMILY BACKGROUND:	Single; father: Albert; mother: Mary Nunziato; brothers: Ralph & Lawrence; sisters: Carmela Frolera and Jacqueline Meyers.
CRIMINAL ASSOCIATES:	John Oddo, (blacked out), Carmine Lombardozzi, (blacked out)
CRIMINAL HISTORY:	FBI #120842A. NYCPD #B250889. Record dates from 1947 and includes arrests for dangerous weapon, abduction, possession of a gun,

	burglary, kidnapping and attempted sodomy and felonious assault on police officer.
BUSINESS:	Claims to be manager of Jackie's Charcolette, 108 Beverly Rd, Brooklyn, NY.
MODUS OPERANDI:	Becoming powerful in the Mafia. A strong-arm man and labor goon, suspected murderer and trafficker in small arms and narcotics.

Source: Excerpted from *MAFIA*, United States Treasury Department, Bureau of Narcotics, 2007.

Selected Bibliography

Publications

"Accused of Four Murders." *New York Times*, May 12, 1907.

"After 24 Years on Death Row, Clemency Is Killer's Final Appeal." *New York Times*, December 2, 2005.

"After the Don: A Donnybrook?" *New York Times*, November 1, 1976.

"Alarming Alliance of Mafia and Street Gang is Broken Up." *New York Times*, December 19, 2007.

"Al Capone Died Here." *Chicago Tribune*, February 15, 2007.

"All Classes Mingle at Colosimo Funeral." *New York Times*, May 16, 1920.

"America's Crusade." *Time*, September 15, 1986.

Anastasia, George. *The Goodfella Tapes*. New York: HarperCollins Publishers, 1998.

"Another Mob Boss Imprisoned for Life." *Chicago Tribune*, February 3, 2009.

"Anti-Cocaine Bill Passed." *New York Times*, March 29, 1907.

"An Archetypal Mob Trial: It's Just Like in the Movies." *Time*, May 23, 2004.

"Armed, Sophisticated and Violent, Two Drug Gangs Blanket Nation." *New York Times*, November 25, 1988.

Asbury, Herbert. *The Gangs of New York*. New York: Thunder's Mouth Press, 1927.

"Attempts to Slay Roosevelt; Wounds Cermak and 4 Others." *Milwaukee Sentinel*, February 16, 1933.

"Bad, Bad Leroy Barnes." *Time*, December 12, 1977.

"Badfellas." *New York Times*, January 18, 2004.

"Barrel Murder Mystery Deepens." *New York Times*, April 20, 1903.

Baum, Dan. *Smoke and Mirrors*. Boston, MA: Little, Brown & Company, 1996.

"Bawdy Business." *Time*, May 25, 1936.

Behr, Edward. *Prohibition: Thirteen Years That Changed America*. New York: Arcade Publishing, 1996.

Bergreen, Laurence. *Capone: The Man and the Era*. New York: Simon & Schuster, 1994.

"Black Hand Manacled at Last." *New York Times*, April 2, 1910.

"Black Hand Suspect Was Bled Himself." *New York Times*, November 13, 1909.

"Blood, Business, 'Honor.'" *Time*, October 15, 1984.

"Blood in the Streets: Subculture of Violence." *Time*, April 24, 1972.

"Blowing the Whistle on Gangsta Culture." *New York Times*, December 22, 2005.

Blumenthal, Ralph. *Last Days of the Sicilians*. New York: Simon & Schuster, 1988.

"Boardwalk Empire: There's So Much to Savor about 'Boardwalk Empire' It's Hard to Know Where to Begin." *Variety*, September 12, 2010.

"Books of the Times: A Don Pays the Price of Carelessness." *New York Times*, May 23, 1991.

"Bronx Boy." *Time*, April 29, 1935.

"Bugging Big Paul." *Time*, June 10, 1991.

"Bugging the FBI." *Time*, March 20, 1978.

"Cancer Closes Case on Vicious Mob Thug." *Chicago Tribune*, July 25, 2008.

"Capone Coup." *Time*, May 27, 1929.

"Capone's Week." *Time*, May 19, 1930.

"The Capo Who Went Public." *Time*, July 12, 1971.

"Causing Talk: Turncoat Mobsters on the Stand in the Racketeering Trial of John A. Gotti." *New York Times*, August 29, 2005.

Cawthorne, Nigel, and Colin Cawthorne. *The Mammoth Book of the Mafia*. London: Constable & Robinson, 2009.

Champlain, Pierre de. *Mobsters: Gangsters and Men of Honour*. Toronto, ON: HarperCollins Publishers, 2004.

"Chicago's Deadly Decade." *Chicago Tribune Magazine*, January 21, 2007.

"A Chronicle of Bloodletting." *Time*, July 12, 1971.

"City Boy." *Time*, July 25, 1949.

"City Prisons Filled with Drug Victims." *New York Times*, June 11, 1915.

"Cocaine Evil among Negroes." *New York Times*, November 3, 1902.

"Cocaine Forbidden in the U.S. Mails." *New York Times*, July 17, 1908.

"The Cocaine Habit." *New York Times*, June 20, 1909.

"Cocaine Habit Horrors." *New York Times*, April 30, 1905.

"Cocaine in Hay Fever." *New York Times*, July 31, 1885.

"Cocaine's Terrible Effect." *New York Times*, November 30, 1885.

"Cocaine User Shoots Seven." *New York Times*, December 6, 1907.

Coen, Jeff. *Family Secrets: The Case That Crippled the Chicago Mob*. Chicago: Chicago Review Press, 2009.

Cohen, Rich. *Tough Jews*. New York: Random House, 1998.

"The Conglomerate of Crime." *Time*, August 22, 1969.

"The Consumers Union Report on Licit and Illicit Drugs." *Consumer Reports Magazine*, 1972.

"A Contrite Salemme Sentenced to 11 Years." *Boston Globe*, February 24, 2000.

Corbitt, Michael, and Sam Giancana. *Double Deal*. New York: HarperCollins Publishers, 2003.

"Criminal Justice; Well-Organized Crime." *New York Times*, March 21, 2004.

"Criminal Mastermind." *Time*, December 7, 1998.

"Crusaders in the Underworld: The LAPD Takes on Organized Crime." First of seven parts. *Los Angeles Times*, October 26, 2008.

"The Curious and the Police Abound at a Wake for Gotti." *New York Times*, June 14, 2002.

"Cyber Scams Are Getting More Personal Thanks to Social Media." *Los Angeles Times*, May 30, 2012.

Dash, Mike. *The First Family: Terror, Extortion and the Birth of the American Mafia*. London: Simon & Schuster UK, 2009.

Davis, John H. *Mafia Dynasty: The Rise and Fall of the Gambino Crime Family*. New York: HarperCollins Publishers, 1993.

"Decline and Fall of an Empire." *New York Times*, January 17, 1999.

De Stefano, George. *An Offer We Can't Refuse*. New York: Faber & Faber, 2006.

"Dixie, Doxie and Dewey." *Time*, February 14, 1938.

"The Don Is Done." *New York Times*, January 31, 1999.

"Dr. Farley Becomes Insane." *New York Times*, February 6, 1886.

"Drug Dealing Was Banned by Mob, U.S. Witness Says." *New York Times*, April 15, 1993.

"Drug Habit Curable, Says Dr. Lambert." *New York Times*, October 7, 1909.

"The Dumbest Don." *New York Magazine*, May 21, 2005.

"An East Side Vendetta." *New York Times*, September 17, 1903.

"80s Plot to Hit Giuliani? Mob Experts Doubt It." *New York Times*, October 26, 2007.

"Enforcer Paints Picture of Gotti as a Powerful Don." *New York Times*, February 23, 2006.

"Extend Drug Law to Guard the Poor." *New York Times*, November 18, 1910.

"Family Guy." *New Yorker*, June 4, 2007.

"Federal Jury Convicts Boscarino." *New York Times*, December 11, 1910.

"Feds in N. J. Bust Illegal Gambling Ring." *New Jersey Star Ledger*, May 22, 2012.

"Finds Drug Evil Pervades the City." *New York Times*, December 5, 1916.

"Five Convicted of Mob Skimming." *Chicago Tribune*, January 22, 1986.

"Five Guilty in Outfit Trial." *Chicago Tribune*, September 11, 2007.

"For a Third Time, a Jury Fails to Convict Gotti." *New York Times*, September 28, 2006.

"A Fortnight under the Pure Food Law." *New York Times*, January 13, 1907.

"Gambino Group Seen as Country's Biggest." *New York Times*, March 31, 1984.

"A Game of Casino." *Time*, January 20, 1958.

"Gangsters Again Engaged in a Murderous War." *New York Times*, June 9, 1912.

"Genovese Family Keeps Its Chin Up: Gigante Becomes Top Don as Gotti Fades." *New York Daily News*, August 12, 2001.

Giancana, Sam, and Chuck Giancana. *Double Cross*. New York: Warner Books, 1993.

"Gigante Sentenced to 12 Years and Is Fined $1.25 Million." *New York Times*, December 19, 1997.

"Glum Gorilla." *Time*, December 19, 1927.

"The Godfathers." *New York Times*, May 5, 1996.

"Goodbye Fellas." *New York Times*, February 27, 2007.

Goodfellas review. *Chicago Sun-Times*, September 2, 1990.

"Good Word for Eastman." *New York Times*, June 21, 1909.

"Gotti Accused of Role in Castellano Slaying." *New York Times*, December 13, 1990.

"Gotti or No Gotti, the Mafia Looks Infirm These Days." *New York Times*, February 18, 1990.

"Gotti's Angry Words Taped in Prison." *New York Times*, December 15, 2004.

"Gravano and Son Plead Guilty to Running Ecstasy Drug Ring." *New York Times*, May 26, 2001.

"Gravano Ends Testimony after 9 Exhaustive Days." *New York Times*, February 18, 1992.

"Gravano Insists He Was Loyal Soldier." *New York Times*, March 13, 1992.

"Gravano Pleads Guilty to Drug Sales in Arizona." *New York Times*, June 30, 2001.

Gray, Mike. *Drug Crazy*. New York: Random House, 1998.

"Happy Birthday to Joe: Mobsters Flock to Margate to Celebrate the Philly Crime Boss's 68th." *Philadelphia City Paper*, August 15, 2007.

"Hard Days for the Mafia." *Time*, March 4, 1985.

"Have No Words of Blame." *New York Times*, October 8, 1892.

"HBO Builds a Mighty, Brutal 'Boardwalk Empire.'" *USA Today*, September 17, 2010.

"He Killed 14 People. He Got 12 Years." *Chicago Tribune*, March 27, 2009.

Hendley, Nate. *Al Capone: Chicago's King of Crime*. Canmore, AB: Altitude Publishing, 2006.

Hendley, Nate. *American Gangsters, Then and Now*. Santa Barbara, CA: ABC-CLIO, 2010.

Hendley, Nate. *Dutch Schultz: The Brazen Beer Baron of New York*. Canmore, AB: Altitude Publishing, 2005.

Hill, Gregg, and Gina Hill. *On the Run: A Mafia Childhood*. New York: Time Warner Book Group, 2004.

"His Life and Crimes." *Time*, January 17, 1969.

"Hitting the Mafia." *Time*, June 24, 2001.

"Hold Lupo as Counterfeiter." *New York Times*, November 23, 1909.

"Hold Nine as Pupils of Lupo the Wolf." *New York Times*, December 2, 1910.

"Informers under Fire." *Time*, April 17, 1972.

"An Inspiration from Death Row." *San Francisco Chronicle*, December 11, 2000.

"Interpret Harrison Law." *New York Times*, June 6, 1916.

"In the Land of the Gigantes." *Time*, July 21, 1997.

"Is the Godfather Insane or Crazy Like a Fox?" *Time*, September 3, 1990.

"Jailing of Crime Figure Called Telling Blow to Mafia in Philadelphia." *New York Times*, January 18, 1987.

"John Gotti Dies in Prison at 61; Mafia Boss Relished the Spotlight." *New York Times*, June 11, 2002.

"John Gotti Jr. Arrested on Murder Conspiracy Charges." *Chicago Tribune*, August 5, 2008.

"Judge: Bring Reputed Mob Boss Back to Chicago Now." *Chicago Tribune*, February 10, 2012.

"Jury Hears Gotti Discuss Organization on Tapes." *New York Times*, February 18, 1992.

Katz, Helena. *Gang Wars: Blood and Guts on the Streets of Early New York*. Canmore, AB: Altitude Publishing, 2005.

"Killers in Prison." *Time*, October 4, 1963.

"Killing That Made the Wolf an Exile." *New York Times*, February 17, 1910.

Kobler, John. *Capone: The Life and World of Al Capone*. Cambridge, MA: Perseus Books Group, 1971.

Lacey, Robert. *Little Man: Meyer Lansky and the Gangster Life*. Boston, MA: Little, Brown and Company, 1991.

Lamothe, Lee, and Adrian Humphreys. *The Sixth Family*. Mississauga, ON: John Wiley & Sons Canada, 2006.

"The Last Don," *Time*, March 22, 2004.

" 'Last Don' Reported to Be First One to Betray Mob." *New York Times*, January 28, 2005.

Lehr, Dick, and Gerard O'Neill. *Black Mass*. New York: HarperCollins Publishers, 2000.

"The Life and Hard Times of Cleveland's Mafia." *Cleveland Magazine*, August 1978.

"Lords of Dopetown." *New York Magazine*, October 25, 2007.

"Low Profile." *Time*, November 4, 1991.

Lunde, Paul. *Organized Crime*. New York: DK Publishing, 2004.

"Lupo Gang Off to Prison." *New York Times*, February 21, 1910.

" 'Lupo the Wolf' Notorious Criminal, Freed by Washington From Ellis Island." *New York Times*, June 12, 1922.

Maas, Peter. *The Valachi Papers*. New York: HarperCollins Publishers, 1968.

"The Mafia: Back to the Bad Old Days?" *Time*, July 12, 1971.

"The Mafia Big, Bad and Booming." *Time*, May 16, 1977.

"Mafia-Run Stock Market Scams More Widespread Than Officials Thought." *New York Daily News*, September 10, 2000.

"Mafia Turncoat Testifies on Gotti Role in Crime Family Power Struggle." *New York Times*, December 10, 1992.

Mannion, James. *The Everything Mafia Book*. Avon, MA: Adams Media Corporation, 2003.

"Merlino Still Runs Philly Mob, Court Document Says." *Philadelphia Inquirer*, May 4, 2012.

"Meyer Lansky Is Dead at 81; Financial Wizard of Organized Crime." *New York Times*, January 16, 1983.

"Mob Boss Admits Insanity an Act, Pleads Guilty." *New York Times*, April 8, 2003.

"Mob Case's First Sentence: 20 Years for Racketeering." *Chicago Tribune*, January 27, 2009.

"Mob Hit Man Gets Life Term." *Chicago Tribune*, January 29, 2009.

"Mob Metaphysician." *New York Times*, May 25, 1997.

"Mobster: Fear Led Me to Kill, Then 'Rat.'" *Chicago Tribune*, June 20, 2007.

"Mobster Gets Life Term." *Chicago Tribune*, February 6, 2009.

"Mobster Recalls Schemes in Days as a Gotti Soldier." *New York Times*, March 1, 2006.

"'Mob Yuppies' Said to Reshape Organized Crime." *New York Times*, April 23, 1988.

"Morphine Victims Sentenced." *New York Times*, November 3, 1900.

"Murder in Gang Haunt; Then Paul Kelly Fled." *New York Times*, November 23, 1905.

Mustain, Gene, and Jerry Capeci. *Mob Star: The Story of John Gotti*. New York: Bantam Doubleday Dell Publishing Group, 1988.

"Must Purify East Side." *New York Times*, August 9, 1903.

Nash, Jay Robert. *Look for the Woman*. London: HARRAP Limited, 1981.

Nash, Jay Robert. *World Encyclopedia of Organized Crime*. New York: Da Capo Press, 1993.

"Nations Uniting to Stamp Out Use of Opium and Many Other Drugs." *New York Times*, July 25, 1909.

"Negro Cocaine Evil." *New York Times*, March 20, 1905.

"Negro Cocaine 'Fiends' Are a New Southern Menace." *New York Times*, February 8, 1914.

"New Jersey Officials Say Mafia Infiltrated Health-Care Industry." *New York Times*, August 21, 1996.

"New Mafia Killer: A Silenced .22." *New York Times*, April 18. 1977.

"The New Poison Squad." *New York Times*, November 1, 1907.

"New York Day by Day; Seeing Castellano's Killers." *New York Times*, December 30, 1985.

Newton, Michael. *The FBI Encyclopedia*. Jefferson, NC: McFarland & Company, 2003.

"Non-Returnable Lansky." *Time*, September 25, 1972.

"Not Entrenched Like Eastern Families: The L.A. Mob: Eking Out a Living Working Streets," *Los Angeles Times*, June 29, 1987.

"Officials Say Mob Stole $200 Million Using Phone Bills." *New York Times*, February 11, 2004.

Okrent, Daniel. *Last Call: The Rise and Fall of Prohibition*. New York: Scribner, 2010.

"One Big Shot." *Time*, November 3, 1930.

"150 Years in All for the Lupo Gang." *New York Times*, February 20, 1910.

"Openings Today in Ligambi Mob Trial." *Philadelphia Inquirer*, October 18, 2012.

"Opium Conference Today." *New York Times*, December 1, 1911.

"Organized Crime: An Offer They Can't Refuse." *Time*, November 25, 1991.

"Patent Medicine Bill to Curb Drug Users." *New York Times*, March 15, 1908.

"Paul Kelly Examined." *New York Times*, December 3, 1905.

"Paul Kelly Found in Cousin's House." *New York Times*, December 2, 1905.

"Paul Kelly's Men Cheered." *New York Times*, April 6, 1905.

"Peter Gotti Is Found Guilty in Murder and Racket Case." *New York Times*, December 23, 2004.

"Phone Executive Admits Conspiracy in Mob Fraud." *New York Times*, January 9, 2005.

Pileggi, Nicholas. *Wiseguy*. New York: Simon & Schuster, 1986.

Pistone, Joseph. *The Way of the Wiseguy*. Philadelphia, PA: Running Press, 2004.

Pistone, Joseph, with Richard Woodley. *Donnie Brasco: My Undercover Life in the Mafia*. New York: New American Library, 1987.

"Police Unearth Cocaine Dives." *New York Times*, September 14, 1908.

"Poorer Drug Users in Pitiful Plight." *New York Times*, April 15, 1915.

"Private Anguish Emerges in Gotti's Conversations." *New York Times*, September 11, 2006.

"Prosecution's Case against Junior Gotti Wasn't Credible." *New York Daily News*, December 2, 2009.

"Prosecutors Shift Attack against Mafia." *New York Times*, January 24, 1993.

"Questions Persist on How to Allot Profit from 'Underboss.'" *New York Times*, October 15, 2003.

Raab, Selwyn. *Five Families: The Rise, Decline and Resurgence of America's Most Powerful Mafia Empires*. New York: St. Martin's Press, 2005.

"Race Riot at Little Ferry." *New York Times*, July 31, 1912.

Reppetto, Thomas. *American Mafia: A History of Its Rise to Power*. New York: Henry Holt and Company, 2004.

Reppetto, Thomas. *Bringing Down the Mob*. New York: Henry Holt and Company, 2006.

"Report: Mob Made $20 Million Since '60s." *Chicago Tribune*, July 23, 2008.

"Reporter's Notebook: What Mobsters Chat About: Glory Days and Bad Teeth." *New York Times*, June 10, 2001.

"Reputed Street Gang Leader Gets 37-Year Prison Sentence." *New York Times*, July 21, 2006.

"Rich Italian Gone; Once Mafia Leader." *New York Times*, December 5, 1908.

Robbins, David. *Heavy Traffic*. New York: Penguin Group, 2005.

Russo, Gus. *The Outfit*. New York: Bloomsbury, 2001.

Saan, Paul. *Kill the Dutchman!* New Rochelle, NY: Arlington House, 1971.

Saan, Paul. *The Lawless Decade*. New York: Bonanza Books, 1957.

"Salvatore Gravano Indicted on Arizona Drug Charges." *New York Times*, May 7, 2000.

"Says Ellison Fired." *New York Times*, June 7, 1911.

Schneider, Steven Jay. *101 Gangster Movies You Must See Before You Die.* Hauppauge, NY: Barron's Educational Series, 2009.

"7 Alleged Southland Mafia Figures Enter Guilty Pleas." *Los Angeles Times*, March 30, 1988.

"Shot By Shot, an Ex-Aide to Gotti Describes the Killing of Castellano." *New York Times*, March 4, 1992.

Sifakis, Carl. *The Mafia Encyclopedia*. New York: Checkmart Books, 2005.

"Slaughter on 46th Street." *Time*, December 30, 1985.

Smith, Denis Mack. *Mussolini: A Biography*. New York: Vintage Books, 1982.

Smith, Jo Durden. *Mafia: The Complete History of a Criminal World*. Leicester, UK: Arcturus Publishing Limited, 2003.

Southwell, David. *The History of Organized Crime*. London: SevenOaks, 2006.

"Special Report: Organized Crime." *Time*, September 3, 1990.

"Telling Tales." *Time*, January 30, 1984.

"10 Dead, 20 Hurt in a Race Riot." *New York Times*, September 29, 1913.

"10 Murders Laid at the Feet of 3 in Mob." *Chicago Tribune*, September 28, 2007.

"Their Thing." *Time*, August 16, 1963.

"Thinks Paul Kelly's a Nest of Floaters." *New York Times*, November 24, 1905.

"13 Alleged Mob Members Arrested for Running N. J. Online Gambling Ring." *Philadelphia Inquirer*, May 23, 2012.

"The 35 Best Shows on TV—Ever." *New York Post*, May 1, 2008.

"Trial on Rackets Delayed in Boston." *New York Times*, July 11, 1985.

Turkus, Burton, and Sid Feder. *Murder, Inc: The Story of the Syndicate*. Cambridge, MA: Perseus Books Group, 1979 (originally published 1951).

"Turncoat Says an Accused Mobster Is Acting Insane to Avoid Prison." *New York Times*, March 5, 1996.

"Uncle Sam is the Worst Drug Fiend in the World." *New York Times*, March 12, 1911.

United States Treasury Department, Bureau of Narcotics. *Mafia*. New York: HarperCollins Publishers, 2007.

"U.S. Attorney Seeks Release of Informer." *New York Times*, February 22, 1992.

"Victims of Cocaine." *New York Times*, May 25, 1886.

"Vincent Gigante, Mafia Leader Who Feigned Insanity, Dies at 77." *New York Times*, December 19, 2005.

"Volk Asks Congress for 'Dry' Inquiry." *New York Times*, January 6, 1921.

"What Elmer Did." *Time*, December 6, 1948.

"What Ever Happened to the South Philly Mob?" *Philadelphia Magazine*, August 2009.

"What's Left of the Mob." *New York Magazine*, May 21, 2005.

"What the Mexicans Might Learn from the Italians." *New York Times*, June 1, 2008.

"Who Wouldn't Be Worried?" *Time*, October 19, 1931.

"Will the Real Mob Please Stand Up." *New York Times*, March 5, 2006.

"Witness Describes Scene at Murder of Castellano." *New York Times*, February 27, 1992.

"Witness Gives Step-by-Step Description of Killing." *New York Times*, April 14, 1993.

"Word for Word/New York Gangs: The Dapper Don and Company Were a Bunch of Copycats." *New York Times*, May 3, 1998.

"Yale Avenged." *Time*, September 17, 1928.

Documents, Reports, and Testimony

"Acting New England Crime Boss Pleads Guilty in Racketeering and Extortion Conspiracy." Peter F. Neronha, United States Attorney, District of Rhode Island, U.S. Department of Justice, September 13, 2012.

"Alcohol Prohibition Was a Failure." CATO Institute Policy Analysis, July 17, 1991.

"The Changing Face of Organized Crime in New Jersey: A Status Report." State of New Jersey, Commission of Investigation, May 2004.

"The Chicago Mafia: Down but Not Out." Federal Bureau of Investigation, June 27, 2011.

"Chronological History of La Cosa Nostra in the United States: January 1920–August 1987." Federal Bureau of Investigation, October 1987.

"Family Secrets of the Murderous Kind." Federal Bureau of Investigation, October 1, 2007.

Finckenauer, James O. "La Cosa Nostra in the United States." National Institute of Justice, 2007.

"Four Gambino Crime Family Members and Associates Plead Guilty in a Manhattan Federal Court—Eleven Gambino Family Members and Associates Arrested Last Year in a National Crackdown on Organized Crime Have Now Pled Guilty." United States Attorney's Office, Southern District of New York, February 17, 2012.

"14 Defendants Indicted for Alleged Organized Crime Activities." United States Department of Justice, April 25, 2005.

"History of Alcohol Prohibition." National Commission on Marihuana and Drug Abuse, 1972.

"Investigative Programs; Organized Crime, Gamtax." Federal Bureau of Investigation, http://www.fbi.gov/about-us/investigate/organizedcrime/cases/gamtax.

"Kefauver Committee Final Report." August 1951, U.S. Senate Special Committee to Investigate Organized Crime in Interstate Commerce.

"Leadership, Members and Associates of the Philadelphia La Cosa Nostra Family Charged with Racketeering Conspiracy and Related Crimes." U.S. Department of Justice, May 23, 2011.

Lonardo, Angelo. Testimony before the U.S. Senate Permanent Subcommittee on Investigations of the Senate Committee on Governmental Affairs. April 4, 1988.

"Mafia Family Fraud: The Case of the Stolen Company." Federal Bureau of Investigation, December 12, 2011.

"Mafia Monograph." Federal Bureau of Investigation, 1958.

"Mafia Takedown Largest Coordinated Arrest in FBI History." Federal Bureau of Investigation, January 20, 2011.

"Mafia Takedown: Philadelphia Boss Charged." Federal Bureau of Investigation, May 25, 2011.

"Manhattan U.S. Attorney Charges 14 Gambino Crime Family Associates with Racketeering, Murder, Sex Trafficking and Other Crimes." United States Attorney's Office, Southern District of New York, April 20, 2010.

Mueller, Robert, III, Director, Federal Bureau of Investigation, Speech to Citizens Crime Commission of New York. New York, NY, January 27, 2011.

Mueller, Robert, III, Director, Federal Bureau of Investigation, Speech to Greater Miami Chamber of Commerce. Miami, Florida, April 4, 2012.

"National Drug Threat Assessment 2011." National Drug Intelligence Center, U.S. Department of Justice.

"National Gang Threat Assessment 2009." National Drug Intelligence Center, U.S. Department of Justice.

"91 Leaders, Members and Associates of La Cosa Nostra Families in Four Districts Charged with Racketeering and Related Crimes Including Murder and Extortion." United States Department of Justice, January 20, 2011.

"Philadelphia La Cosa Nostra Capo Sentenced to 57 Months in Prison." United States Attorney, Eastern District of Pennsylvania, United States Department of Justice, September 17, 2012.

Pistone, Joseph. Testimony before the U.S. Senate Permanent Subcommittee on Investigations of the Committee of Governmental Affairs. 1988.

"Report on the Enforcement of the Prohibition Laws of the United States." National Commission on Law Observance and Enforcement, 1931.

"26 Charged in $10 Million Gambino Organized Crime Family Gambling, Loan Sharking and Prostitution Operation." Richard Brown, District Attorney, Queen's County, February 7, 2008.

"Two Alleged Members of the Philadelphia La Cosa Nostra Family Charged in Second Superseding Indictment." United States Department of Justice, April 26, 2012.

"United States v. Nicholas W. Calabrese, James Marcello, Joseph Lombardo, Frank Calabrese Sr., Frank Schweihs, Paul Schiro, Michael Marcello, Nicholas Ferriola, Anthony Doyle, Thomas Johnson, Joseph Denezia and Dennis Johnson." United States District Court, Northern District of Illinois, Eastern Division, August 2006.

Valachi, Joseph. Testimony before the U.S. Senate Permanent Subcommittee on Investigations, 1963.

"World Drug Report 2011." United Nations Office on Drugs and Crime.

Websites and Online Articles

American Film Institute. "Top 10 Gangster." http://www.afi.com/10top10/gangster.html.

AmericanMafia.com. http://www.americanmafia.com.

BBC News. "Mafia King on the Straight and Narrow." March 29, 2008. http://www.bbc.co.uk/news.

CBS Detroit website. "Organized Crime in Detroit: Forgotten but Not Gone." June 24, 2011. http://detroit.cbslocal.com/2011/06/24/organized-crime-in-detroit-forgotten-but-not-gone.

Centers for Disease Control and Prevention. http://cdc.gov.

CNN.com. " 'Dapper Don' John Gotti Dead." June 11, 2002.

DRCNet Online Library of Drug Policy. http://www.druglibrary.org.

Drug Enforcement Administration. http://www.justice.gov/dea/index.shtml.

Federal Bureau of Investigation. http://www.fbi.gov.

Film.com. "And the Amy Award Goes To . . ." Posted July 18, 2008. http://www.film.com/tv/and-the-amy-award-goes-to.

The Guardian TV and Radio blog. "The Guardian's Top 50 Television Dramas of All Time." Posted January 12, 2010. http://www.guardian.co.uk/tv-and-radio/tvandradioblog/2010/jan/12/guardian-50-television-dramas.

Henry Hill website. http://henryhill90290.tripod.com.

History News Network. "Civil Rights: Let 'em Wiretap!" October 22, 2001. http://hnn.us/articles/366.html.

Los Angeles Police Department. "About the Vice Division." http://www.lapdonline.org/detective_bureau/content_basic_view/1987.

National Institute on Drug Abuse. http://www.drugabuse.gov.

Officer Down Memorial Page. http://www.odmp.org.

PBS.com. "The Opium Kings: Opium throughout History." Aired May 20, 1997. http://www.pbs.org/wgbh/pages/frontline/shows/heroin/etc/history.html.

Slate.com. "Modern Mafiosi: How Does the Mob Make a Living These Days?" Posted January 21, 2011. http://www.slate.com/articles/news_and_politics/explainer/2011/01/modern_mafiosi.html.

United States Marshals Service website. Visited August 5 and 6, 2012. http://www.usmarshals.gov.

WPRI-12 website. "The History of New England's Mob Bosses: A Rhode Island Legacy of Mafia Dons." Published November 24, 2008, updated March 26, 2012. http://www.wpri.com/dpp/news/local_wpri_underworld_bosses_rhode_island_20081124.

Index

About the Author

NATE HENDLEY is a Toronto-based writer. He lives with a placid cat and next door to Jeanne Enright, world's finest girlfriend. His published works include Greenwood's *Bonnie and Clyde: A Biography*, ABC-CLIO's *American Gangsters, Then and Now, Crystal Death*, and *Steven Truscott: Decades of Injustice*, and several other titles.

Nate's website is located at http://www.natehendley.com. He manages a blog about crime writing at http://crimestory.wordpress.com and a blog about creative motivation at http://motivatetocreate.com.

Nate can be reached at nhendley@sympatico.ca.